# Life *of a* Mystic

## EMBRACING PATHWAYS TO CONSCIOUSNESS

By

# TANIS HELLIWELL

# Other books by Tanis Helliwell

The Dragon's Tale

The Leprechaun's Story: As told by Lloyd to Tanis Helliwell

Good Morning Henry: an in-depth journey with the body
intelligence

High Beings of Hawaii: encounters with mystical ancestors

Hybrids: so you think you are human

Summer with the Leprechauns: a true story

Pilgrimage with the Leprechauns: a true story of a mystical
tour of Ireland

Decoding Your Destiny: keys to humanity's spiritual transformation

Manifest Your Soul's Purpose

Embraced by Love: Poems

# Life *of a* Mystic

EMBRACING
PATHWAYS TO
CONSCIOUSNESS

## TANIS HELLIWELL

Published by Wayshower Enterprises

Library and Archives Canada Cataloguing in Publication

Title: Life of a mystic : embracing pathways to consciousness / by Tanis Helliwell.

Names: Helliwell, Tanis, author.

Identifiers: Canadiana (print) 2025029267X | Canadiana (ebook) 20250292718 | ISBN 9781987831641 (softcover) | ISBN 9781987831658 (Kindle) | ISBN 9781987831665 (EPUB)

Subjects: LCSH: Helliwell, Tanis. | LCSH: Spiritual biography—Canada. | LCSH: Mystics—Canada—Biography. | LCGFT: Autobiographies.

Classification: LCC BL73.H45 A3 2025 | DDC 204.092—dc23

Cover photo by Yvonne Vruggink. Icons by: Muhammad Atif, Flaticon and Smashicons from www.flaticon.com. Cover and book design by Maywood Design.

tanishelliwell.com

# Dedication

*To my dear brother Mark Harvey Helliwell.*
*Remembered with love.*

# Contents

# Introduction

This book began 30 years ago and documented my life until age 46. Then it stopped. Every decade, I would revisit it, but felt unable to change anything or move forward. Now, at last, the time is right to continue.

As we reach our elder years, it is valuable to reflect on our lives. Every experience has helped shape the person we have become. By examining the events we have chosen and those that have been imposed on us, we can better understand our purpose and let go of old hurts. It's healing, and perhaps we even find humor in situations that were once painful. Over time, we come to see that our significant disappointments were, in retrospect, relatively minor. They have endowed us with admirable qualities such as forgiveness, tolerance, patience, and a deeper compassion for the suffering of ourselves and others. Additionally, reviewing our experiences gives us an opportunity to celebrate our accomplishments. More importantly, reflecting on our lives enables us to evolve as we consider the question, "What has my life contributed to others and the world?"

I wrote this book not simply to reflect on my life but to gain deeper insight. My hope is that my spiritual journey might open doors for you. While each of us is unique, we encounter certain predictable challenges on the journey to Self-realization. For example, we all must confront and overcome our fears. Also, we need to let go of all attachments, such as those to people, money, possessions, or the roles we play.

At the same time, we receive support from Spirit in learning about our strengths and growing our specific talents. This may entail learning about our past lives, spirit guides, masters, and meeting allies along the way. Both dark nights of the soul and gifts from Spirit awaken pathways to consciousness in us. Just as we physically change throughout life, we have the opportunity to evolve emotionally, mentally, and spiritually based on our choices and how we respond to the situations we face.

One of the spiritual pathways for me is nature. We are part of the natural world and our life mirrors the three stages a flower goes through—from a bud to a full bloom, and finally to producing a seed, a fruit. As a bud, I discovered my gifts and experienced the right environment to grow into a strong plant. Some teachers and situations were like the sun, nurturing these gifts, while others were like strong winds and storms, helping me become resilient.

Although still influenced, as we all are, by our environment and surrounding circumstances, in the second stage, the flowering, I began to share my unique combination of talents in both mainstream and spiritual fields. This was like rooting deeply into the soil to withstand any situation, desired or not, that I might encounter while growing into a healthy, mature plant.

The third stage, the fruit, has been about deciding what to grow and letting go of what did not serve my soul's purpose. While in the flowering stage, the focus was more on developing both my personality and soul to create a soul-infused personality. In the fruit stage, the motivation has been on using my gifts to feed others in service to the Divine.

Currently, we are poised to make a quantum leap in consciousness where we will be able to perceive beings previously thought to only exist in our myths. Since childhood, I have been fortunate to observe higher realms. I've written books about the inhabitants of these worlds, including elementals, merpeople, and dragons. Many individuals have reached out to me over the years, expressing how beneficial it has been for them to learn about these beings and how to communicate with them. As we walk our pathways to consciousness, we begin to experience these higher realms. Hopefully, this book will inspire you to reflect on the spiritual paths you, too, have taken and to see paths calling you on the next step of your wonderful journey.

# The Bud Unfurls

*Let me be a rose*
*inviting you to visit,*
*a mirror*
*to see yourself clearly,*
*and a doorway into your soul.*

# 1

# Mystical Child

I was born conscious. There was a Being with me whose job was to help humans make choices for their next incarnation. This Being oversaw and assisted with human evolution. It had an all-knowing presence infused with tolerance and love that completely knew and accepted my true Self. This Being brought me to my mother and father and, as we hovered in the ether, I chose them as my parents.

"Are you ready to go back?" asked the Being without words.

"Yes, it's time." I answered by thought.

"How do you feel about returning?" the Being asked.

Inside, I felt the rightness of my decision and realized the Being knew my feelings. Looking down at my prospective parents, the path of my future life was revealed. It didn't appear very difficult…from up there. There was no coercion from the Being beside me. I chose this life of my own free will. It was simply time to get back to work. Working on Earth brought joy, and a warm and hopeful feeling enveloped me at the thought of incarnating again. I do not recall saying goodbye to the Being, so perhaps there were days, or even months, of unconsciousness.

The next thing I remember was being inside my mother's womb. She was in the final months of her pregnancy, feeling very nervous and even fearful. She had many worries, including an impending fear of delivery. However, she also questioned whether she was making the right decision in having a child. She and my father had been married for seven years and had not intended to have children. I was an accident. Still, beneath her fear and ambivalence, I felt loved and accepted. I sent her telepathic messages of reassurance, letting her know that we would have a wonderful time together. This vision was of being friends with my mother as an adult, not as a child. This vision became reality many years later and it was an early learning that some 20 years needed to pass for this to happen.

My mother went into labor and began to panic. I sent continuous messages of comfort, but she wasn't receiving them. Deciding that the best way to help her was to be born quickly, I turned toward the light at the end of the tunnel and descended. At first, there wasn't much progress, but when my entire body was finally inside the tunnel, things progressed rapidly. The walls of the tunnel squeezed, expanding and contracting. The opening was very near now. One last squeeze and someone's large, rough hands caught me. The light was blinding and painful, and the voices were like cannons booming in my ears. The physical sensations were most unpleasant.

"This may be more difficult than I anticipated," was my initial thought upon emerging.

Whether I consciously shielded myself from hypersensitivity to my environment or did so instinctively is not known. The result was the same: I closed down my higher spiritual centers to experience relative physical and emotional comfort in the material world. My life purpose became hazy as I adopted the outer garments of the child others saw. However, there were moments in childhood when the other world, my real home, enveloped me again, but I couldn't find the way there when I wanted it. This left me yearning for something inexpressible.

Sometimes, especially during the early years at age two or three, expanded feelings of joy would wash over me. A connection to a flow of energy that had no name. This would happen more frequently when alone in the bath or lying on my belly in the warm shallows of a wading pool. Often, it occurred outside in nature when I united with the life of the trees, grass, and flowers. Nature was a pathway and I cherished those moments and accepted them as part of my everyday world. It did not occur to me that adults and perhaps other children did not experience these moments.

Growing older, these ecstatic experiences decreased. By age eight or nine, I knew there was another world—a magical place—where I wanted to go, but the pathway had disappeared. Sometimes, however, that world and my concrete, physical one overlapped. This happened less and less, and those times of expanded awakening were very precious.

By this time, I had learned that parents, grown-ups, and even other children didn't talk about that special place. Through their example, I realized it was not acceptable to even know about this place. Still, in dreams, I visited this place and could do things that were not possible when awake. There it was possible to fly, walk on water, breathe in the depths of the sea, and meet exciting beings: faeries, dragons, and such. Wouldn't it be amazing to do this while awake? There was no point mentioning this desire to my parents, as they would not have approved or understood. Yet, two events occurred around this time, giving me hope that this wish could come true. The first of these involved an organization for children called "Brownies."

Like many other girls, I attended Brownies, where we earned badges by tying knots, collecting plants, and doing chores for our mothers. This was not particularly exciting, but I studied hard. Our leader, Brown Owl, said that if we earned enough badges, we could fly up to the next level— "Guides". Finally, an adult was promising to teach us to soar into that special and thrilling world of my dreams. On the day when "it" would happen, I sat perched and ready. Somehow, I managed to get through the school classes with Miss Bonham and raced home to find my mother ironing the Brownie uniform for the last time. How carefully I polished the shoes. How quietly I stood while she tied the tie.

It was a rainy, dark fall evening when I stepped out of the front door of our apartment above our family's hardware store. Brownies and Guides met at the nearby Anglican church around the corner. Since it was close, my mother didn't come with me; besides, she was busy working. I tiptoed around the puddles, making sure my shoes would pass inspection. Once inside the large oak doors of the church, I took off my coat, straightened my uniform, and tilted the tam slightly to the side of my head as I had been taught. Finally, I ensured the Brownie pin was perfectly centered on the tie.

Ready, I entered the hall. Nothing had changed. The place looked the same as it did every week—cold and bare. My heart sank. There was no long red carpet or a yellow brick road like Dorothy had in *The Wizard of Oz.*

"Don't rush to conclusions," echoed the words my mother had said many times. "I'm sure there's an explanation."

Scanning the hall, I saw the Guides, dressed in blue, clustered together at one end. The Brownies were at the other end, their group forming and unforming like an amoeba about to split in two. Some of them, like me, were going to fly up, while others were too young and had to remain in Brownies. Walking over to join the older Brownies, I silently hoped that the inauspicious setting would miraculously transform upon flying up.

The guide leader entered and started organizing her squad. Two by two, her girls lined up and formed an arch. She signaled to Brown Owl, who quickly mustered the senior Brownies into a line at the beginning of the arch. My heart pounded with anticipation. I needed to go to the toilet but held it in. I must have stopped breathing because I felt dizzy. What if I fainted? That would be terrible, and they'd never let a weakling fly up.

Inside my head, my father's voice said, "Pull yourself together," and somehow, I did.

Brown Owl cleared her throat, and silence reigned. She started talking about how well we had performed as Brownies and that we had earned the right to become Girl Guides. That was all she said; it was a brief speech. After Brown Owl finished speaking, the guide leader, who stood at the other end of the arch, instructed us to extend our arms and fly up to her.

I waited my turn and then, putting my whole soul into it, stretched out my arms and, flapping them, ran through the arch toward her.

"Welcome," she said, moving me aside to make room for the next ex-Brownie.

Nothing had changed. They had promised we would fly, but it was a lie. In that moment, the realization dawned that they were unable to go to the magical place I yearned for.

Returning home that evening, Mother asked, "How was it?"

"Fine," I replied, not meeting her eyes.

I never told her about my deep disappointment and how my heart had been shattered. She had enough worries on her plate, trying to raise two kids while working full-time with my father in a small, struggling hardware store on a busy street in the heart of Toronto. However, that was the last time I went to Guides.

Although deeply disappointed, my great dream persisted. There was a magical land, and if I could find the key, I could go there. This remained a strongly held belief. Maybe it was reading a book about Peter Pan or watching the movie. Neverland, Tinker Bell, and Peter Pan beckoned like a precious gem shining in a dark room. Like Peter Pan, I wanted to stay forever young and have exciting adventures fighting the evil Captain Hook and keeping the other children safe. But most of all, I dreamed of being sprinkled with fairy dust and flying.

How to go to Neverland? The key was in the story. I was like Wendy, the older child taking care of her younger brother and being responsible. My parents, like hers, were absent, as they were always working. I waited eagerly for Peter Pan to come and rescue me. He didn't come. Brown Owl hadn't helped, and now Peter Pan had let me down. Obviously, you couldn't count on others to help you get your dreams.

Still, this wasn't as upsetting as it could have been if I hadn't held the key to Neverland. And what was the key? In the story, Peter Pan told Wendy that if she believed she could fly, then she could. Well! My belief was strong. Every night while asleep, I'd fly to Neverland. I soared over the treetops and glided with the birds. Many interesting beings, including animals, spoke in these places. Life during the day wasn't nearly as fascinating as nightlife.

The desire to fly during the day kept building until one day I decided to try. My parents were downstairs working in the store and my younger brother, Mark, hadn't come home from school yet. I was alone. Flying must be one of those things you're not supposed to do or others would do it. It had to be secret. Anyway, only children could do it. It said so in the story. I went to the bedroom and shut the door.

The sun streamed through the skylight in the ceiling, casting rays that created streamers in the air. Perhaps sunbeams were like faerie dust. I quietly glided across the floor to avoid disturbing the beams, which welcomed me with their warmth, flooding over and through my body. Closing my eyes,

I imagined myself filled with holes through which the faerie dust flowed. I was full of air, like a balloon, and like a balloon, floated.

"Imagine yourself lifting off the floor," I said to myself.

My body felt very light, yet my feet were still on the floor. Why wasn't it working? Right. You needed a launchpad.

Holding on to this light feeling, I pushed the old wooden dresser into the sunbeams. Gazing through half-closed eyes, I climbed onto the top of the dresser from the bed, moving closer to the sky, closer to the sun. Nonetheless, it was a long way down to the floor. Nervously, I tried to regain the peaceful light feeling. Opening myself to the sun, that feeling returned. With closed eyes, an opening to another world appeared. The certainty that I could fly coursed through me. Holding still and allowing the feeling to grow, a strong inner rightness enveloped me. In that ecstatic state, I leaped off the dresser...and fell to the floor shocked back into the physical body.

Something was wrong. Maybe I hadn't wished hard enough. Attempting to keep belief intact, I climbed back on top of the dresser. Calming the fluttering butterflies in my stomach, I opened my arms allowing the sunbeams to fill me. With unwavering belief, I envisioned myself taking off from the dresser and soaring around the room, out through the bedroom door. Then, I exited through our front door and floated down the street, higher now so no one could see me and bring me back. My raised arms transformed into wings, and I glided off the dresser...then crashed to the floor.

Devastated, I lay there wondering about this failure. The only thought that made sense was that I was too passive and weak to let all those sunbeams inside me. Maybe I could try being strong and demand to fly. Half-heartedly, I crawled to my feet, but somewhere inside, the knowing grew that I wasn't going to succeed.

Remembering my father's words, "If at first, you don't succeed, try, try again," I struggled onto the dresser and, holding back tears, steeled myself to try again. It must work. It must. Please let it work. Clenching my teeth, waving my arms up and down in birdlike mockery, I closed my eyes and jumped. Crash! I got up and climbed onto the dresser again.

Close eyes. Wave arms. Jump. Crash. Get up. Climb onto the dresser. Jump. Crash. Again and again, I did this until, bruised in spirit and body, I lay on the floor. The bedroom door opened.

"What are you doing?" my mother asked, frowning and gripping the door handle. "We can hear crashing downstairs in the store."

"I was trying to fly." She had trained me to answer politely when asked a question, but something was dead inside. Her eyes traveled around the room, reconstructing the scene.

"You'll have to stop now," she said gently, as an understanding of my disappointment came to her. "We can hear you downstairs. You didn't hurt yourself, did you?"

"No, I'm fine," I replied, providing the answer she wanted.

"Good." She closed the door behind her.

I never tried to fly again, although the belief that it was possible continued. Something was wrong with me. Maybe, like Wendy, I was too old to go to Neverland. My childhood ended, and this dream slept. It was time for me, like Wendy, to grow up.

Now, as an adult, I wonder about the secret lives and deep wishes children have that they never share with their parents. And if they do share them, do their parents brush them aside and say, "You'll grow out of it." Many children have friends in other realms, like elves and gnomes, which their parents call "imaginary." Parents dismiss their children's friends as impossible because they have lost the ability to see these beings themselves. They often forget that, long ago, when they were children, they had a faerie friend. If parents remain open-minded and respect their children's experiences, their children will learn that they can speak freely about anything with their parents and that they can trust them to listen. What a wonderful gift that is for anyone, but especially for a child.

Also, deep-seated desires of children can reveal talents, goals, and even a person's life purpose. This was true for me, as it may be for others. In fact, I was destined to see other worlds…just not as a child. If parents take these childhood desires seriously, they may even be able to support their children in pursuing their life purpose.

It was a sunny Sunday. Dad and Mom were upstairs in the apartment getting ready to go to Grandma and Grandpa's. My younger brother Mark and I were already dressed and supposed to behave. We had been told not to wander off, so we were playing tag on the sidewalk in front of the store. Perhaps I tripped or was pushed too hard when tagged, but the outcome was the same. I fell headfirst into the sharp corner of the building. My forehead split open where the third eye was and blood streamed down onto the Sunday clothes. Knowing my parents were going to be cross, I started to cry, both from the pain and because the more I was hurt, the less angry they'd be. Children intuitively know how to get sympathy.

Dad arrived. "What's going on here?" he bellowed. "Can't we leave you two alone for a minute without you getting into trouble?"

"Daddy, I'm hurt. Mark tripped me." Yes, another childhood trick is to blame a sister or brother. I was quite adept at this.

Dad saw me then. Blood flowed freely down my face…which I made no attempt to remove…hence more sympathy. Concern filled his eyes as he swept me into his arms and carried me upstairs.

Mark chased after us, shouting, "I didn't trip her; she fell."

Mom took one look and rushed to the fridge for ice to stop the bleeding. Dad called the doctor. This was back when doctors still made house calls.

Dr. Pretty was an English gentleman with a lovely, gentle manner. We had gotten to know each other quite well through chickenpox, two bouts of measles, multiple cases of flu, and a tonsillectomy. Usually, I did what he requested, but this time I disagreed.

"Tanis, this is a deep cut. I need to stitch it up," he said.

"Please don't," I cried, partly from pain and partly out of annoyance at his suggestion.

"If I don't stitch it, you will have a scar between your eyebrows for the rest of your life."

"I don't care about the scar. I don't want you to stitch it."

Mom and Dad looked at me with frustration. I was not behaving well.

"Dear, Dr. Pretty knows best," cajoled Mom. "He's come all this way on his day off to help you." Standing a little back and allowing the doctor to tend to his work, Dad remained silent.

"Please, Dr. Pretty," I pleaded, looking straight into his clear blue eyes, "I don't want you to stitch it, but you can bandage it if you'd like." By giving a concession, I was proving what a nice, agreeable child I was. Yup…another strategy for getting what I wanted.

He turned to my parents for their decision.

"It's her decision," said Dad, looking at me.

I smiled at him in gratitude for being allowed to decide for myself.

I am still grateful today that Dr. Pretty didn't give me stitches. Although I couldn't have expressed my feelings in words as a child, I had a strong inner sense that the opening between my two eyes served a purpose. Years later, I learned that in many ancient cultures, such as Egypt and Mesoamerica, procedures were performed on initiates to open their third eye, enabling them to perceive other dimensions. I believe that the accident opened my third eye and, in doing so, kept a gateway to the magical world open. At the same time, it compensated for the closure of my throat chakra.

There were things I wasn't supposed to talk about for fear of hurting or disappointing Mom and Dad. My continual sore throats and colds, which led to a tonsillectomy, were a direct result of shutting down the throat chakra. By now, I had learned not to speak about my desires or other realms, as I knew by then that these topics were off-limits. Why? First, because my parents were poor and couldn't afford to send me to camp or give me treats like other children might have had. Second, in my secret mystical life, they and others seemed to lack the abilities or interests I possessed. I didn't want to cause them pain by asking for something they couldn't provide or do.

I'd kept these mystical gifts a secret since I was about six or seven. One day, I was walking to school with two friends. One girl liked me, while the other thought unkind things about me, even though she spoke nicely to my face. I asked her, "Why do you say one thing and think another?"

and repeated her exact thoughts. She was shocked, and now even the other girl was afraid of me and no longer wished to be my friend.

That night at dinner, I experimented with my parents by saying one thing and thinking another. To my horror, I discovered that they could not hear my thoughts. This difference from other children and adults took root. From then on, I made efforts not to listen to others' thoughts and attempted to be like them to fit in. It's wonderful to develop an ethical sense as a child, and I believe many children have an instinctive goodness where they don't share parts of themselves that might cause others discomfort.

Growing older, I realized that my ways of seeing, hearing, and perceiving were not physical. Lying in bed at night with the door closed, my astral body traveled to the living room, where I'd listen to my parents' conversations. This was particularly true if they were discussing me or a topic that intrigued me. One moment I could be in bed, and the next, be in the living room with Mom and Dad, observing them and listening to their discussion. Then, I'd return to my physical body and call out responses to what they were talking about. In a split second, I'd be back in the living room, smiling as they whispered like children caught in a secret.

"She's at it again," Mom would remark to Dad.

Then either Mom or Dad would call out to me, "Go to sleep, big ears."

Big ears became my nickname. It was a game to me that they didn't know I could see and hear them. Still, a part of me didn't want to be a snoop, so I would only do this when they weren't sharing secrets with each other. It would be unfair to discover private thoughts by using my gift, so I confined myself to what was within the bounds of acceptability. My parents didn't treat this as unusual and said I had "very good hearing."

My brother and I shared another habit that suggested budding psychic powers. We both sleepwalked and later had only a vague memory of it. One time, while he was sleeping, Mark packed a bag full of books, walked out the front door, and was later found wandering along the highway, rummaging through garbage cans…still asleep.

My behavior lacked his drama. Asleep, I would pull out the drawers from the dresser and call Mom to come and take them. She would do so

Margaret and Eric Helliwell, my mother and father

Mystical Child

Showing my younger brother, Mark, something

and lead me back to bed, where she engaged in detailed conversations that I couldn't recall the next morning. Sometimes, when Mom told me about this the following day, I would hazily remember that it had happened. It was like trying to recall a dream that lay just below the surface of consciousness.

Mark and I exhibited trance-like psychic behavior, akin to Edgar Cayce, but my parents were unaware of such matters. They attributed it to our being troubled in our waking life, which, of course, we likely were. Mark was briefly taken to a psychiatrist for help. The garbage can incident on the highway frightened them. Not wanting to be fixed, too, I was able to stop myself. I learned early on to conceal any paranormal abilities that seemed different...even hiding them from myself.

Many children feel the need to hide their true gifts to stay safe and loved, and sometimes to protect their parents. Perhaps my story reveals something—a talent, a gift—that you, too, hid as a child. For various reasons, this gift might have been unacceptable for a child to show, as it was in my case, so it was better not to draw attention to it at that time. The personality vessel needs to mature as a child to support the timely unfolding of gifts.

# 2

# Discovering New Gifts

On the verge of becoming a teenager, we moved from Toronto to a new suburb in Georgetown, a small town in Ontario. Here, Mom and Dad opened a larger hardware store and bought a bungalow. Mark and I were finally able to have our own rooms, and we were allowed to paint them any color we wanted. Mine was lilac. Mark's was brown.

Our parents sold turtles and birds in their store, and we, like most kids, were eager to have pets. Mine was a darling bird, a parakeet named Perry, whom I taught to speak. He'd fly around the house calling out, "Merry Christmas, pretty bird, pretty Perry." Perry loved butter, and while we ate breakfast, he would take off from his perch, land on our heads, and dive into the butter for a good feed. Mark also had a bird, but it died. I felt a strange combination of sadness and elation that my bird survived while his didn't. On one hand, I must have been developing a moral conscience—one can only hope—and my sadness for Mark was a result of this. On the other hand, because I had so few things I wanted, I was jealous of anything my brother received. It's not a nice thing to admit, but it's common not only with children but also with adults who live their lives with feelings of scarcity.

I no longer tried to escape to a magical land and instead focused on being normal in the everyday world. I accepted my parents' view that we were an average family. So, whenever I excelled at something, it surprised me completely. I don't think Mom and Dad expected or even believed that either Mark or I would be particularly good at anything. Please understand that they were good parents and did not abuse my brother or me. Still, they were physically and emotionally absent because they worked long hours to put a roof over our heads and feed us. There were no extras in our lives, and they called us "gentile poor." This meant we knew which fork to use and not to put our elbows on the table, and to say "thank you" in almost all situations.

Nothing unusual occurred during the first year in our new home, but two events at age 13 shook the underpinnings of the belief that I was mediocre without any talents.

It was the last year of primary school. Happily, I was quite popular due to my friendly personality, which attracted and retained friends, and my average marks at school were acceptable to both me and my parents. Unhappily, however, I was shorter and skinnier than other kids my age. To make things worse, recently I'd had a large stye on my right eye and a boil under my arm that reinforced feelings of unattractiveness at a time that boys had become a preoccupation.

In early June, our teachers organized a track and field meet. The entire school was set to compete in running, high jump, broad jump, and relay events. This was not something I relished doing. I didn't want Lynn—my first crush from afar—to notice my skinny legs and flat chest. Moreover, I had developed a perspiration problem. Baby powder and heavy deodorants didn't help. I even wore two sweaters in June to prevent anyone from seeing the wet stains under my arms. The last thing I wanted was for the boys, especially Lynn, to see me in a soaking wet blouse.

As if having to participate in field day wasn't bad enough, Janice, the tallest and most athletic girl in our class—the one who was expected to clean up the field alongside the rest of us—publicly challenged me in front of the class. Janice behaved as if she hated my guts and often did unpleasant things, like pulling my hair. Why was this? Perhaps it was because she was not as popular as me, or perhaps she had a crush on me. These are my reflections as an adult, but my 13-year-old self didn't have this perspective and viewed her treatment as unwarranted personal persecution.

Field day arrived. Glancing out the bedroom window, I saw a heat haze rising over the neighborhood. It was a sunny day, unfortunately. It would be a real scorcher, which meant I would sweat a lot. After slathering on three layers of underarm deodorant, I put on my whitest T-shirt because Mom said underarm stains were less noticeable in light colors. Skipping breakfast and, with my head hung low, I closed the front door behind me and set off for school. I felt sick to my stomach and trapped by Janice. Because of her public challenge, everyone would be watching us. She was a head and a half taller than me and played every sport going. How could I expect to win or even make a decent showing?

Dragging my feet, I arrived at school. The teachers were prepared with stopwatches and chalked starting lines. The high jump and long jump pits had been dug, and the pole was already in position for the high jump. Some of the boys were practicing. The whistle blew.

Mr. Allen, our eighth-grade teacher, called out, "Senior girls, 50 yards, take your places."

Shaking, I took my place in line. Janice slid in next to me.

"I'll wait for you at the finish line," she whispered, looking down at me with a smirk.

Something in my stomach tightened. I resolved to do my best and quietly prayed to God for help in winning.

Mr. Allen's voice echoed in my ears, "On your mark…Get set…Go."

Time barely moved. Seconds existed between each of his words. Every cell in my body pulsed with energy. Each muscle was stretched like an elastic band. When he said, "Go," I catapulted forward like an arrow in flight. My feet scarcely touched the earth. I was like wind guided by will. In this superconscious state, I easily won the race and returned to physical reality to find Janice hovering over me.

"I'm onto you, Helliwell. You won't win next time," she hissed.

I felt a pang of sympathy for Janice. Sports were her sole strength, and I was about to take that away from her. A worried thought arose that I was creating an enemy. Yet, another part of me was elated and proud of my victory. The 100-yard race was next.

"Line up. Take your places, girls," said Mr. Allen.

I waited until Janice had taken her place, then went to the opposite end of the line. When Janice saw where I was, she left her spot and shoved in beside me. Saying nothing, she scowled as if intending to beat me up. I was frightened but also angry to be subjected to this nasty treatment. The anger fueled my strength and willpower. The whistle blew and I took off down the track neck and neck with Janice. Pumping my little arms as fast as possible, I brushed past the finish line a few inches ahead of her. Panting, she stared at me in disbelief.

Friends came up to congratulate me. I was smaller and less athletic than most girls, and my win astounded all of us. In this superconscious state, I felt exhilarated and expanded, both larger and greater than usual. No longer did I feel like a kid but more knowing, which now, many years later, I recognize as the soul state.

Next was the senior girls' high jump. I walked over slowly and joined the line. Janice was already there, a black cloud settled over her. The high jump began at two feet, and everyone cleared it. At three feet, the number of competitors dwindled to half. By three and a half feet, we were down to three girls: Janice, me, and another girl. The other girl knocked the bar down at three feet nine. Janice and I remained. By now, the entire school had gathered to watch. Most of the boys couldn't even jump that high.

I remained in an altered state while simultaneously sensing everything. Sweat rolled down my arms, and a gentle breeze fluttered beneath the intense heat. My heart beat strong and determined in my chest. There was no fear and only a profound sense of Self and power. I easily left my body and observed it from above. It appeared taller, more mature. Janice knocked the bar down at four feet, and I soared lightly over it.

After a break to rest, the long jump competition started. Janice should win this, but she should have also won the high jump and races. Her legs were a foot longer than mine, yet, seeing her slumped shoulders, you could tell her spark was gone.

I walked over to Janice and, standing beside her, said quietly, "I've been lucky today. You're a far better athlete than me. You're going to win this long jump."

Janice turned her head and looked at me. I smiled and reached out my hand. She took it, smiled, straightened her shoulders, and began running toward the chalk line. She made a fantastic jump. I finished in third place. Later that day, we stood together for a photo in the local paper. Janice competed in every sport possible in high school and did very well. I, on the other hand, never took part in another competitive sport.

One part of me couldn't believe what had happened that day, and I definitely didn't know how to reproduce the experience. By now, it was clear that the magical world appeared unexpectedly at certain times, but it couldn't be relied on. Revisiting this experience now, I realize that it was the first time I recall calling on God for help. Mom and Dad never went to church, and although they had sent Mark and me to Sunday school, we didn't pray, meditate, or speak of God at home. Asking God for help was definitely a way to awaken a spiritual gift, but I found it almost by accident, and I didn't actively call on God again for many years. Excelling at anything didn't match my mediocre self-image. It was easier and less painful to stay invisible and, therefore, safe. This message was reinforced during a heartbreaking occasion that same year.

Every Friday, our class had a visiting singing teacher. Mr. Harrison was chubby and balding, wore glasses, had beautiful, fluid hands, and a wonderful voice. He also wanted us to sing perfectly. For one term, we practiced for the public recital at the end of the year. We had learned most of our songs fairly well when he announced on a Friday that he would choose the soloists. As we sang, he walked by each student, cocking his head near their mouths to listen to their emissions. It was unnerving as he moved closer. I was caught between wanting to be chosen and not wanting to be chosen. Delivering my fate to the wind, I sang as normally as possible. In other words, I entered a neutral state and felt non-attached to whatever happened. He must have liked my neutral emissions, for he chose me.

No one had ever complimented me on singing before, and even though I enjoyed it, I did not consider myself a good singer. I was convinced Mr. Harrison had made a mistake, and that when he discovered how bad I was, he would be angry. I was afraid to spoil his recital. The gap between my desire to please and my inability to do so widened. I was certainly no longer non-attached to results. He gave me the Irish song, The Rose of Tralee, to sing. I practiced in the shower, in the basement by the furnace, and on long walks in the field across from our house. I even asked Barbara, the girl with the lovely voice who was singing another song, to help. She listened and said it sounded fine.

The night of the recital found me in utter despair. I was more convinced than ever that I would be terrible and embarrass not only myself but also Mr. Harrison. Mom and Dad couldn't come because they had no one to help in the store, but Mom bought me a frilly white blouse for the event. It was see-through, so you couldn't see perspiration stains.

The moment arrived, and the lights in the auditorium were turned off. Mr. Harrison's final words to us before we took the stage were, "It's a full house. I'm sure you'll do well, just watch me."

Being soloists, Barbara and I were placed in the front row. Mr. Harrison raised his graceful white hand to gain our attention. He gave us our note from the pitch pipe, and we started our first song, Danny Boy. That went quite well, resulting in polite applause for our efforts. Song after song followed in the program, and the closer we got to my solo, the more terrified I became. Mr. Harrison signaled me to step forward. Standing alone in front of the audience, the stage lights beat down on me. I couldn't breathe and panted for air. Mr. Harrison's hand was arched in the air, waiting for me to start. Down it came. I went blank, forgot the words, and froze in horror. A hush fell over the audience, and Mr. Harrison turned a critical eye towards me. He started mouthing the first line of my song before raising his hand again.

"The pale moon was rising" emerged from my mouth, and the words, accompanied by gasps for breath, kept flowing during the first verse. By the time I reached the chorus, I was nearly adjusted. Mr. Harrison appeared more relaxed, and just after thinking the torture would end, I forgot the lines of the second verse.

I shot a look at Mr. Harrison that clearly said, "Help!" His beautiful tenor came in softly, singing the first line and, continuing with him, I managed to get to the end of the song.

This event caused trauma related to singing that lasted for years. In fact, it permeated every area of performance. As a child and teenager, it was safe to be part of a group and relatively anonymous, but completely unsafe when all eyes were on me. I was torn between two conflicting desires: one desire was to be exactly like others, while another part was proud and happy to excel at something and to be distinguished from the crowd. These conflicting feelings stayed with me into middle age and served as great teachers.

It's rare that we go through childhood without experiencing a painful or even traumatic event. Our karma, both positive and negative, brought in from past lives, usually begins to unfold early in life. Traumas are not accidental and often serve as lessons that wouldn't be learned otherwise. However, it's not easy at the moment, and it can take years before we understand what we were meant to learn from them. For example, our own pain might help us learn forgiveness, humility, or compassion for others' suffering. It might also lead us on a healing journey to understand "why" we fear something, such as speaking or singing in public. Perhaps, in another life, we were killed for sharing opinions different from others.

Looking back on childhood, I am grateful to have experienced visions and gifts from other realities. Now, I understand more fully why they were not regular occurrences. Living in that mystical world for extended periods as a child would have been difficult. It might have unsettled me emotionally and led to instability, especially in the Western world where I grew up. I lacked spiritual teachers or even supporters for my mystical gifts, and awakened teachers are still sadly absent in our Western society.

Many children possess spiritual or other talents that are often deemed unacceptable or misunderstood in Western society. They frequently cannot express these gifts and, when they do, risk being sent to professionals for normalization. Instead of recognizing the genius and diverse intelligences among them, many children are stifled, which leads to a lack of diversity and excellence in our culture.

Nevertheless, even as a child and teenager, my environment was perfect for my soul and personality development. I was not born in India to parents who practiced meditation. My parents were hardworking, relatively poor, and honest and they were respected in their community and embodied small-town Canadian values. Even now, I am thankful for this upbringing, during which I received positive reinforcement for being helpful to others. By age 13, I was helping my parents in their store and also did housework for Mom on Saturdays. Like my parents, I was responsible and dependable in interactions with others.

I was no saint. I fought with my younger brother, as many teenagers do, and I had a bad temper whenever I thought Mark was receiving more of something than me. Fortunately, I developed a greater concern for others as I grew older, and this initial seed blossomed into compassion in adulthood. Each of us possesses different strengths. I was born with more wisdom than love. Through my family and childhood upbringing, I began to cultivate compassion for others. The Divine Spirit, working in conjunction with my soul and karma, had given me a supportive family and circumstances that allowed me to learn this.

In early years, I didn't understand the importance of karma as the foundation on which we must awaken pathways to consciousness. I mainly learned by living through experiences and becoming conscious of what worked and what didn't in my life. It was a period of unfolding, of budding, of discovery.

# 3

# Stepping Forward
# and Near Death

With only average grades in primary school, I was placed in a commercial stream in secondary school. Our first class was home economics, in which the teacher showed us how to make jello. Most of the girls in the class wore lots of makeup and were drooling over football players. I, on the other hand, found the studious boys, who were not in my class, more interesting. More than ever, I felt different from my classmates but didn't know how to fix the situation.

One day, I overheard Sherry, one of the girls in my class, say to another girl, Ann, "I'm going to study hard and get into the academic stream next year."

Ann replied, "Me, too."

Eureka! The solution to my dilemma. "I'm going to study and get into the academic stream too," I told them.

Sherry looked at Ann, and they both burst out laughing, clearly finding it hard to believe that I could pull it off. Just like when Janice challenged me publicly in the athletic competition, when mocked and dismissed as inadequate, my willpower took over. After improving my grades, I entered the academic track the next year, where I continued to be an average student. Biology, English, and Ancient History were my favorite subjects, with the expected result of not doing well in other classes. The five years in secondary school went by without major ups or downs, but one part of my final year at age 18 was truly enjoyable: I participated in a musical revue called Spring Run Off that toured southern Ontario.

My boyfriend, Mike, was the talented musician behind this musical and dramatic production. He took on the roles of producer, director, and conductor, and our cast was made up entirely of high school students. I sang and acted in the chorus but had no desire for further glories. When Mike asked me to sing the song "Summertime" as a solo, I, still clinging to the memory of the singing trauma five years earlier, was quick to refuse. My grades suffered because of involvement with the revue, but I had no regrets. We had a good time, and it was a great learning experience. Additionally, it served as a diversion from thinking about what to do after graduation.

Dad recommended taking a one-year secretarial course. He had left school at just 14, and by the time I graduated, he was 64, belonging to an older generation when women did not attend university. University was not part of his mindset. Mom, on the other hand, believed that becoming a flight attendant was the ideal path. That had been her big dream, and it would let me travel the world and live an exciting life—the life she hadn't lived. Instead, she started working in her aunt's hardware store at 16 to support her family financially.

There were no role models for university in my immediate or extended family. I applied because my female friends were going, there weren't many interesting options, and studying mysticism to develop spiritual gifts wasn't among them. My parents supported this decision. They didn't always understand my choices, but they backed whatever I decided to do. They trusted my judgment, and I, in turn, tried not to disappoint them.

I was accepted into a general arts program at the University of Toronto, but was denied residence due to my grades not meeting the required standards. Going to see Miss Carmichael, the Dean of Women at Victoria College, I appealed to her to reconsider.

"Why are your grades so low?" she asked, sounding dubious. "Do you have a reason that would justify allowing you into residence?"

"My grades are low due to my involvement in the musical Spring Run Off," I replied. "Additionally, I was working part-time during the school year to save enough money for university, since my family cannot afford to send me."

"I've heard of Spring Run Off. Only students performed, right?" she asked, impressed.

Pausing to reconsider, she finally said, "I have one spot available in a small shared room at the oldest women's residence, Annesley Hall."

"Thank you so much. I appreciate it," I replied, overjoyed to be accepted into a residence with an old tradition. As a first-year student, a freshie, it would be easy to blend into anonymity and settle into my new group's sense of security. This thought quickly faded with her next words.

"However," she continued, "I have a favor to ask. Could you speak on behalf of all first-year students in being welcomed to the university. Will you do this?"

How had I, the one with the lowest grades in residence, been chosen for this? It suddenly became clear. Miss Carmichael must have thought that I, an "almost" professional actor, would perform well in front of a large group of people. How mistaken she was. Owing Miss Carmichael a favor, I acquiesced and would, terrified though I was, repay her.

The man overseeing the welcoming ceremonies was Northrop Frye. At that time, I didn't know that Dr. Frye was considered the world's leading expert on the Bible and a giant in literary criticism. We were seated next to each other at the dinner preceding the ceremony. As a dinner companion, he was kind and encouraging, sharing that he played the organ. Although he seemed shy, I did my best to keep up my end of the conversation. After dinner, we were chauffeured to a large lecture hall where a vast number of people had gathered. We were shown to our seats on stage, and the ceremony began.

I was almost catatonic with fear. This could be The Rose of Tralee revisited. The same panic I had felt so many years ago while singing a solo in primary school returned. The words of my speech disappeared from memory. I forced my attention back to the room. Northrop Frye was nearing the end of his welcoming talk. He looked over and began to introduce me. I rose from my chair and made the long walk to the podium. Only fragments of the speech remained in consciousness. Holding onto one of these fragments, I leaned into the microphone and started to speak. My heart raced in my chest. I recited as much as I could remember and hopefully strung the words together in a somewhat acceptable order. Once finished, and through blurred vision, I found my seat again and, immobilized, waited for the evening to end. I hadn't done it perfectly, but I had been adequate.

Although only 18, I began to wonder why the universe kept pushing me into public view. When I say I wasn't a particularly good athlete, singer, or speech giver, it's true. Others were more talented and sought the accolades, while I avoided visibility. Why, then, did this pattern continue? At that time, I was too young to understand that my destiny would require me to step forward with my mystical gifts. I was still trying to hide them and be like everyone else—whatever that meant. The universe gives us opportunities to recognize a pattern in our lives that serves our soul's purpose, but it may be decades before we recognize what that pattern is.

Fortunately, this moment of visibility with Northrop Frye passed, and I fell back into the old pattern of being an average, anonymous student. This continued for the next three years of majoring in English and minoring in Psychology. University, like primary and secondary school, was largely about rote learning of information that could be repeated verbatim on exams. It did not appeal to my inherently experiential, creative, and intuitive way of viewing and learning from the world. The traditional educational system favored left-brain dominance, leaving my right brain starved by that system.

Why did I stay, you may wonder? Simple. I couldn't think of anything else to do. After the first year, I applied to be a flight attendant (Mom's dream) with the idea of traveling the world. However, being too short—at least that's what they said—I was not accepted. There was no other career path beckoning; thus, for lack of positive alternatives, I continued at university.

I excelled in one thing there: I became the residence hippie. My skirts were shorter than most and my straight hair was down to my waist. I tried marijuana—unlike most politicians who deny it—and belonged to both The Beatles and The Who fan clubs in Britain. When The Who came to North America, I managed to get friends in to meet them. Despite my genuine adventurous nature, another part of me was quite traditional.

For two years, I dated Simon, a young man from secondary school. He was studious, clever, and serious, embodying those qualities for both of us. I helped him open up socially and brought playfulness and love of the Earth into our relationship. Although we loved each other, it was fortunate for both of us that we didn't marry, as we needed to pursue our personal destinies. Fortunately, we are still friends and supportive of each other's life choices.

Simon taught me through marrying a more traditional woman that loving someone, because he did love me, is not the main reason to choose that person as a lifetime partner. This was a painful lesson, realizing I wasn't the right fit while trying so hard to be like others. You may have fallen in love in your teens, early 20s, or even later and not been chosen by your beloved, so you know how heartbreaking this is. Now, I know that significant people in our present lives have been important in our past lives, and we're likely to know them in future lives. When we meet again, both they and you can make different choices.

Spirit, or cosmic consciousness, or the Creator, or God—if you prefer those terms—oversees our destiny. It steers us, both unconsciously and consciously, in the direction it wishes us to go. As a child and young adult, I was mostly unaware of Spirit's guidance. My spiritual gifts were inherent and intuitive; I was not conscious of Spirit directing my life. However, when something happens repeatedly, I learned to pay attention. This realization brought Spirit's influence in my life into my conscious awareness. Still, this deep knowing took decades to fully mature. Along the way, I learned that we have the free will to choose to follow Spirit's guidance and to gracefully accept what we would prefer not to happen, but this was not always an easy lesson.

By marrying, having children, and working in a traditional job, I would not have fulfilled my soul's purpose. It was necessary to remain open to unknown realities. However, I might have chosen the conventional if I had not experienced spiritual realms earlier in life. During the secondary school years, I lost touch with the spiritual current that had given me so much joy as a child. But something happened in my first year at university that reconnected me to that life-spring of spiritual energy and reminded me of what was possible.

One weekend, my brother Mark invited me to go downhill skiing with him. Mark had taken up skiing that year and had become keen about it. I had never tried skiing before and felt a little nervous, but he assured me that it would be easy and fun. I thought it would be nice to do something together to grow closer to Mark and repair our somewhat strained childhood relationship.

Sunday was beautiful; it was cold and clear under a blue winter sky. We set off early to reach the hill before the crowds. The morning began well. We rented skis, and Mark taught me to snowplow and how to glide down the baby hills. I spent more time upright than horizontal, so he suggested we try the bigger hill. The ski hill was not large and had a rope tow instead of a chair lift.

Turning to me, Mark said, "Keep your skis together, and when the rope comes by, grab it with your right hand and let it pull you up the hill. Once you reach the top, let go and wait for me."

Preparing for the first run, I stood as Mark instructed and grabbed the rope with my right hand as it passed by. The rope began pulling me up the hill. My eyes were fixed on the skis, ensuring they stayed together. At first, I was a little nervous about falling, but, nearing the top, I began to relax. Taking my eyes off my skis, I noticed a sign that read, "Prepare to disembark." Loosening my grip on the rope, my neck jerked forward. Shocked, I realized my scarf had twisted around the rope. Passing the next sign that read, "Disembark," I was lifted by my neck into the air. Quickly, I grabbed the rope with my right hand again. Instinctively, I knew to support my weight or risk breaking my neck. Then, I placed my left hand on the scarf to prevent it from tightening and strangling me. All of this happened in a split second, and it felt as if time had slowed almost to a stop.

I existed and was conscious in ordinary time and no time simultaneously. There was no fear of dying, although I recognized that serious injury was possible. This thought caused no concern. In this slowed-down time, this extended pause, I was completely aware of each thought and every action. My heart thundered in my chest while, at the same time, I watched it pumping the blood. On one level, I knew my body's physical reality and, on another level, understood how it was connected to universal life. The breeze, clouds, and earth beneath my dangling feet were kin. They all saw and knew me, just as I did them.

Hanging by my neck, I was filled with immense gratitude and joy for my life. In that brief yet fully expanded moment of joy, I also sensed my parents' pain if anything bad were to happen to me. Compassion for them touched me deeply, yet living and non-living were equal for me. I had no preference and knew I had free will to stay or leave this world. In this timeless state, I glimpsed a future where, if I chose to stay, I'd be 28 before my real work could begin; I chose to stay.

In my mind's eye, I envisioned Mark standing at the bottom of the hill, watching in horror at the unfolding events. Although feeling emotionally detached from both my danger and his fear, I wanted to reassure him. I called his name to let him know I was thinking of him.

"Mark!"

Having done so, I calmly surveyed the options. I was hanging approximately 40 feet in the air and moving towards a pulley on top of a large wooden pole. The scarf had to go around the pulley. My arms were immensely strong, much stronger than they were in everyday life. Lifting myself by my right arm, I discovered there was less than a foot of scarf between the rope and my neck. With sure, calculated movements, I adjusted my hands so the scarf would strike the pulley first. Having done everything possible to ensure I would live, I, still with no emotion but with complete consciousness and acceptance of Divine will, waited for the impact.

When my head struck the pole, I was knocked unconscious. The scarf was severed, dropping me to the ground. From far away, still in a superconscious state, I heard Mark, with great fear in his voice, calling out. I opened my eyes to find him leaning over me, an expression of both deep love and profound pain on his face. Smiling to reassure him, I shakily got to my feet and suggested we call it a day. It was difficult to speak. Ripples of the Oneness still lingered, but I chose not to talk to anyone about the beauty of the experience. By this time, I had learned that others did not share these insights, and discussing them would only confuse and possibly disturb my family and friends.

I could have sued the ski lift company for having defective equipment that could not be turned off during emergencies, but decided against it. Despite a slight weakness in my neck, I was unharmed. Many benefits followed. Because of that near-death experience, I have little fear of physical death. Experiencing transcendent consciousness at a young age reinforced a knowing that other realms awaited. Furthermore, knowing how deeply my brother loved me catalyzed a deeper love for him. All childhood jealousy disappeared forever. Lastly, in those precious moments hanging by the rope, I understood that my life purpose was to help and love others.

Each stage of life offers lessons. At 19, I was not yet prepared to teach spiritual truths. First, like other young adults, I needed to master the world of our day-to-day existence. This is the realm of the ego and personality. We must overcome ego temptations to avoid using spiritual gifts for self-serving purposes. This phase lasted until I was 28. During childhood and early adulthood, I learned how to not only survive but also thrive in this material world.

In this initial stage, I caught glimpses of otherworldly light and possibilities absent from day-to-day reality. After the experience on the ski tow, I no longer believed I had to choose between the everyday and mystical worlds. I embraced both as realms I was ultimately meant to understand and inhabit. As a child, teen, and young adult, the spiritual realm was a place I could only visit on special occasions. The ski tow experience, when all time stopped, held a promise: the door to spiritual realms would open when Spirit, the Source of All, thought the time was right.

# 4

# Brushes with the Underworld

Entry into the adult world was abrupt. It began the summer after graduating from university. I worked both day and night as a waitress to earn enough money to travel for a year in Europe. One evening, still in the waitress uniform and returning from a shift, a stranger approached me in the subway.

He was polite and mentioned that he was a musician who knew no one in town.

"Would you consider having coffee with me?" he asked.

Thinking about how I might feel in his place, I agreed. We went to a nearby restaurant and had a pleasant conversation.

"Where do you live?" he asked.

I told him.

"What a coincidence! My boarding house is on the same street. I'd be happy to walk you home. Would you mind listening to some of my music first? After all, we are passing right by my house."

I agreed.

Now we're in his room. I'm sitting on a chair beside the table, while on the far side of the room is a bed.

"Would you like a drink?" he asked.

"Thank you, that would be nice," I replied.

He put on some jazz music, went into the kitchenette, and returned with two drinks in hand. We drank and talked, and I started to feel strange.

"Did you put something in the drink?" I asked, trying to keep a growing sense of panic out of my voice.

"Acid," he replied, smiling—the expression of a wolf who had trapped a lamb.

Shaky inside, bravado outside, I protested his action and hastily rose to leave.

"Sit down," he said firmly, moving towards the door.

The lock clicked shut. Key in hand, he pulled his sweater over his head. Reality blurred. Was this happening, or were the drugs affecting me?

"Stop. I have to go," I said, racing for the door.

"You're not going anywhere."

His hands restrained me. I was lifted and dropped onto the bed. My uniform was pulled over my head, trapping my arms so I couldn't see.

"Please don't, I'm a virgin," were the last words I remember saying.

He didn't stop. I became hysterical and started to cry. After that, I recall nothing that transpired. There is no memory of how I got home. I regained consciousness several hours later, sitting on the sagging couch in the apartment I shared with another student. My roommate, Joan, her hair disheveled from sleep, entered the room wearing her granny gown. Light streamed through the window. Her eyes traveled over me.

"Tanis, why are you in your coat and uniform? Haven't you been to bed?"

She sat down beside me and took my hand. Joan was not a touchy type of person.

"I must look bad," I thought, amused by her unfamiliar action. Fleeting memories from the night washed over me. Tears streamed down my cheeks.

"I think I've been raped," I choked out the words. "I need a bath."

Joan took me by the arm and led me down the stairs to the bathroom on the floor below that we shared with two other girls. Still numb, I sat on the stool where she put me. When the bath was ready she helped me undress and then left me alone in privacy. Part of me was afraid to look at my body. What would I find? Another part was a detached, curious observer. My breasts looked fine. Down further, just below the navel, there were scratches. Maybe his zipper ...? A knock on the door brought me back.

"Are you alright?" asked Joan.

"Yes. Fine," I replied, providing my usual response in difficult situations.

"I called Jo-Anne, as she has a car. She will take you to the health clinic."

Drying off, I dressed and waited for Jo-Anne. At the clinic, the doctor examined me coolly while she reprimanded me for my poor judgment.

"Do you want to press charges?" she asked, while writing notes.

"No," I replied. Aside from the minor scratches on my stomach, I was unharmed.

I didn't tell my family about this experience for several reasons. First, I was unhurt, so why worry them? Second, they might feel angry, sad, or powerless about what happened, even though there was nothing they could do. Third, although I did not consciously know about archetypal experiences at that time, I intuitively knew there was a positive purpose behind the rape. Furthermore, my family would not understand because the intuition that there was a positive purpose for the rape lay in the same realm as the other inner secrets and knowings. Several years later, this inner sense of rightness  was confirmed. I'd unconsciously re-enacted the Greek myth of Persephone and Hades.

In that myth, Persephone is an eternal girl—innocent, trusting, and devoted to her mother, Demeter. Hades, the god of the Underworld, abducts Persephone and takes her to his realm to become his wife. While in the Underworld, Persephone eats pomegranate seeds, which means she can no longer return full-time to her mother's world of Light. From that point on, Persephone spends half her year in the world of Light and the other half with Hades as the Queen of the Dead and of the Underworld.

Myths and archetypal gods and goddesses can shed light on the events we go through in life. Recognizing how we unconsciously reenact myths is an important path to consciousness. Learning about the Persephone myth has been eye-opening for me. At the time of the assault, I was 21, still a virgin, and, like Persephone, was innocent and trusting—the eternal girl. Like Persephone, I had a strong bond with my mother. The stranger was a perfect Hades—he was black, forcibly dragged me into the Underworld, and drugged me. I entered a dark, unknown world.

Although I did not consciously choose to be raped, it marked a time to embrace both my womanhood and the hidden parts of myself. Before this incident, I was a girl. There was little connection between my nice girl personality and the powerful Queen of the Underworld within me. I had flirted with sexuality but never acted on it. I chose nice young men as boyfriends who allowed me to live above the waist. But it wasn't only sexuality that existed below the waist; it was also the roots of my tree of life. Living only from the waist up, I lacked the roots needed to anchor my spiritual self in this everyday world.

Occasionally, spiritual gifts surfaced during times of stress. However, it was time to consciously explore my shadow and unconscious, in which my power and full potential lay. Otherwise, my entire life would be one of unmanifested potential as a psychological and spiritual virgin. My unconscious chose this man, this Hades, as a catalyst to begin ripening me both as a complete human being and as a woman.

This viewpoint may be difficult for many women who have been raped to accept. Moreover, I'm not implying that all women who have been raped are unconsciously seeking that experience to connect with a deeper part of themselves. However, I do believe that this can be true for some women, as it was for me. In any case, I find it most instructive to examine all painful events in our lives to discover if there is a positive lesson—an opening to a greater part of ourselves—that emerges from any pain.

The journey into the Underworld continued after leaving Canada for Europe. A year earlier, I had met Bill and we had become friends. After the rape, we started to date and became intimate. It was a time of freedom. Bill was a stocky, blond, good-humored and extroverted guy. He loved to play the guitar and sing, and he was kind and well-liked. Telling him of my travel plans—a year in Europe—he decided to meet me when he finished university in three months. Saying a temporary goodbye, I left for England myself.

Elizabeth, an older acquaintance from secondary school, was living in London. Writing ahead, I asked whether it was possible to stay with her for a short time. She replied with a qualified yes, for a week. I felt both excited and anxious on my first morning in London. Queueing up, as others were doing, I stepped onto a red double-decker bus. Climbing the spiral staircase, I took a seat as close to the front window as possible. A Cockney driver started up the aisle, calling out, "Fares, please."

Balancing perfectly on the swaying floor, he leaned over and asked, "Where are you goin', luv?"

Quietly, I stated the destination.

"Where you from, luv? The States?" he asked in a booming voice.

Sinking further into the seat and convinced that everyone was watching the tourist, I answered politely, "Canada."

"Just got here, did ya?" he continued loud enough for the entire bus to hear him.

"Yes," I replied, cringing against the window.

So much for the comfortable desire for anonymity! During the week, I tried to look English. Mimicking the cadence of British voices, I cultivated colloquialisms, and bought a Mac raincoat. Increasingly, I passed by strangers unnoticed, but the week was drawing to an end.

One evening, Elizabeth suggested that we visit two English friends with whom she had traveled around India. "Sheila and Patti have more space than I do. Maybe you can stay with them," Elizabeth said.

Sheila's first words revealed she was a lesbian. Smiling at me, she turned to my friend and said good-naturedly, "You subject us to your male friends and then you keep her for yourself."

When Sheila and her partner, Patti, invited me to stay with them, I accepted. I was not as comfortable with these new hosts as with my Canadian friend because their world was foreign to me. They were both British and many years older and wiser in the ways of the world. Moreover, all their friends, except for Elizabeth, were gay. Their idea of a fun night out was to go to an all lesbian club where some of the women, unsuccessfully, I might add, hoped to convert me away from men. This was quite an adjustment for a small-town Canadian in a foreign country, but there was more to come.

Sheila was a witch who worked with the dark side. Her journey to become a witch is a fascinating story. According to her, when she was 16, she met and began living with an older man. Soon after, she started having dreams about being taken to places where strange people performed rituals on her. When Sheila told her older friend about these dreams, he laughed and told her not to be silly. One morning, she woke up with painful welts on her back. Confronting the man, he confessed to hypnotizing her and taking her to covens at night. At that moment, she decided that to survive, she must go to the covens as an active, rather than a passive, participant. She did this, and 12 years later, when I met her, she was still doing so.

Sheila was one of the most powerful and charismatic people I have ever known. She was the first person with whom I could share my mystical experiences. She understood because she had similar gifts. Because of this, I initially hoped she would teach me.

"Could you teach me the mystical arts?" I asked her one day.

Her face became sad. "I recommend you read Ouspensky and Gurdjieff, but avoid witchcraft. Once you start along that path, you won't be able to leave it."

Sheila was speaking about herself, yet she radiated an essential goodness. She never did anything to harm me and was considerate in her interactions with everyone. Although some of her stories about the rituals she had participated in made my hair stand on end, she only showed me the positive use of her talents.

One day, I badgered Sheila for proof of the gifts she claimed to have. There was a box of Smarties on the table. Taking her scarf from around her neck, she handed it to me.

"Blindfold me and scatter the Smarties on the floor," she said.

I did as she asked. The Smarties came in many colors, including orange, pink, blue, green, mauve, yellow, red, and dark brown. Blindfolded, Sheila picked out all the dark brown Smarties for herself and all the red ones for me. This demonstration was an innocent parlor game, a display that could be overlooked, but one day she revealed her talents more dramatically.

Patti and Sheila had both been kind, but the time was approaching when I needed to meet Bill in the Netherlands. I was unsure whether to stay with them or go to the Netherlands. Sheila's world was the Underworld. Yet, she might help me develop mystical and even spiritual gifts, for which I had never had a teacher.

Bill's world, on the other hand, was the Upperworld—the one I had lived in for 21 years and had some mastery over. I had worked weekends and every summer through secondary school and university to pay for my education. Doing various jobs, such as picking berries, babysitting, working on the Ford factory assembly line, being a telephone operator, supermarket cashier, and waitress, had honed my ability to adapt to most situations. Now, I wanted to play. With Bill, there would be new experiences such as exploring museums, zoos, meeting people, and visiting markets across Europe. It would be a much-needed vacation.

I had written to Bill a few weeks earlier, expressing my confusion about which path to take. One morning, the postman brought his reply. Bill's letter revealed deep hurt and rejection. He was a kind person, and it saddened me to have caused him pain. I went for a walk to clear my head and decide on the best course of action. I strolled for miles without a destination in mind, wandering through rows of London council houses, and finally arrived at a park.

When confused or troubled, nature has always offered me a quiet environment to listen to the inner voice of Spirit. Walking through the park, my feet crunched the autumn leaves, and the scent of warm decay filled my nostrils. Taking in the aroma, I wandered until I finally reached the center of the park. Sitting on the ground, I waited for spiritual guidance. Before long, I sensed eyes on me and, looking up, saw Sheila heading straight toward me. Both Sheila and Patti had been at work when I left the house, so neither of them would have had any idea where I was.

"How did you find me?" I asked, shocked by her appearance.

"I sensed something was wrong, so I came," Sheila replied. "I always know your whereabouts. I could locate you anywhere in the world at any time."

I knew this statement was not an idle boast. I'm grateful to Sheila for discouraging me from taking the black path. To be clear, witchcraft itself is not a black path, and I have known wonderful witches who are healers and committed to the Source of All. The black path, however, exists within all spiritual traditions. It is the path of ego and self-service, leading away from, not toward, Spirit. In contrast, the path to Spirit involves the continual surrender of one's ego.

Sheila is one of several individuals on the warrior path of power who, for some reason, have wanted to protect me. I perceive the core of goodness in people's souls, and respond to it. Perhaps this is why even those on the black or warrior paths of power look out for me. They safeguard this perception of their pure souls. At 21, I would not have had enough power or will to withstand the darker forces that Sheila was aware of. Therefore, I'm grateful she never introduced me to anyone else on that path.

As I reflect on those early days, I think about young people experimenting with drugs, sexuality, and risky lifestyles. For those with a strong sense of themselves, exploring new ways of living can be liberating during youth. However, for those who are less secure and more vulnerable as they transition from childhood to adulthood, these explorations can be dangerous.

A fledgling bird's first attempts at flight are clumsy and fraught with danger. Yet, without embarking on this stage, the bird will never learn to fly and fulfill its true potential. Experimenting with various ways to live is a crucial phase in personal growth. If we don't engage in it while young, we may reach middle or later age longing to relive missed opportunities of our youth. I am grateful for a series of experiences, both in my youth and early adulthood, that allowed me to stretch my wings in uncharted territory. This journey has given me a deeper appreciation of the many paths that others have chosen. Hopefully, I've gained more tolerance, compassion, and understanding than I would have otherwise.

What these brushes with the Underworld have also taught me is discernment, which is an essential tool on the pathway to awakening. Through discernment, we learn to choose and to take responsibility for our choices. It's not easy to learn discernment through comfortable sameness. Meeting people with different values, preferences, and lives affords us the opportunity to reflect on our own choices and to review them to see if they are still those we wish. We stretch beyond former boundaries and gradually find ourselves embracing the world.

Leaving London, I met Bill in the Netherlands. We had a wonderful year hitchhiking across Europe, where we stayed in youth hostels and camped. We encountered people from various walks of life, and I could share stories from that year, but it would sound like a travelogue. I simply enjoyed learning about our diverse world and its people: how they lived, the way they thought, how different foods tasted, and what the various markets, churches, and museums looked like. We traveled with one principle: "Treat people well, and they'll give you their best." This opened up many wonderful opportunities for us.

Through this year of traveling, I overcame many fears and outdated beliefs from my early life. Many life changes are subtle and unfold over time as we meet new people and encounter different situations. However, some changes are dramatic and remain vivid in our memories. Three significant opportunities for growth stand out in my memory. Bill and I had been traveling for about nine months and were hitchhiking across Tunisia when I developed a severe cough and a congested chest. We stopped in a small town to rest, but my condition worsened.

When I became delirious, Bill and a young local man carried me, one on each side, to the local clinic. The clinic was a rundown, once-white building, slightly larger than its neighbors. There were dogs prowling through the garbage, dragging off blood-soaked rags and other items I carefully avoided identifying. Bill's arm tightened under my shoulder as they hurried me through the door.

A man signaled for them to take me into a small room off to the side. Inside, a stooped middle-aged man with a stethoscope hanging from his neck sat at a very dusty desk cluttered with bottles and instruments. Bill and our young friend were asked to wait outside, and I was directed to a stool. The middle-aged man explained in French that he was a doctor who came once a week to assist the local people.

The message was clear: "This may not be your ideal clinic, dear, but be thankful you're here."

The doctor checked my temperature and listened to my breathing with a stethoscope. The diagnosis: double pneumonia. After placing pills in my hand along with instructions on when to take them, the doctor helped me to stand and opened the door to the next room.

There were about 20 people waiting in line. The line led to a man standing beside a chair in the center of the room. When the people reached the man, they pulled down their pants, bent over the chair, and received a needle in their rumps. Probably penicillin. I was not pleased to see that the same needle was being used repeatedly, and even less happy to be at the end, not the beginning, of its history. However, being very ill, when my turn came, I bent over the chair, pulled down my pants, and received the injection. Good news, in less than a week, I was well enough to travel. Packs on our backs, Bill and I set out for the next town and the Algerian border.

Border crossings are pretty much the same around the world. The faces and uniforms of the guards change, but their attitudes are similar. Most guards exhibit a surly demeanor that automatically places me on the defensive. The guard at the Algerian border was no exception. He wore khaki army fatigues and knee-high black boots. Black reflective sunglasses concealed his eyes. Given his appearance, it was a pleasant surprise how quickly he stamped our passports out of Tunisia.

"Do you have any Tunisian money?" he asked in French.

"Yes," we admitted willingly.

"Hand it over. It's illegal to take it out of the country."

We had previously inquired at the bank in town about taking money out of Tunisia and were informed that we could. The guard intended to pocket our money.

Bill and I were furious. Full of self-righteous indignation, we left the guard and walked back into town. We found the local market and spent the remainder of our Tunisian money on food. Self-satisfied and righteous, we returned to the border. Men in military regalia milled about. Some entered a hut off to the side where, through the door, we observed a card game in full swing. We continued to the customs check. The same guard we had encountered earlier met us.

"Surrender your Tunisian money," he said without preliminaries.

"We don't have any; we bought food with it."

His face reddened, his torso puffed up, and he declared angrily, "You can't cross the border."

As he had already stamped us out of Tunisia, he could not legally refuse us. Furious at the injustice. I picked up my pack, climbed over the fence, and started hiking towards Algeria. Bill, probably through common sense, waved goodbye. I kept marching. It took a few minutes for the guards to catch on to what I was doing. It was even a few more minutes for them, clutching their machine guns to their chests, to load into their jeep. I was halfway to Algeria when they finally caught up to me.

There were four guards, and the one in front insisted I get into the jeep. While defending myself in somewhat imperfect French, I kept walking. I was a Canadian citizen who had been mistreated and insisted on speaking with their commander if I got into their jeep. We argued back and forth for a few minutes in the no-man's land between Tunisia and Algeria. Finally, I agreed to return with them.

The commander awaited me. He led me into the room where the card game had taken place just minutes earlier. All traces of the game had vanished. Instinctively I knew that anger was not the right approach with this man. He possessed the cool, calculating gaze of a predator, ruling over his domain. He and his men could not afford to lose face. Choosing to disarm him with innocent charm, I attempted a Persephone approach.

"My French is not good," I began, exaggerating my girlishness. "The guard mentioned we couldn't enter Algeria with Tunisian money, so we spent it. Now the guard claims we've done something wrong. Surely you, commander, must recognize that there's been a misunderstanding."

The commander calmly listened to the story. His intelligent eyes weighed the options.

"You and your friend may leave," he said, ushering me out of the room and toward the border.

I was exhausted both from the recent illness and this ordeal. Bill and I checked into a small pension in the neighboring Algerian town. There, we met a woman who had attempted to cross the same border with two male companions a few days earlier. One of her friends had been carrying hashish and was detained when it was discovered. She and her other friend were let go and had waited for their friend in Algeria. Half an hour later, they heard a gunshot. They never saw their friend again. She was convinced he had been killed.

In this way, we learned firsthand that many countries neither have the same laws nor show the respect for human and individual rights that we take for granted in North America. This hadn't been a consideration when acting; I only thought of the other untenable option. If we couldn't cross to Algeria, we would have needed to retrace our steps back through Tunisia and then cross the sea back to Europe. That alternative seemed much less appealing than the one I chose. This was not the only time when my intolerance for injustice sparked self-righteous anger, encouraging me to act in ways quite contrary to my usual behavior of complying with powerful authority figures' wishes.

Many years later, a Cherokee medicine man named Swiftdeer told me that to catalyze your power, you often need to confront a formidable tyrant. By standing up to that tyrant, you can harness his or her power to enhance your own. This is precisely what I did with the border guards.

During that period of my life, and for several years afterward, I encountered many powerful tyrants. In protecting both myself nd others in these situations, the universe provided many opportunities to bolster my strength. It was a lesson that I, embodying a girlish Persephone archetype, needed to learn in order to mature and deal with the darker aspects of the Underworld.

Maybe you've stood up to a tyrant in your life, whether it was an authoritarian father or mother, an unfair boss, or a selfish friend. The tyrant could be self-pitying, bossy, a know-it-all, guilt-inflicting, or angry. There are many ways to face a tyrant, and the best approach depends on what kind of tyrant they are. You need to adapt your strategy to suit the situation. Remembering how freeing and empowering it was to take this stand—even if you feared the consequences at the time—strengthens you to confront both inner and outer tyrants in the future. Standing up to "teaching tyrants" is a path to awakening.

Another experience in the Underworld stands out from that year abroad. Bill and I took a boat from North Africa to Spain, hoping to find work. We each had only $1000 to last the year, and our money had almost run out. We went to Torremolinos, a small fishing village on the southern coast that was expanding due to tourism. A friend from secondary school knew a young woman named Barbara who was working there, so we went to meet her.

Barbara, an attractive redhead, shared a simple two-bedroom Spanish dwelling with a man named Paco.

"We have an extra bedroom and could use help with the rent. Also, Paco works at a bar. He got me a job there and can get you one too," said Barbara, smiling.

"Wonderful! I'm in. What's the job?" I inquired.

"It's easy. You sit on stools, and tourist guys, mainly from England or Northern Europe, buy you a drink. Paco gives you a Coke or ginger ale and charges them for alcohol. You receive a cut from every drink."

"And why would they want to buy me a drink?" I asked skeptically.

"Because they're on holiday, looking for company, and you speak English. Additionally, you are expected to dance with them and show them a good time," Barbara replied.

"And what about Bill? Can he work in the bar too?" I asked, thinking he could deter any overly interested men.

"No, it's mostly single guys who come in, and if there are single women, they are more interested in meeting a Spanish guy like Paco. Bill, being blond, looks too much like their guys back home."

"But first," Barbara said, continuing, "do you have a miniskirt?"

"No, it's not ideal for hitchhiking," I replied.

"Fine, I'll show you how to make a leather one," she said, pointing to the one she wore.

So, it was all set. A day later, ensconced in a leather miniskirt, I had my introduction to being a bargirl in Torremolinos. Being shy and uncertain in the situation, I didn't look at any guys and sat staring at the wall. That's when Paco stepped in.

"If you want to make money, you need to smile at the guys and gesture toward the dancefloor with your eyes," he demonstrated, wearing an inviting come-hither look.

Come-hither looks were not part of my repertoire, so I studied how Barbara did it and went to the bathroom to practice. Standing in front of the mirror, I tried to emulate Paco's come-hither look and burst out laughing at my rolling eyeballs. Closing my eyes, I visualized Marilyn Monroe's drooping lids and gave it another try. Better. With only $200 left, Bill and I had no time to waste. On the third try, I added a little smile. This was as good as my come-hither was going to get without years of practice. Nervous, I returned to the bar and plopped down next to a man sitting alone. "This is one of my favorite songs," I told him, bending the truth and glancing towards the dancefloor.

Off we went for a few dances, and he invited me back to the bar for a drink. I don't drink hard alcohol, but recalling Paco's recommendations, I ordered the smallest drink with the most alcohol, knowing the drink would be ginger ale. This way, I could keep drinking all night. My first, second, and third nights passed without incident. By then, I'd met the other bar girls, many of whom were older than me, Spanish, and looked as though they'd had a hard life. They were welcoming but kept their eyes on the customers and often left with them.

Then came night four. I was dancing with an older, proper English gentleman who sought more than just dancing. He was having a hard time accepting "no" for an answer.

"But that's what you girls do, isn't it?" he asked. "You go with guys for a fee who want to spend the night with you. Those women," he said, nodding at the older Spanish bargirls, "are here to meet clients."

The light went on. This was turning into an interesting year. First, I became friends with a gay witch and now I was dealing with prostitutes. I told the keen Brit to try those ladies and from then on passed overly-interested guys to that end of the bar where my new friends were happy to accommodate them. Having become more observant, I recalled that I sometimes saw Paco around town arm in arm with older women tourists. I decided to talk to Barbara about this.

"I've noticed that Paco often goes out with other women. Doesn't that bother you?" I asked.

"It's business," she replied. "They're here for a hot Spanish lover, and Paco has some regulars who return every year."

Hearing that Paco was a gigolo was shocking. My parents were set to arrive in a week to visit. It was their first time away from Canada, and it was a big deal. Their well-behaved daughter had now become a bar girl living with a gigolo. Oh no, not good.

I must have shown disgust as Barbara looked at me sternly and said, "In Spain, there are few choices for young men to make money if they're poor. Paco does what he can to get money so he can buy his own bar. He is kind to those women, and he is kind to me."

"You're right," I apologized. "I'm being a prude. He is a lovely guy, and those women are lucky to know him. Still, my parents won't be ready for this."

When Mom and Dad arrived, Paco rented a car and went out of his way to give them a tour and ensure they had a good time. They appreciated everything Paco did for them, and I never mentioned his other vocation. Barbara and Paco helped me overcome the sexual prejudices acquired from my family and small-town life. Like my experience with Sheila, working as a bar girl in Spain expanded my understanding and increased my tolerance for life choices that are often viewed as unacceptable in mainstream culture.

If you have traveled abroad as a young or even older person, you will likely encounter broadening experiences. When facing unfamiliar circumstances, it's important, as you probably learned, to cultivate an open mind and heart to embrace new learning. Failing to do so only leads to pain and dissatisfaction. Traveling is a wonderful way to deepen and expand perspectives while fostering tolerance and non-judgmentalism, both of which are necessary if we are to become conscious.

# 5

# Lessons in Manifesting

After a year of traveling, Bill and I returned to Canada. It was incredibly difficult to adjust to coming back. When friends asked about our year abroad, I discovered they only wanted a quick, superficial account and nothing deeper. Often in Europe I'd felt like an outsider and now home no longer felt comfortable. The central problem was that, although I still loved my old friends and family, we no longer held the same life views. This left me feeling more isolated and different than ever.

Bill was happy to attend teacher's college to become a teacher, but no profession called me. Faced with a significant decision, I asked myself, "What should I do?" I decided to be as acceptable as possible in what my family, friends, and the mainstream world valued while waiting for Spirit to provide further direction. During my near-death experience on the ski tow, I was told that my real work wouldn't begin until age 28, so there was some time to put in.

I decided to go back to university to upgrade my bachelor's degree to an Honors in English. Having gained confidence and maturity during the year abroad, I now had the strength to confront my inner tyrant: the old belief that I wasn't very smart. As an undergrad, I had never faced my fears of failure and only did the bare minimum to graduate. It was time to change that. My goal was to achieve 80 percent, the magic number to be accepted into the Master's program in English at the University of Toronto. Did I reach this goal? No. I ended up with only 78 percent and was not accepted. The door to an academic career closed. But the good news was that these grades showed I was smarter than I had thought. My respectable score went a long way in curing me of feelings of intellectual inferiority. Today, I'm glad the academic door closed, but back then, I had no idea what to do next.

Seldom do we get through our 20s without experiencing a similar disappointment when a door closes on a goal we hold, whether it be to become a professional athlete, actor, mother, or doctor. Amid the pain, it's essential to trust that Spirit knows best how to unfold our unique genius. It's crucial to have faith in the journey and to recognize that even if we don't reach our goal, we have received other gifts from our efforts.

Bill had taught secondary school for a year, earning a good income, enjoying vacations, and liking his job. Therefore, lacking a better option, becoming a secondary school counselor and English teacher seemed like the obvious choice. Counseling came naturally to me. Finally, at age 24, I found a job that let me use my well-developed intuition. Often, I knew why students sought counseling even before they told me. This helped me ask questions that saved us both time and allowed students to start discussing their problems much earlier. My code of ethics regarding the use of intuition was to only look as deeply as a person wanted to be seen. I honored the students' inner privacy. My motivation was to help, and they must have sensed it because I was highly sought after by students.

Non-academic and somewhat tough teenage boys were my favorites. This surprised other teachers because, with hair down to my waist, I still looked 18. We connected well because I genuinely cared about them and treated them with respect. Although outwardly girlish, travel had made me streetwise. They knew I was no pushover, but also that I would stand up for them. One of my goals was to help these teenage boys to smooth out their rough edges so they could succeed while keeping their inner integrity. We teach and preach what we are learning ourselves.

Although most of my work involved counseling, I taught two English classes: one for eighth grade and one for eleventh grade. With these students, I experimented with different learning methods, as much as possible within the constraints of a traditional school system. For example, knowing how even the word "speech" induces fear, I suggested that the eleventh grade students give a "presentation." This allowed everyone, not only the academic students, to excel and built self-confidence in non-academic students.

Each student chose something they were passionate about, such as motorcycles, baseball, dog grooming, music, baking, etc. They could bring in pictures or props and, if needed, even have another student help them. Then, their peers evaluated their work and provided feedback on what they did well and suggestions for improvement. This process taught discernment and critical thinking to the students, and since I made peer grades account for 50 percent of the final grade, the students understood that I valued their opinions.

However, sometimes my teaching experiments went awry. I took the grade eleven students to contemporary theatre productions at a time when the curriculum primarily focused on Shakespeare. Our evenings out usually went smoothly, but once, I nearly got into serious trouble. Here's what happened: I called a favorite playhouse in Toronto.

"Is your play about men in prison suitable for 16-year-olds?" I asked. "If it is, I'll bring my class of 30 students."

"Oh yes, they'll love it," replied the ticket seller. Later, I realized that I should have asked for more details.

Looking forward to the play, we arrived and seated ourselves. The first act consisted of every swear word you could imagine, nudity, and masturbation. By intermission, I was in shock and already visualizing being called into the principal's office and given my termination papers. The principal and I were not fond of each other, and he would have relished a reason to fire me. It was his first year as a principal, and having just transitioned from the army, he believed that everyone should fulfill his requests unquestioningly. Early on, he had jokingly—let's give him the benefit of the doubt—asked me to sit on his lap and I had refused. You can see how we came to loggerheads. Five years later, he was dismissed for unethical conduct, so karma did come home to roost.

During intermission, the students gathered around and thanked me profusely for bringing them to the play. The class toughs, nudge nudge, wink wink, were especially eager to say how much they were enjoying the performance. This was a bad sign. The second act continued much the same. Sleep, not surprisingly, eluded me that night. The next morning, I entered the office anxiously and was greeted by the principal's secretary. Her daughter was one of the students who had been with me the previous evening.

"My daughter said it was a wonderful play," she said, smiling. "It was very kind of you to take them."

A sense of well-being washed over me. The students appreciated what I was doing for them, and their silence was a way of showing it.

Jim Gollert, the head of the counseling department, encouraged my initiative. For example, when I suggested that morale in the school was flagging and that the teachers and students needed a play day together, he said, "Why don't you organize it!" So I did. We closed the school for a day, and 1600 students and teachers chose activities they wanted to do together, including bowling, art gallery, museum, classical concerts, pottery making, Italian cooking, and many other options. This was only one of the many events where Jim supported new projects I was able to initiate for the school. I remain grateful to this day for his encouragement of a young teacher in her first full-time job.

Over the next three years, I earned a Master's degree in Counseling and Adult Education, studying at night and during the summer while continuing to work in the secondary school system. During this period, I gained skills that would be useful in the future, such as speaking in groups, teaching, and organizing events. I learned and practiced the essential rules for surviving and thriving in our Western culture.

Still, it was impossible to fully develop or use my greatest gifts by continuing to work within the school system. It was too restrictive, so I submitted my resignation. This dilemma may confront many of us when we realize we can do a good job in a profession but are not fulfilled. Our talents and interests lie elsewhere.

There's one more thing that Bill and I accomplished during that time. We had little money, but thanks to Dad's proud co-signature on the bank's mortgage, we managed to secure two mortgages to buy a house. We lived on one floor, slept on a mattress in the dining room, and the bathroom was in the unfinished basement. We rented out the second floor to cover

Simon Llewellyn my first love

The secondary school teacher

Practicing my come-hither look as a bar girl

the mortgage payments, and somehow, we swung it. This experience, even more than teaching, made me feel like a responsible adult. This stage of my life felt complete and finished.

Let me explain. Before we can fully develop our spiritual selves and answer our soul's call, it is necessary to master our material world. This can happen in many ways. It may entail working in a traditional job where we test our skills. This was my path, but it could just as easily mean devoting yourself to raising a family. If you are a musician, it could involve developing your style and then marketing your work. What is common to each of these paths is that we learn the rules by which our society operates, ensure we can financially support ourselves, foster healthy relationships, and learn to balance our needs with the needs of others. This period of development typically lasts until approximately age 30, although this may vary depending on the personality and soul gifts of the individual.

These predictable stages of development are referenced in many spiritual traditions. For example, Jesus did not commence his spiritual ministry until he was 30 years old. Similarly, Gautama Siddhartha was a husband and father before he renounced his physical riches, became an ascetic, and began his search for the Divine. He was approximately 28 at that time and 35 when he attained enlightenment as the Buddha.

Sometimes, there may be a dramatic break between the first stage of our lives and our second, as there was with Siddhartha. Other times, we can continue to live and work within both the traditional and spiritual worlds. We need to learn the practical skills of surviving and even thriving in our culture while developing a strong, well-integrated personality before embarking on our spiritual journey. I began my soul's quest to discover and fulfill my spiritual purpose at age 28.

Over several years, I grew increasingly interested in spirituality and signaled to the universe my willingness to embark on a spiritual journey. This happened in two ways. In 1966, during the first year at university, I attended a lecture by Maharishi Mahesh Yogi, the guru of The Beatles. At that time, I knew Transcendental Meditation (TM) was a path I would pursue later. After starting teaching and establishing a regular schedule,

I began practicing TM. Hungry for spiritual growth, I was immediately drawn to meditation, discovered the peace and calm that TM offers, and looked forward to my twice-daily sittings.

Also, since my early 20s, I have been an avid reader of books about inner mysteries and other dimensions. The writings of Rudolf Steiner, Leadbeater, and Edgar Cayce served as my introduction to this subject. My reasons for meditating and reading books on these topics were to become enlightened and to develop as a noble human being. Through meditation, I sought to purify my negative thoughts, feelings, and actions so I could be more compassionate toward others. I also wanted to understand more about the mystical experiences that had come to me unbidden, on and off, since birth. Spiritual hunger attracts the notice of Spirit, but until this time, I was pursuing my interest independently and had not sought help from other teachers. Still, knocking on heaven's door awakens Spirit's interest in helping us along the path to consciousness. This may happen in surprising ways.

# 6

# Beyond Limits

Bill and I put on our backpacks to travel again. Our journey lasted 20 months through Mexico, Central and South America, the South Pacific Islands, Australia, New Zealand, and Southeast Asia. Traveling for long periods serves many functions in my life. By reducing possessions to what is possible to carry in a backpack, simplifies priorities. Additionally, by traveling on local buses, staying in simple accommodations, and eating with the people of each country, I discover—as much as an outsider can—the values of diverse cultures. I empty my Western values, strip down to the basics, and fill up with new insights about different ways to live a meaningful life.

So many new things were learned on that journey. For example, to push past my physical boundaries and survive, and to be humble, witnessing the love showered on us by those less fortunate. Finally, my intuition was increasing, and I knew it was connected to my soul's purpose. That said, there was no clarity on how to use these spiritual gifts, as they were not accepted in our Western culture. One situation, which I call the Amazonian endurance test, taught me all of these lessons.

We were in Quito, Ecuador, when we heard about a trip up a tributary of the Amazon River to visit an aboriginal community that had been headhunters in the previous generation. Being avid followers of National Geographic, this idea appealed to us. We set out by local bus and traveled through increasingly remote countryside until we arrived at the small village from which the trip departed. There, we met a native guide, Hector, who conducted these adventures. The cost for three days, including food, was $18. This low price raised cautionary flags for me, as did a book of comments Hector showed us, written by "survivors" of previous expeditions.

"Only for individuals in A1 physical shape."

"Definitely not for females."

"The most physically grueling experience of my life."

I suggested to Bill that we back out, as all three comments excluded me. But Bill, raised on Tarzan as a child, was gung-ho. He spoke with others who were interested in going, and they thought the comments must be exaggerated. That night, my dreams were filled with premonitions of disaster.

A beautiful sunrise greeted us the next morning. After a quick breakfast of stale bread and instant coffee, we set out in a dugout canoe with a motor attached to the back. The water was calm and the sun warm. Gradually, I relaxed as we moved deeper into the jungle. Sinking into a state of well-being, I was roused some hours later when our bow ground to a halt on the muddy shore. We disembarked, and our canoe departed. We waited for the chief of the local tribe who was supposed to guide us to their village, but he never showed up. After an hour, Hector informed us that our boat would not be returning and that we would have to walk to the village, which was over 35 kilometers away.

My worst fears confirmed, I decided to keep my "I told you so's" to myself and lifted the pack I was given onto my back. Hector did not walk; he loped. He was tall for a native, taller than me. He might have been anywhere from his late 20s to 40, but my guess was early 30s. He spoke a few words of English, a few more of German, quite a lot of Spanish, and we were able to converse through these combinations. Members of our group included a Japanese mountain climber, a Swiss scuba diver, a Canadian hockey player, an American physical education instructor, and a British equestrian. Bill and I were, without a doubt, the least fit.

We struggled to keep up, wading up to our waists through bogs filled with leeches. We walked along fallen trees that spanned crevices which, if we slipped, would drop us hundreds of feet. My frayed nerves finally gave way when I had to swing on a vine over a raging river. Tarzan had never been one of my heroes, and I didn't make it to the opposite bank but swung back to the middle and dumped. Fortunately, the group was able to rescue me and drag me to the other side. During the last three hours, I had been falling further and further behind.

"We're going on ahead," Hector told me in halting Spanish and, pointing at a boggy path, added, "You walk in that direction."

After they left, I collapsed in tears. Bill, who had stayed with me, raged at being left behind and expressed his anger at me for not being able to keep up. We kept on walking. The next few hours were a nightmare, and just as the last light of day faded, we finally stumbled into the camp where the group was spending the night. The dinner for the eight of us consisted of one small can of sardines mashed into a mound of rice. Dessert was the mushy, water-soaked cookies I poured from my pack. Sleep did not come easily.

"I can't go on," I announced to Hector the next morning after a night spent trying to sleep in the open with a wet sleeping bag. "I'll wait for you to come back."

"We're not coming back this way and you must come with us," replied Hector, growling like a jaguar and slashing his throat with his hand. Much as I enjoyed seeing jaguars on TV, meeting one by myself in the jungle was not on my bucket list. My decision was easy.

"The village is not far. Eighteen kilometers."

Maybe not for a local man in A1 physical condition. However, there was no choice but to continue.

Hector put me behind him and, without another word, loped off into the jungle, leaving me to keep up. The rain began, and my running shoes slipped with every second step. I fell into the first two rivers we encountered, but somehow managed to pick myself up and keep going. I swore to myself and cursed Hector's back. Finally, entering a superconscious state, I alternated between walking and loping. My body moved on its own, and I observed it in amazement. I could continue for hours in this state; pain and exhaustion ceased to exist, allowing me to easily keep pace with Hector. My body moved correctly and automatically while my emotions and mind shifted into neutral. In this superconscious state, it was a surprise when the jungle thinned, revealing a clearing. We'd arrived at the village.

People emerged from their thatched huts to welcome us. They were captivating and friendly. Both men and women had elongated earlobes decorated with exotic jewelry. The men wore loincloths, while the women had exposed breasts. Their village was called Tajuno, and they called themselves the Aucas. We had brought sweets for the children, along with soap and matches for the adults. The children filled their mouths with candies and, with swollen cheeks, begged for more. It made me reflect on how much I had compared to how little they had, and yet they were happy and cheerful. All the gifts were appreciated.

Feeling someone's attention on me, I turned and saw a tattooed old woman watching me from the edge of the crowd. She noticed me noticing her and smiled a toothless grin. She knew what I was thinking and feeling, just as I knew hers. We did not speak the same language, but communicated through gestures and by listening to each other's thoughts. I called her Grandma.

Our visit was a cause for celebration, and shortly after arriving, we were invited to dinner. We were guided to a large, thatched hut in the middle of the village. There was a cooking fire in the center of the hut over which a pot simmered. Amid much laughter and joking, we were encouraged to sit down around the fire. The women scooped the pot's contents into wooden bowls and passed them to us. Nothing was recognizable except for the grit from the river water, which was the soup base. I caught Grandma's eye.

"What are we eating?" I asked her with sign language.

She laughed mischievously, mimicking a monkey scratching itself while the men shot at it with a blow gun.

It must have been an old monkey because it was quite tough. I ate both out of courtesy and to build up strength for the return journey. After dinner, we were shown to a small hut where we could sleep. Lying awake and reflecting on the experiences of the last two days, I finally drifted off while listening to Grandma singing the songs of her people. I felt blessed and protected.

The chief returned from hunting the next day and agreed to take us halfway back to our starting place. We boarded dugout canoes and were paddled for several hours by his men. There was such grace and rhythm in their movements that I drifted into a blissful state. This peaceful state ended as the canoes landed on the shore and we were told to get out. After goodbyes were said, we were left alone in the jungle once again.

"We must walk six hours to get to the place where the boat comes," Hector said in a combination of Spanish and English. Looking at me, he added. "We must walk fast or we miss the boat."

With those words, he set off with his usual lope, leaving me to follow. Taking deep breaths and counting steps, I quickly entered the same trance state as on the way to the village. It became easier to induce this superconscious state where my body performed acts of endurance and strength beyond what would have been possible previously. Many years later, I discovered that I was practicing a tantric meditation called *"lung-gom-pa,"* used by Tibetan monks in the Himalayas to cover large distances with minimal effort. Lung-gom-pa means "wind-concentration" or "mind over matter," and it involves allowing the breath of life, the prana, to rise in your body until you feel almost weightless.

After several hours of strenuous walking, Bill collapsed from exhaustion. The soles of his shoes had come loose and were flapping.

"I can't go on," he said in tears.

The others left.

Standing over Bill and still in a neutral trance state, I said calmly, "Bill, you have to get up. Everyone will leave you if you don't."

"Sit down for a minute and stop marching," he cried, his voice filled with anger and hopelessness.

"I've hypnotized myself, and if I sit down, I might not be able to get up again," was my answer, while still marching in time.

Picking up his pack, I started walking up the next hill. He got up and followed. Several hours later, we finally arrived at the place where the motorized dugout canoe would pick us up. Returning to ordinary consciousness, my exhausted body collapsed onto the nearest stone.

By the time the boat arrived to take us back to Misahualli, Bill and several others were complaining of stomach cramps. That night, everyone except me had developed dysentery. Two individuals were taken to the nearest hospital for infections, and the hockey player was flown back to Canada with serious abdominal problems.

Many lessons came from the Amazonian endurance test. First, it was interesting that, although physically the weakest person, I emerged from the experience in the best health. Second, when the others abandoned Bill and me—not out of cruelty, but because they had no energy left—it pushed both of us to go beyond what we thought we could handle physically. I discovered a previously unknown inner core of physical strength. Additionally, I learned how to induce a superconscious state to access this energy reserve. It was similar to what I had experienced as a child when I tried to fly like Peter Pan and again during field day in eighth grade.

Perhaps you have also had an experience, or even multiple experiences, where you were able to physically, emotionally, or mentally go far beyond what you felt capable of. Patterns often recur in life; however, until they occur several times, we may not be consciously aware of them. That was my experience. By examining these repeated patterns or fractals, we can learn to avoid negative ones that lead to pain, while implementing positive patterns that foster happiness and success.

During the 20-month trip, other spiritual gifts were also emerging. In Buddhism these gifts are referred to as "realizations." Two events stand out that reinforced the growing awareness that my intuitive and even prophetic abilities were increasing. In the first instance, while sleeping on the floor of a wooden shack on a beach in Costa Rica, I awoke in terror of something dangerous in the shack. I lay there unmoving for some time, attempting to talk myself out of this fear.

"There's no one in the room but you and Bill. Don't be silly," I repeated to myself again and again.

Finally, unable to ignore this inner knowing and remaining completely still, I spoke to Bill.

"Bill, wake up and light the candle," I whispered until he finally heard me.

"Be careful and get up slowly. There is something dangerous in the room."

"That's crazy. Nothing is here," he mumbled groggily.

"Please light a candle. I don't want to move without light."

He slowly climbed out of the sleeping bag, found the candle, and lit it. Inches above my head was a gigantic scorpion on the wall. Cautiously rolling away and standing up, my fear subsided. Known danger is often less frightening than unknown danger. Bill sent the scorpion into its next life. Perhaps this was not honoring all life, but we wanted to be able to sleep safely for the remainder of our stay.

There is an intriguing addition to this story. Upon returning to Canada, a close friend said that at the exact moment this event occurred in Costa Rica, he awoke from sleep, sensing I was in danger, and sent energy to help. I wasn't intentionally reaching out to him, but was indeed sending a signal for help. It's not uncommon for friends and family to pick up telepathic messages when their loved ones are in danger or dying. These vibrations resonate more strongly in the ether than those of joy or happiness and, therefore, are more easily heard. Furthermore, people can more readily receive messages in dreams because their conscious mind is disengaged.

If nothing more than the scorpion incident had occurred, I might have lumped it within the growing portfolio of my usual spiritual gifts. However, a second incident took place a few months later, revealing that these gifts were transcending the confines of both time and space. They were entering the realm of prophecy.

Bill and I often joined other travelers for short periods, which relieved the pressure of being together 24 hours a day. For this reason, we teamed up for a few days with two brothers, Bruce and Colin, in Mexico City. Something about them, especially Colin, felt like family. We helped them find accommodation, visited sites, and had dinners together before going our separate ways. Neither they nor Bill and I knew where we were going next or when we would arrive, so we didn't expect to see each other again. Still, we exchanged addresses at parting with the words, "If you're ever in Toronto," which were reciprocated with, "If you're ever in Edmonton."

Two months later, Bill and I found ourselves in Guatemala City, preparing to fly to Tikal the next day to see the Mayan ruins. Not sleeping deeply and caught in that in-between state between sleeping and waking, I saw Bruce and Colin sitting at the top of the largest pyramid in Tikal. I knew with certainty that, as predicted, we would encounter the brothers.

In the morning, I shared the vision with Bill. Based on their last known itinerary, he was skeptical and shared many hypotheses about where Bruce and Colin might be. Unconvinced, I stayed silent and waited with curious anticipation. After all, within hours, the truth would become clear. If this vision was accurate, then what was expected of me by Spirit? Wanting and not wanting this gift alternated. The old fears of being different from others resurfaced.

We flew to Tikal, disembarked, and made our way through the jungle to the pyramids. Bill walked faster than usual as he was probably wondering if the vision would be correct. Breaking into the clearing, we paused to get our bearings.

"Tanis. Bill," a voice called from above us.

We looked up. Bruce and Colin were at the top of the largest pyramid, just as I had foreseen. Bill turned to me and laughed, but I caught a slight unease behind his eyes and his thought: "Oh my God, how did she know?"

We shared a lovely few days with Bruce and Colin before parting ways. Since we were traveling at different speeds, neither of us expected our paths to cross again.

Several months passed. Bill and I were in Peru, on our way to Cusco to attend an ancient Incan ceremony, the Festival of the Sun. The night before the festival, another vivid vision occurred between sleeping and waking. I saw that we would meet Bruce and Colin at the entrance to the festival. The next morning, I shared this vision with Bill, and this time, he was no longer skeptical.

Cusco was very crowded. Thousands had come for the festival. We proceeded through the crowd to the pre-Incan fortress of Sacsayhuaman, where the ceremony would take place. I felt tense with anticipation both for the festival and meeting with the two brothers. As we passed through the entrance of the main gate, preoccupied with these thoughts, I ran straight into Bruce.

Recognizing that these prophetic gifts were not a one-time occurrence, I felt unsure about what to do. I was hesitant to admit to others, even myself, that I possessed them. Since the age of 12, I have kept journals, including one during that trip. Years later, when I reread these journals,

I found that there was very little, if any, mention of spiritual events recorded. Up to this point in my life, my journals are filled with trivial details about everyday life. I wrote about meals, the prices of things, and made to-do lists. It's as if, by documenting only ordinary events, I was unconsciously hoping to keep myself anchored in the physical world. The spiritual world was locked away in a secret place, so much so that I didn't even trust my journal with that knowledge. I didn't mention my first vision of meeting Bruce and Colin in Tikal, and only briefly touched on the second meeting.

My reluctance to discuss these transformative spiritual experiences, even in my journal, stems from a fear of being different—a fear rooted since childhood. After going through these events, I realized that confronting this fear and actively exploring these precognitive abilities were crucial for my soul to fully integrate into my daily life.

Not all precognition ends happily. People often predict sad events because the vibrations of tragedies are recorded more strongly in the ether. Also, foreseen events can take a long time to happen. It wasn't until after Bill and I returned from our trip when I foresaw the deaths of several family members that actively seeking to open the doors to these spiritual gifts became a priority.

The first event took place on our way home as we were visiting my aunt and uncle in Los Angeles.

"Have you heard any news from home?" asked Uncle Wilton as part of the conversation.

"It's too bad about Aunt Bootles' death," I replied without thinking.

"I didn't know she had died. Why didn't anyone call us? When did it happen?" he asked.

"I can't remember who told me, Wilton. I believe it was some time ago and painless."

Wilton called every relative on the West Coast to share the news. Afterward, he called my father and gave him a piece of his mind for not informing him.

"But Bootles isn't dead," my father replied. "Where did Tanis get that idea?"

Wilton picked up the phone and called back all the relatives to inform them of the mistake. He and my father were not pleased. I'd been sure she was dead and was just as confused as they were about the source of this information. Bootles died within six months. This situation established my reputation within the family. The "kiss of death" became the new nickname. Although they said this with affection, they often visited the doctor for reassurance before my visits.

Although not remembering where or when the precognitive message came, I knew the information was true as clearly as if someone had told me directly. Additionally, I found—not just in theory but in practice—that knowledge exists outside of time and is difficult, if not impossible, to limit to a specific moment.

The second example of precognition that stands out occurred in a dream. Dreams are often the first point of entry for precognitive experiences, so if you want to develop this skill, start by paying attention to your dreams. Precognitive dreams usually carry a stronger energy than regular dreams, and if you've ever experienced a precognitive dream, you can easily notice the difference. It's precisely because I recognize this difference that the following dream was very painful to receive.

At the time of the dream, Joan, a close friend, was seven months pregnant with her first child and had asked me to be the godmother. In the dream, Joan was in labor, and I was helping her deliver the baby. I laid the baby on a narrow bed and was surprised at how large the newborn was, resembling a six-month-old. A plastic bag appeared around the baby's feet and began to rise up the body until the baby was fully enclosed in the bag. In the dream, I tried to rip off the bag so the baby could breathe, but it kept growing back. I woke up from the dream horrified at the thought that Joan's baby might be born dead.

I awaited Joan's delivery with a sense of impending doom. One day, the call came—Joan had delivered a healthy baby boy whom she named Jesse. What a relief. Concluding that the dream was nothing but fears for Joan, I tried to push the original foreboding out of my mind. Months passed, and Joan set a date for the christening. Looking for a gift for my godchild, I decided to have Jesse's horoscope cast. But as I listened to the astrologer's reading of Jesse's life, the old foreboding returned with a vengeance. He had chosen a difficult life. The next day, Joan called—Jesse had died of crib death the night before. He was six months old.

Jesse's death was just one in a series of losses. My father, grandmother, and Bill's father also passed away during that time, and I foresaw all these deaths to the extent my subconscious allowed. My subconscious protected me, but at the same time, it aimed to prepare me for these painful losses. It understands how much information our conscious self can handle without suffering overload or trauma, which could lead it to shut down and possibly never open again.

The superconscious soul, the conscious personality, and the subconscious unknown parts of ourselves are all One. They are all aspects of Spirit, of cosmic consciousness, of the Source of All. Therefore, it is truly Spirit that knows how much we can handle at each point in our lives. We must trust Spirit's guidance. Spirit is our best friend who oversees every step on the path to awakening.

# 7

# Assistance and Pitfalls
# on the Path

The deaths of loved ones, following on the heels of precognitive dreams, finally catalyzed me into action. Until then, I hadn't studied with anyone, and these spiritual gifts had emerged by themselves. It was time to intentionally develop them. Being successful in work, relationships, and homeownership, I had mastered the material world to the extent that I was interested in at that time. However, I felt dissatisfied with my spiritual progress.

Age 29, astrologers refer to as the Saturn Return. Astrologically, it's a time to reflect on the first part of our lives, let go of what no longer serves us, and consider what we want to pursue next. Entering the third decade, a period when many start to realize their unique talents, signals from both Spirit and personal interests continually pointed to my spiritual gifts. It was time to act. Reading books on esoteric subjects and meditating no longer sufficed. I wanted to learn from those who shared similar experiences and enrolled in courses to explore my dreams and spiritual abilities.

One of the first dream workshops was sponsored by the Association for Research and Enlightenment (A.R.E.) in Virginia Beach. It was led by Elsie Sechrist, a friend and colleague of the trance psychic Edgar Cayce. This course provided tools for analyzing dreams and emphasized the importance of maintaining an active dream life.

While at the A.R.E. something surprising happened! They had developed a test for Extrasensory Perception (E.S.P.) and I took it to see how strong my E.S.P. was. The test showed I didn't have any special psychic abilities. This was both amusing and confusing. If not psychic gifts, then what did I have? Since then, I've learned that there is a difference between being a psychic and being a medium. A good psychic can scan 360 degrees around a person's astral body and tell you what you ate for breakfast and how many children you have. A medium, on the other hand, connects to the higher frequency of the mental plane from which thoughts that create our emotions and physical bodies derive. For example, a psychic might say you have cancer, while a medium would identify the mistaken thought in this or other lives that caused the cancer.

Above the frequency of the mental plane is the causal plane. By accessing the causal plane, a medium can perceive a person's past lives and read the history of humanity, sometimes called the Akashic Records or the Book of Life. As we develop our consciousness, our vibrational frequency increases. Consequently, psychics can become mediums if they eliminate incorrect thoughts, emotions, and actions. Moreover, a person who is not exceptionally psychic can still be a medium.

Although I don't advertise myself as a medium, I fit that definition. The A.R.E. tested individuals for psychic, not mediumistic, abilities. The test involved one person looking at cards while a second person described what they saw. The more accurate responses given, the more psychic the person was considered. This type of test didn't appeal to me because I am not interested in cards. However, if someone had a physical or emotional problem, the spiritual eyes and ears—located in my etheric body—would open out of a desire to help.

For me, hearing and seeing in this way is almost as clear as if you were sitting in the room talking to me. I don't even need to have my eyes closed and can talk to you while still listening with my etheric ears. This way, I can hear your words as well as the thoughts you don't express. This clairaudience allows me to hear and communicate with beings in other dimensions. With clairvoyance, these spiritual eyes enable me to see the future, past lives, and beings in other realms too. During these moments, I feel larger and more porous than when confined to my physical body. Everyone can develop this ability, and like any skill, the more it's practiced, the stronger it becomes. These abilities develop naturally on the path to consciousness.

Bill Menzo and I celebrating Christmas

With Mom and Dad in later years

Me with local children, Lake Toba, Indonesia

While focusing on dreams, someone handed me a book titled "*Ross Peterson, the New Edgar Cayce*" by Allen Spraggett. Since Ross Peterson was teaching a two-week course in Cancun, it felt like a sign from the universe to enroll.

Upon arriving at Cancun airport, I spotted a somewhat paunchy man with striking white hair and immediately knew it was Ross Peterson. In his late 50s, he wore white pants paired with a Hawaiian shirt. What set him apart from other American tourists was a hint of eccentricity and his eyes. He had seer's eyes—the kind that would have identified him as a witch in the Middle Ages. These were the types of eyes I had come to associate with psychics.

Many times, when experiencing new spiritual gifts, I've been fortunate to find someone who confirmed my vision and gift. Ross did this for me. Ross Peterson was a talented trance psychic, and during several evenings of the course, he entered a trance to analyze the dreams of the participants. One night, he interpreted a dream that had troubled me ever since it happened a few months after my father's death.

In the dream, my father was in a burning place controlled by highly intelligent, mechanical robots. Everything around him glowed with the orange-red hue of Mars. The air was thick with sulfur, and flames flared from the smoldering ground. He saw me and called for help.

"Tanis, I'm in hell! Please get me out of here. I want to come home with you."

At his words, I envisioned him sitting in his favorite chair in my parents' living room. In the dream, Mom and Mark were there, but when I pointed out Dad's presence, neither of them could see him. They quickly lost interest in what they thought was my imagination.

"Only you can see and speak to me," Dad said.

I was distressed about the responsibility of helping him escape from hell and began looking for a solution. Suddenly, a book appeared in my hands, and opening it, I started reading sections aloud to him. It was a holy book, and its main message was to contemplate God, emphasizing that Mom, Mark, and I all loved him. As I read these words, he started to fade. I woke up in a sweat, fully aware of the reality of the dream and despairing that my father was in such a terrible place.

In a trance, Ross agreed that the vision was accurate and that my father was in his own version of hell. Dad had not been a religious man, and when he realized he had died, he believed he must be in hell. Ross said I had given Dad the key to escape his hell and that I could communicate with beings who were dead.

Since that day, I have communicated telepathically with Dad on several occasions, as well as with others who have passed away. I have never initiated these contacts. It's important not to interfere with the work that non-physical beings are doing in the astral plane by tying them to the physical world. Yet, sometimes, during dreams or when I feel a conscious presence nearby, I pause and listen to the message the being wants to share.

Several years later, this occurred with my father. During that time, my mother was befriending a man who was dying of cancer.

One morning, I spoke with her and asked, "How is Val doing?"

"I visited him today," she said. "He was eating, and we had a nice visit."

In other words, Val was conscious and a long way from dying.

That night, while ascending the stairs at home, I sensed a presence nearby. My first thought was that it might be an aunt who had died a few weeks earlier. It's not unusual for those who have crossed over to reach out to me. They often want to convey a message to their loved ones and choose me as a messenger. Rarely do I inform their grieving families that I have had direct contact; instead, I tend to find words that comfort them. Upon reaching the top of the stairs, I entered the meditation room and sat down. I was astonished to see my father and even more surprised by what he shared.

"I've come to inform you that I've just received Val. Please tell your mother that he's fine."

Dad looked to be in his mid-40s, much younger than the 76 years he was when he died. He radiated energy and self-confidence.

"What's your job where you are?" I asked Dad.

"I welcome souls as they arrive and help with their placement."

As he spoke, I had a clear vision of him doing his job. The spirits of the deceased were passing by him. He was guiding them toward their chosen destinations, as long as those wishes aligned with the Divine plan. Dad was not traditionally religious in his lifetime, but he was a good man and a skilled organizer, and I was pleased that he had found a useful function.

"How's Fred?" I asked, inquiring about Bill's father, who had passed away the same year as Dad.

"I don't see him very often because he mostly hangs out with the Dutch crowd. He has taken up golf."

We both smiled at the thought of Fred playing golf, and in the distance, I saw him with others. Fred didn't sense my presence, and I had no wish to disturb him. At the same time, Dad wanted to leave, so I thanked him for the message and said goodbye.

"Look after your mother," were his final words.

Early the next morning, Mom called. "Before you say anything, Mom," I said, "I know Val passed away last night."

"That's right! How did you know?" she asked, puzzled.

I told her about Dad's visit, and she was happy to hear about his current work. I mentioned Val's death before she did to show that Dad was taking care of Val, since I knew this information would comfort her.

Sometimes, people tell me, "I'm afraid that if I explore spiritual matters, I'll face something terrifying, like ghosts, and I'll never be able to shut the door again."

Although this might be a slight detour, please allow me to address this concern. Why? Because if we are afraid to explore our spiritual gifts, they won't develop, and we will remain trapped in the endless cycle of birth, death, and rebirth.

I've never encountered or experienced anything that Spirit did not believe I was prepared for. The door between this reality and other dimensions has opened and closed at the appropriate times. Spirit, or the Source of All by another name, has always protected me. I believe this is common for others as well. However, this does not mean we should be careless or irresponsible when exploring other dimensions. Hallucinogenic drugs, for example, often open the door to other realities which, in some cases, we are not ready for. In my view, hallucinogenic drugs should only be used by those who lack other spiritual access and/or who have strong egos to handle the shock of this new perception while receiving professional support.

Watching Ross Peterson clarified which paths to take and which to avoid. Although respecting Ross's gift as a trance psychic, I did not think it was desirable to become one then, and still do not think so now. Surrendering your will to another, which often happens with trance psychics, is not a good practice. First, how can you be sure that the being trying to communicate through you is ethical and on a high spiritual level? When a being dies, they do not automatically become an angel. Instead, they retain the level of spirituality, good or bad, that they had while alive. Second, the path to Self-realization/enlightenment involves learning to access higher realms consciously, not unconsciously. Third, unlearning the habits of being a trance psychic can be difficult, making conscious access to higher realms challenging. Ross Peterson was attempting to do this and was experiencing significant difficulty.

Furthermore, after the trance ends, you haven't made progress. The fears and resentments that existed before the trance still remain. What benefit does this bring to your waking life? It is better to consciously work on cleansing your mental, emotional, and physical imperfections. By doing so, you become a being of light who can intentionally work with other dimensions.

# 8

# Past Lives and Spirit Guides

During this same two-year period, another person greatly influenced my spiritual growth: Dr. Helen Wambach, a psychologist from California who wrote *"Life After Life."* She led a workshop on past life regression and connecting with our spirit guides.

Before attending Helen Wambach's workshop, glimpses of some past lives had arisen on occasion. Snippets arrived in dreams, while others surfaced when encountering someone who seemed familiar. However, there wasn't a systematic way to access these past lives. As with dreams, I had been a passive rather than an active receiver of information from other realities.

One of my past life regressions with Dr. Wambach is worth sharing. It illustrates how our left brain, which is dominant for most of us in Western civilization, may attempt to sabotage the information that our right brain receives in order to maintain control. We must overcome this resistance and ensure that both hemispheres are equal partners in gaining and processing information. This represents one of the stumbling blocks we might encounter on the path to consciousness.

You might recall situations from your past where this was the case. Perhaps your intuition once warned you, "Don't trust that person," while your rational mind argued, "Don't be silly, you don't even know her." Your left brain convinces your right brain to dismiss its intuition, and two days later, that person does you a dirty. Instances like these increase our trust in right brain knowing. Helen Wambach's workshop helped boost my confidence in trusting my right brain and sharing its intuitions with others.

In the workshop, the lights were dimmed, and we lay on a carpeted floor, cozy and warm in our blankets. Dr. Wambach explained that there are three levels of hypnosis. Most of us experience the first level every day. For example, if we're watching TV and it's time for bed but we lack the energy to turn off the TV, we might be in a hypnotic state. Another example of first-level hypnosis happens when we're driving on the highway and realize we've been driving for 20 minutes without fully recalling our actions.

In the second level of hypnosis, we remain conscious but can access awareness levels that are usually unavailable. At this stage, we can meditate, connect with spirit guides, and explore past lives. The third level of hypnosis is accessible to only ten percent of the population who can enter trance. Both Ross Peterson and Edgar Cayce experienced this, and they were unaware upon returning to waking consciousness of what they had said or done during their trance states.

Helen Wambach helped us access level two hypnosis, allowing us to recall our past lives. She slowly counted us down from ten to one to induce this state. Once we were relaxed but still conscious, she asked us to visualize roses and our house to activate our right brain. From these images, she guided us through tunnels and rooms into our past lives.

In the first past life regression, I hovered over the continent of India and saw a light in the north beckoning me. I descended and found myself in a desert surrounded by sand. My left brain immediately discounted this information.

"This can't be India. India isn't a desert," my left brain remarked.

My inner vision observed my male body in that life—the sandals, robe, hands, and finally eyes, which were a striking green.

"This can't be right," my inner critic remarked. "Whoever heard of Indians with green eyes?"

Dr. Wambach continued her questioning. "What are you doing in that life?"

I stood in the sand, watching men on horseback race back and forth while playing a game. They held long sticks, using them to hit a skull that rolled across the ground.

"This is obscene," my left brain declared in disgust.

"Now you are embarking on a journey," she continued.

I saw and felt myself on a camel's back. My stomach turned queasy, and it became clear that my motion sickness in this life originated from that moment. Not to be silenced, my left brain was busy sabotaging this inner knowing, saying, "Is it camels or horses in that place? It can't be both!"

None too soon and still feeling nauseous, I arrived at my destination: a beautiful white city that rose on the edge of the desert. I had come to attend a Muslim religious event.

"Indians are Hindus, not Muslims," my inner critic interjected.

Dr. Wambach's voice pulled me back. "It's time to confront your death in that life. If this is distressing for you, you can go to sleep and awaken when it's over."

I didn't go to sleep and was amused to hear people snoring in the dimly lit room. At the same time, while being aware of them, I was also conscious of my past life. I lay in a tent with a wound on the left side, being tended to by a woman dressed in black. She was my wife, and that same woman was my mother in this life. They didn't look the same, but their essence and vibration were the same. It was not a surprise to discover that I had known my mother before.

The regression ended, and I returned to full waking consciousness, remembering everything. Although the experience felt true, the questions my inner critic had raised still bothered me. These questions were soon answered. That very week, I had lunch with two women from India and decided to tell them about the recent regression experience. They listened intently to the story and, when I finished, confirmed its accuracy.

"There is a tribe of desert dwellers in northern India who are Muslims and have green eyes," one woman offered.

"Not only that," said the other, "this tribe did indeed play the game you described, and it is from this game that polo is derived."

Their comments went a long way in encouraging trust in my inner knowing. They also reinforced the validity of other guided visualizations that Helen Wambach facilitated for us. In one of these sessions, I met spirit guides.

Lying on my back, relaxed, and deep in meditation, I heard her say, "Ask your spirit guide to come into view."

The feet appeared first, belonging to a man wearing heavy sandals, a poncho, and a sombrero hanging by a cord down his back. He looked Mexican, with dark hair, and his eyes sparkled with mischievous intelligence. He was about 40 years old.

"What is your purpose in my life?" I asked him.

"I'm helping you develop wisdom, but your wisdom is in quite good shape," he replied. "So, I won't be working with you as much as your other spirit guide."

With his words, a middle-aged woman from India appeared. Her black hair was pulled back, and she wore a colorful ruby and gold sari that cascaded gracefully to the ground. She had a gentle yet confident smile.

"What is your purpose in my life?" I asked her.

"I'm helping you develop love," she said.

I liked both guides; however, after our initial contact, I rarely spoke with the man. Nevertheless, I sensed him working with me without my conscious awareness. It was more important to learn from the Indian woman to cultivate greater love and compassion.

You might wonder what a spirit guide is. Spirit guides are disembodied human beings who have not completed their cycle of physical incarnations. Their role as spirit guides is a choice they make between their earthly lives. They possess certain well-developed talents, such as love, wisdom, creativity, and peace, and they assist an incarnated being who needs to develop these qualities. Spirit guides do not work alone but are guided by the Great Beings, including enlightened Masters like Christ and Buddha, who oversee human evolution.

We can connect with our spirit guides through guided visualization, dreams, and meditation. Some people have one guide, while others, depending on the qualities they are developing at any given time, may have more than one. These guides can change as we learn what they teach. As a result, we might receive a different guide or a Master. A Master is a Self-realized being who has completed his or her physical, astral, and causal incarnations. Jesus and Tara are both considered Masters, but thousands of other individuals also work with these great Beings and are Masters.

Working with my dreams, spirit guides, exploring past lives, and meditating all served as awakening pathways for me. I believe they are important for others too. These tools created a deliberate connection to the spiritual world, shifting my journey from being passive—allowing spiritual experiences to happen to me—to actively seeking a deeper connection to Spirit, to God.

For three years, I worked with my Indian spirit guide and incorporated her recommendations into my morning meditation and daily life. One morning, while meditating in a hotel room in Calgary, this suddenly changed. For a while, it had become harder to meditate, and I hadn't spoken with her for several days. With that thought, I called her, and she appeared.

"I've come to say goodbye. My work with you is complete. You've learned everything I can teach about love," she said.

Her words filled me with joy, yet also sadness, as I would not see her again.

"Please tell me your name then," I asked.

When she told me the name of my Transcendental Meditation (TM) mantra, I realized that my six-year practice of TM had also ended. Doing something twice a day for six years and trusting its benefits makes it unsettling to think of it ending. Although I rarely spoke to my other spirit guide, I now turned to the Mexican man responsible for teaching wisdom.

"Are you going to teach me now?" I asked hopefully.

"No, brother. I'm taking you to our Master."

It was amusing to be addressed as brother instead of sister. One part of me thought good-humoredly that he was having trouble recognizing I was female. Perhaps he'd been in the spirit world too long. Another serious part realized he was emphasizing our shared bond in service to humanity.

At the Mexican guide's words, a man I call The Great One appeared. I recognized him immediately from a past life in Atlantis. In that life, I was a man skilled in using a crystal rod for diagnosis and healing. A talented healer, but bored and lethargic, The Great One reprimanded me for not putting enough love into my work.

The Great One is a Master who assists humanity in evolving. In Atlantis, he appeared in a somewhat rounded, middle-aged form. He radiated love, but also disappointment and sadness about my current state. In an instant, I saw our past relationship in Atlantis and knew our current purpose. For several years after this experience, I met with him daily on the inner plane for guidance and direction.

After meditating in the hotel room in Calgary, I congratulated myself on progressing from working with a guide to working with a Master. However, I made the ego-centered mistake of asking for a test of my love. This was the first and last time I had the hubris to request a spiritual test. You will understand why shortly.

Feeling positive about the world, I went downstairs to pay the hotel bill. Due to the lengthy meditation that morning, I was running late to catch my flight. However, I could still catch the plane by acting efficiently. I handed the credit card to the front desk clerk to settle the bill.

After a few minutes' delay, he returned without the card and said, "Your card is invalid. We are withholding it. You'll have to use another form of payment."

"That can't be," I replied, shocked. "There must be some mistake."

"There's no mistake," he said, frowning. "Your account is overdrawn, and we are confiscating your card."

My feeling of love vanished. "I want to speak with your manager," I insisted.

When the manager came, I explained, "My account is never overdrawn. There must have been a computer foul-up."

"I wouldn't know about that, Madam," the manager replied curtly. "All I know is that your card is invalid, and we have confiscated it."

"I need the card. The plane to Toronto departs in one hour. What use will my card be here in Calgary? It will take weeks to get a new one," I proclaimed with righteous indignation to the growing crowd.

"Besides," I added, "I don't have another way to pay."

"You can't leave until you pay," the manager threatened.

Irritation, which had shifted to annoyance, was now replaced by fury. "I will send you a check from Toronto," I said, grabbing my bag and storming out the front door into a waiting cab.

"To the airport quickly," I instructed the cab driver, then sat back, trying to cool off.

"That was your test in love," I heard internally. Remembering the glaring failure, my heart ached. This was the last time I asked for a test to confirm any spiritual progress. It doesn't matter that Visa apologized for the misunderstanding and sent a new card. It doesn't matter that, upon returning home, I paid the hotel bill by check. Confirming these facts doesn't make the handling of the situation right. All trials, whether we think they are fair or not, are opportunities for growth. The universe makes it obvious until we learn this lesson.

Self-righteous indignation at being wrongfully accused or mistreated is my Achilles' heel. This theme has driven me to angrily defend myself since childhood. There is a midpoint between passively accepting erroneous accusations from others and aggressively defending ourselves. Neither strategy correctly utilizes power. In both cases, we identify too closely with the little self, the ego, and fail to comprehend the lessons that the higher Self, the soul, is attempting to impart. Spirit, the Source of All by another name, points an arrow at the area where we can achieve the greatest progress by changing an undesirable pattern.

We need to learn different things at various times in our lives. In my 20s and early 30s, strengthening yang energy to stand up to tyrants and succeed in the world was necessary. However, this was not what I needed to learn in my mid-to-late 30s. During that period, softening and developing compassionate, loving yin energy was key. In doing so, my yang strength became an adversary because it didn't want to lose the control it had gained.

By handling the situation with the hotel clerk in a defensive and aggressive manner, I was not acting lovingly. My ego sought to prove I was right by showing that the clerk and the manager were wrong. If my soul's goal was to be compassionate in all situations, I certainly did not accomplish this with that attitude. The hotel staff were not attacking me personally; they were acting based on the information they had. Gradually and painfully, I learned that staying neutral and being nonattached to the outcome was the most helpful inner attitude to respond best in difficult situations.

Writing these words, I am reminded of the Dalai Lama, who was only 15 when the Chinese took Tibet. Rather than counterattack, he has devoted his entire life to returning to Tibet peacefully. Although he has not achieved this goal, he has accomplished much more. He brought Tibetan Buddhism to the West and became an international spokesperson for peace. I wanted to become more like him.

# The Flowering

*Do not second-guess Spirit;*
*your lists of preferences*
*mean nothing.*
*Spirit is not interested in your comfort,*
*but in breaking you apart*
*until your shell crumbles*
*and you are reborn as love.*

# 9

# Spiritual Allies

Transitioning from a spiritual student in my early 30s to a spiritual teacher in my 70s didn't happen overnight. This process unfolded over many years and only became clear in hindsight. Still, there were signs in my early 30s that I had entered a new, more mature phase of life. It was the moment for my developing gifts to blossom.

In this next stage, I studied with Masters on the inner plane. They helped me strengthen my spiritual gifts and act from the heart and soul, rather than from the solar plexus and ego. In the outer world, I met advanced spiritual souls who possessed specialized knowledge and were dedicated to helping others develop consciousness, and we became friends and colleagues on the path. Also, I no longer taught teenagers; I began to teach adults.

After returning from my 20-month trip through South America and Southeast Asia, finding a job proved impossible. Although it was a fertile time for exploring my dreams, past lives, and meeting spirit guides, I was chomping at the bit to apply what I had learned in both spiritual and personal growth. Unfortunately, it wasn't as easy as I hoped. I no longer fit into any of the jobs I applied for. After six months of facing only closed doors, I decided to start my own company to teach what had helped me in my spiritual and personal development. Three paths to consciousness emerged from these interests. During the week, I worked as a management consultant; on weekends, I taught spiritual courses; and in between, I ran a counseling practice focused on spiritual transformation. Helping others became a source of profound personal and spiritual growth for me.

The dictionary defines a teacher as an "educator, preceptor, trainer, mentor, coach," and teachers "impart knowledge and guide others." Although I have always been a spiritual student, my pattern is to apply what I learn in both personal life and work. As these interests evolve, what I teach changes, but I continue to teach.

Initially, to build confidence in "doing it right," I taught what I had learned from Helen Wambach, Ross Peterson, and A.R.E. Soon, however, I developed my own method to regress people to their past lives and guided them back to Atlantis, Lemuria, and even further to their earliest Earth incarnation. The results were fascinating. Some participants saw themselves living in caves or resembling Neanderthals, while others envisioned themselves as immaterial, etheric beings in a hazy world filled with water vapor and dim light. The similarities in their experiences of Atlantis, Lemuria, and early Earth were remarkable.

Journeying to future lives, the visions of many individuals regarding clothing, transportation, communication, relationships, food, and gender bore strong correlations as well. An interesting fact was that some individuals were more spiritually evolved in earlier lives than in later ones. This was true for me as well. I emphasized gathering all information, whether pleasurable or painful, and using it to improve their present lives. Individuals may begin their spiritual explorations out of curiosity, but for lasting impact, the lessons require application to their current lives. This is the real goal.

In addition to conducting past life regressions and future life progressions, I also guided individuals to the start of their current lives. They revisited childhood scenes until they saw themselves hovering above their mother's body at the moment of conception. My questions helped them determine their life purpose, why they chose their parents, and the patterns they carried into their present life from past lives. Many were surprised to find that their consciousness entered their mother's body not at conception but much later—often seven or eight months into the pregnancy.

Participants remembered how their mother felt about having them and everything she thought while they were in utero. Later, they were able to verify these perceptions with their mother. Dr. Thomas Verny, a Toronto psychiatrist, was researching similar topics. He sent his assistants to these workshops to examine my techniques and conclusions. His book, *The Secret Life of the Unborn Child*, confirms many of my findings.

I conducted these workshops across North America and in Germany. They were called Exploring Your Unconscious, and the content varied as different topics piqued my interest. Past life regressions evolved into future life progressions, analyzing dreams was replaced by healing oneself and others, and meeting spirit guides changed into meeting an Ascended Master. This period was marked by remarkable productivity. Along with offering group workshops, I used these and other traditional techniques in my counseling practice focused on spiritual transformation to help individuals discover their soul's purpose.

However, this was only half of my work. My other role was as a management consultant. Initially, no one wanted to hire me. So, with nothing to lose and suspecting that others value what they pay more for, I tripled my rates. By the end of the year, there was more work than I could handle. It was interesting to learn that, in our Western society, people tend to believe that charging more money indicates better quality. While this idea might be erroneous, it is useful to understand what works and what doesn't in the world.

Clients included universities, government agencies, social service organizations, banks, accountants, resource companies, and mental health facilities. The workshops across Canada were on assertiveness, career and life planning, the dynamics of change, counseling techniques for therapists, time management, stress and burnout, and customer service. I also led a study to assess the training needs of the Civil Service Commission, which was the largest training organization in Ontario, Canada.

For the first five years, both corporate workshops and spiritual ones were equally enjoyable. I only had to imagine teaching a topic, and someone would want it. It was an exhilarating time, being rewarded financially along with people's gratitude and respect for what I loved doing. The common thread during this period was learning to balance personality needs to succeed in the world with the desire to serve others. Although I continued working as a management consultant for 30 years, in those first five years, I felt like a fledgling, trying her wings for the first time and exploring new lands.

To prevent complacency and avoid resting on this success in the outer world, Spirit arranged to deepen my inner spiritual world. Bill and I were on vacation traveling through western Canada when we arrived at a place that was part motel, part spiritual center. While checking in at the office, we noticed a bulletin board advertising various healing courses in the area.

Looking at one of the brochures, we asked the motel owner, "Reiki, what is that?"

"It's a Japanese healing technique," she replied. "You place your hands on different areas of a person's body and allow the universal energy to flow through you to heal them."

"That sounds interesting. Unfortunately, the course has already started," we said.

"Don't worry," the woman replied. "Wanja Twan is teaching the course, and she's very flexible. She'll probably let you in."

We drove to where Wanja and her two young daughters had erected a tepee for the summer. From behind the flap, a large, motherly woman, beaming like the sun, emerged. Bill and I liked her immediately and asked if we could still attend her course.

"You've missed half, but it's not a problem. We'll catch you up," Wanya replied, smiling.

On the surface, Reiki involves laying hands on a sick person's body to allow healing energy from the universe to flow through you. However, many interesting phenomena occur with Reiki. Individuals who initially come to receive something for themselves often leave wanting to give to others. Furthermore, healing is not confined to the physical body and can also help heal the erroneous thoughts that created the physical or emotional illness.

Reiki did not appeal to my mystical interests. Unlike the more mystical aspects of past lives, spirit guides, and dreaming, Reiki felt very simple, almost ordinary. However, developing mystical gifts were worthless without deepening love and compassion for others. And blessings upon blessings, my heart opened more when giving Reiki to others.

Before Reiki, my spirituality was mostly mental and abstract. Reiki connected me to the healing aspect of spirituality. I've never felt drawn to focus on hands-on healing in my work, so I've never taught Reiki, although I was made an honorary Reiki master a few years later. Still, I'm grateful to have met and built friendships with many Reiki masters. Without this practice, there was a danger of becoming an esoteric spiritual teacher and overlooking the importance of physical contact and healing the body.

The fall after taking the course, I organized a Reiki workshop for Wanja in Toronto. Serving others is an important way to develop spirituality, and participating rather than leading a course is an excellent way to learn humility. Therefore, for many years, I organized workshops and talks for other teachers, from which I have benefited. Without respect for those who came before us, we may develop an inflated sense of self-worth. Jesus showed us how to humble ourselves when he washed the feet of his disciples.

After the workshop ended, Wanja suggested we meet a Tibetan Buddhist monk at a center in Toronto. His name was Zasep Tulku Rinpoche. Tulku signified that he was a reincarnation of a previous lama, and Rinpoche means "precious one" and indicates that he is a high lama. These are honorary, not personal, names.

I knew very little about Buddhism but was eager to meet this monk, and decided to wear a burgundy dress with yellow-orange trim and an amber necklace. We arrived at the Buddhist center and were welcomed by Zasep Tulku Rinpoche, who wore an outfit that closely resembled mine. Actually, that's an understatement. Unbeknownst to me, I had dressed not only in the same traditional colors as a Tibetan Buddhist monk but also in the same fabric. Thinking back, I remembered that I had bought my conservative dress in a Tibetan shop. I felt embarrassed that he might think I was mocking him, but he immediately put me at ease with his warm smile and kind words.

"This is what women wear in Tibet when they are to be married," Rinpoche said, his intelligent, sparkling eyes glancing at my amber necklace…the only part of my outfit that did not resemble his.

Going upstairs, we sat cross-legged in a small circle. Rinpoche sat at an angle to me, interviewing two friends who had accompanied us. While he was doing this, I decided to conduct a mind probe to assess his integrity. I have met many powerful, talented individuals, but before allowing them to influence me, I check their integrity for the protection of myself and others. This probe involves consciously merging with someone's aura. It gives me a deep knowing about someone. Individuals do not need to be present, as I can read this information in the ether simply by thinking of them. Because I can easily maintain a conversation at the same time, no one has ever been aware of me doing this. Therefore, Rinpoche's reaction was a surprise.

I had just entered his aura when he turned around and looked at me with both interest and a telepathic request to stop. I felt slightly chastised but more intrigued that he could sense my light touch on the surface of his mind. I knew nothing of Tibetan Buddhism then and only later discovered that Tibetan monks practiced many of the spiritual gifts—realizations, as Rinpoche called them—that I had developed over the years.

At the end of the interview, he invited us back for an evening meditation. During the meditation, Rinpoche did his own mind probe where he thoroughly explored my chakras, energy field, and motivations. I did not resist but allowed this to happen. In fact, I followed him during his investigation.

When he was finished, I asked him telepathically, "Was it my imagination or were you really inside my mind and energy bodies?"

He smiled and replied telepathically, "It was not your imagination."

I felt naked but also elated. Finally, there was someone with whom I could have telepathic conversations. From him, I sensed both gratitude that he had found a friend in the West who had similar gifts and a slight puzzlement about how I'd learned to do this.

A few weeks later, during a group meditation at Rinpoche's place, he asked us to meditate on Buddha. Trying to follow his instructions, Maitreya appeared instead of Buddha. A little shaken, I approached Rinpoche after the meditation and began to explain what had happened. Rinpoche erected an invisible mental barrier around us. He began bombarding me with questions that shocked me into a state of mental blankness while still being fully aware. The answers that emerged from my mouth were stripped to pure truth. No longer did the personality speak; it was the soul, my higher Self. This test lasted several minutes before I returned to my normal consciousness.

"When you ask to see Buddha, what does Maitreya say?" Rinpoche asked for his last question.

He says, "Look again," I replied.

Rinpoche smiled, amused, and said, "Maitreya is the Buddha of the future."

He added four words before dismissing me: "You are a teacher."

By saying this, he affirmed my inner knowing, experiences, and soul's purpose. Some years later, I saw a film about the training of Tibetan monks. In the film, a senior monk stands over a junior monk holding a whip. He fires questions at the junior monk, and with each question, he cracks the whip. This technique puts the monk in higher soul consciousness, and the senior monk assesses his progress. This is what Rinpoche did to me.

Zasep Tulku Rinpoche's center, Gaden Choling, is devoted to Mahayana Buddhism, whose basic tenet is service to all sentient beings. Practitioners are encouraged to develop compassion and open their hearts to assist others. This is what I was attempting to cultivate as well. Most Tibetan practice involves a great deal of ritual, chanting, and visualization of various deities. This combination of heart, wisdom, and mysticism appealed for many years.

I participated in many initiations with senior monks and even took two Vajrayogini initiations with the Dalai Lama. This initiation focuses on self-transformation, healing, and enlightenment—all goals I pursued. Ultimately, however, I found Tibetan Buddhism to be overly mental and opted for a simpler, meditative practice. As with TM, I don't want to diminish the importance and validity of these spiritual practices, but merely am stating that they did not resonate with me personally in later years.

Both Wanja and Zasep Tulku Rinpoche were spiritual allies. They both offered wisdom, support and assisted in my spiritual growth. Rinpoche seemed like a brother, as if we had known each other in past lives when I was also a Tibetan monk. The Dalai Lama felt like an older brother. In one vision, I saw The Dalai Lama leading a group of us from Sirius, the brightest star in the night sky, to help establish life on Earth.

In addition to meeting Zasep Tulku Rinpoche, another significant event transpired because of Wanja. A few years after meeting Rinpoche, Wanja asked, "Could you guide me in a past life regression, Tanis? Then I'll do you."

There was nothing in particular that I wanted to explore, but was pleased to help her. After we had explored her past life, Wanja led me in a visualization. Immediately, a Master appeared.

"What's his name?" Wanja asked.

An answer sprang to mind. "Adonis," I replied, recalling the Mesopotamian story of Adonis.

Adonis comes from the Canaanite word meaning "Lord." Tammuz-Adonis was a god of fertility who was beloved by Ishtar-Aphrodite, the mother goddess. When he died and descended into the Underworld, Ishtar followed him and assisted in his ascension. This Mesopotamian narrative of death and rebirth predates the Christian story of Jesus's death and resurrection. By referring to himself as Adonis, this man implied that he was an Ascended Master and that his ascension was ancient in human history. These thoughts and more took just a millisecond to process.

"He wants to take me above the Earth to see the beings helping with humanity's evolution," I told Wanja.

"Go ahead," she encouraged me.

In a superconscious state, I saw Christ. With outstretched hands, he received energy from the Sun, which he transformed and sent to 12 beings below him. These 12 beings received the energy, transformed it, and passed it on to 144 more below them. These levels of beings formed a vast living grid of energy surrounding our planet. More levels, in a hierarchy of evolution, extended downward until the final circle rested at the Earth's center. There, beings not of human evolution received the energy and sent it upward to the planet's surface for use by humans, animals, and plants. In this vision, it was disheartening to see that all levels of beings were energy givers except for humanity. We were the only takers. It was humbling to witness the incredible love and dedication they showered upon humanity. Furthermore, I felt ashamed of our human race and the parasitic relationship we maintain with these beings.

During this superconscious state, the energy in my body increased dramatically, like being plugged into an electrical socket. I was partly paralyzed and could barely speak while every cell in my body vibrated. At the same time, I felt expanded, as if there were no boundaries between my body and everything else. It was an ecstatic experience, better than an orgasm, and the ecstasy was sensual rather than sexual. The kundalini fires rose through all chakras, which were opened, cleansed, and balanced, while the dross of negative thoughts, feelings, and actions was burned away. My frequency increased, and I ascended to a higher level of consciousness. During this experience, sighs and groans of ecstasy escaped from my mouth, as if they came from someone else. These sounds seemed significant, as if my throat chakra was opening.

The experience lasted for a while before returning me to everyday life. Although it was a deeply personal experience, sharing it with Wanja was comforting. This rise of kundalini energy has happened multiple times since then, always leaving me in awe of its beauty. I don't actively seek these experiences because their beauty can be addictive for me. Still, I am grateful when these ecstatic moments happen naturally on my spiritual journey.

There are methods to stimulate their occurrence through breathing techniques, body postures, and working with a sexual partner who has a similar energy level. I have studied some of these techniques in Tibetan and Native American traditions. However, based on my experience, it is better to purify our ego before awakening the kundalini energy, the coiled serpent that rises through our chakras. Failing to do so could lead to mental illness, uncontrolled emotions, and, more commonly, sexual cravings. All of these can obstruct an individual's spiritual progress. The main goal, if we want to achieve Self-realization and liberation from this pain-filled world of illusion, is to become non-attached to sensual and material pleasures. Bliss will naturally follow from that.

Receiving this vision of co-creating with the hierarchy of Ascended Masters aligned with reading books about El Morya. I sensed a deep connection to El Morya and to Els, who had come from Sirius. There seemed to be a strong relationship between The Great One and El Morya, but I was unsure if they were the same being for several reasons. The Great One had a more rounded body and radiated love, while El Morya was more slender, mental, and emanated will.

It might be helpful to mention a few words about Els since they are little known. Els have assisted humanity since early times. The Old Testament of the Bible mentions them and even refers to them as the Elohim. Els are form builders who work closely with angels, who imbue these forms with essence. Although originally an El, I felt that El Morya had entered human evolution to help us. These questions led me to a third important person in my life: Alma Bell Brown.

A few years earlier, I attended a talk by Alma Bell Brown at the Total Health Conference in Toronto. Believe me, her talk bore no outward resemblance to health. She spoke of angels and Ascended Masters. She was "the real deal," as she likes to say. Hoping she could shed light on the beings with whom I was speaking, I asked to visit her.

Alma would have been in her early 70s at that time. She had short hair she cut herself and wore no-nonsense clothes she made herself. She was about my height, meaning short, with the well-padded body shown in prehistoric art of Earth Mothers.

"Have you come to sit with me?" she asked, radiating love.

"Sit" means to lie on the floor and be guided by Alma through a visualization. Unsure about sitting, I replied, "I thought maybe we could talk."

"Better to sit so I can check you out. I want to see who you're meeting and where you're going," Alma replied straightforwardly.

Alma had been sitting with people for about 20 years, and trusting her, I lay down on the floor. In her guided visualization, I saw beings I'd been working with, others I'd only heard about, and some I'd never heard of. I journeyed through various planes of existence and gateways to other realities. Two hours later, exhausted, I returned to everyday reality.

"I've never seen anyone do what you've done, especially not on the first time. I want to make you a minister," Alma said without preamble.

I continued lying on the floor, trying to absorb what she said. Finally, I sat up and responded, "I don't know, Alma. It's an honor to be asked, but I've always followed what feels right for me and am cautious about joining a church with rules."

"Don't worry about that," she replied. "It's my church, and I give you full permission to do whatever you want. It would be good for you to be a minister since you can legally marry people and officiate at funerals."

Hesitating, I replied, "Thanks, but please give me time to think it over."

I went home, meditated, and called Alma the next morning to accept. I became Reverend Tanis Helliwell, a minister in the Universal Cosmic Light Society. [1]

I sat with Alma for many years and celebrate her unwavering devotion to the Divine. She would cook for you, hem your pants, take you to meet Masters, and do anything she could to care for you.

Although I never used this legal status, accepting this ministerial title from Alma, a spiritual ally, was an honor. This gift felt like a recognition by the universe that I was manifesting the Creator's will. It also signaled that one stage of my life was ending and another was beginning, even though I did not know that until a month later.

One lifelong habit is to seek out an expert—whether a book, a person, or an organization—to deepen my understanding of my transmissions and visions. This curiosity about Ascended Masters, Angels, and Elohim led to a convention in Lake Louise hosted by The New Age Church of the Christ. [2]

There, the similarity between what I and their mediums were seeing gave me a deeper trust in communicating with Ascended Masters. I needed this immediately because, during the final meditation, Archangel Michael instructed me to go to Lake O'Hara for my 35th birthday.

Checking out early the next morning, I asked the clerk on duty, "How would I get to Lake O'Hara?"

"It's closed for the winter," he replied. "It's higher than Lake Louise and it's already gotten snow."

I believe our actions on our birthday set the tone for the year ahead and the next day was my birthday. So, having been told to go to Lake O'Hara, I wasn't going to start the year by saying "No."

Trusting that everything would work out, I approached a local man for transportation. He agreed to drive me to the foot of the road leading to Lake O'Hara. He left with this warning.

"It's a 16-kilometer uphill walk. I don't think you'll make it in those high-heeled boots. Even if you do get there, the lodge is closed for the season. So, where will you stay?"

Not exactly good news. If I hadn't been buoyed up the last week by the confirmation of what the Masters were telling me, I might not have gone. It was frightening to start up the unplowed road that morning. But it was a beautiful winter day, with a blue sky, crisp mountain air, and glistening snow. Fear soon evaporated, replaced by happiness to be alive. I started singing and laughing at my own crazy, reckless action, throwing caution to the wind and trusting fully in Spirit. A few hours later, I heard a truck coming up the road.

"What a break," I thought, signaling the driver to stop. My high-heeled boots had become uncomfortable.

The young driver, clad in a lumberjack shirt, leaned out of the window. "Where are you going?" he asked.

"To Lake O'Hara. Could I please get a lift with you?" I said.

"I'm taking some wood up to the youth hostel down the road a piece. The lodge at the lake is locked for the season," the young man replied, looking concerned for my well-being.

"If you could drop me off at the lake, that would be great," I asked again, reassuring him that I genuinely wanted to go to Lake O'Hara.

"Hop in then."

"Well, that's good news. There's a hostel not far away if I get stuck," I thought to myself as we drove up the road.

"Yeah, everything's alright, yeah," I hummed Mary Magdalene's song from the musical Jesus Christ Superstar as we pulled up to the lake.

"Thanks for the lift," I said, getting out of the truck.

"Just make sure you're at the hostel before dark," the driver advised, eyeing my city clothes. "It gets really cold up here at night, and you're not dressed for it."

I thanked him once more as he drove away.

"What should I do next?" I said to myself, scanning the surroundings. "Let's go check out the lodge."

The lodge was set back a bit from the edge of the frozen lake. Walking to the lodge door, I tried it. Locked. Option one was eliminated, but option two remained. Around the lodge were a few cottages. Would any of them be open? I was fairly certain that Archangel Michael's message meant for me to stay at Lake O'Hara and not down the road at the hostel. Wandering past the cottages, I tried each door in turn, only to discover they were all locked. Running out of options, I reached the last cottage and read the name on the door. It said T.H. Mission. Amazing. The initials of my first and last names and the purpose for being there. I knew the door would be open. It was.

Obeying the laws of this world, it never would have occurred to me to enter another person's property without permission. However, following the higher spiritual law, I was both expected and welcomed. There was some wood in the basement and matches beside the fireplace. The owners had left a quilt, candles, and a few crackers in the kitchen. Overjoyed at my good fortune, I took a walk before dark and strolled along the lakeside and then, feeling the need for more physical activity, hiked up the mountain to view the lake from above. It was one of those perfect days that will always stay in my memory as a moment of complete harmony with nature and the Creator.

As the sun was setting, I returned to the cottage and started the fire, ate the crackers, lit the candles, and waited for midnight. I would like to share with you what happened next, but it's not possible. Attempting to write about that night, the computer experienced numerous problems that lasted for three days until I finally accepted the message. I prefer not to seem secretive, but Spirit does not want me to reveal this experience. Discernment is one of Spirit's great teachings: knowing when and what to share, and what not to.

The next morning, I walked down the mountain and returned to civilization. One stage of my life had ended, and another had begun. For five years, I had been able to grow in both the outer and inner worlds and offered workshops on corporate and spiritual topics. After that night, it was clear that my inner life was set to change dramatically, but how this change would impact my corporate work had not sunk in.

Naively, I thought it would be possible to offer corporate workshops that incorporated my new spiritual self. That's what had happened in the past. However, this was not to be. It's often at the peak of success that we face what seems like a setback, but in hindsight, it actually signifies a deepening of our undeveloped strengths. If you reflect on your life, you might find that this is true for you as well.

# 10

# The Dark Night of the Soul

Until my 35th birthday, experiences with Spirit had mainly been positive, full of joy, meaningful encounters, opportunities, and spiritual growth. I approached this exploration with enthusiasm and felt blessed in all areas of life.

Corporate work had been fulfilling. Financial security, love and belonging, status and achievement, and even self-actualization came easily. The corporate work was both stimulating and meaningful, as it helped others grow personally and professionally. Furthermore, I continually created and taught new workshops on spiritual topics. There seemed to be no limits other than my own imagination about what I wanted to do. In my personal life, Bill and I had lived together for 15 years, and our relationship was characterized by mutual support, respect, and good-humored companionship. I was also blessed with wonderful friends and family.

In retrospect, I see this younger Tanis as an enthusiastic person bringing humor, goodwill, and learning to others. However, she lacked depth. Her knowledge had not been fully internalized or transformed into deeper wisdom and compassion. For this to happen, it was necessary to move to what is often referred to in common parlance as the Dark Night of the Soul.

This path involves stripping away all that the ego has built. It is a descent into the dark, the Void, the Nothing—a state of being no one and doing nothing. It requires the dissolution of all roles to which we are attached. It involves the absence of knowing and, for me, the absence of spiritual beings who had previously helped me. In doing this, I understood, although still dimly, that my deeper purpose in this life would become clearer. Although I had been growing in compassion, especially over the last few years, it had not yet been transmuted in the fire of my own pain. During this next stage, it would be.

The Dark Night of the Soul was challenging and painful, but I would not exchange it for the younger me. During the joyful times leading up to it, I learned to manifest my desires in this world; however, without releasing attachments, it might have been tempting to manifest only for myself. Through the Dark Night of the Soul, I gained deeper compassion for others, and my main purpose became serving them. It's important to note that previous happy, positive years also included moments of the Dark Night of the Soul, such as the deaths of many beloved family members. Additionally, the years spent in the Dark Night of the Soul contained their share of joy and celebration. The paths intertwined, as periods of great pain and grief were often followed by times of creativity, insight, and productivity.

At a later time—which will be discussed in due course—a third path, that of creative outpouring, emerged for me as it does for others. This path arises from an integration of the learning from positive and negative experiences and transcends both. In the third path, we take the lessons learned from both positive and negative times in our lives and bring them back into the world, transformed to create new realities for ourselves and others. It is a commitment to use our talents to the fullest extent that our love, wisdom, and power will allow.

Spirit knows the specific combination of positive encounters and challenges that each person needs to be guided toward their transformation, meaning my path may differ from others. What is common among most individuals is the necessity of experiencing a Dark Night of the Soul on their spiritual journey. This often occurs during middle age, but it is not limited to that period. Additionally, the Dark Night of the Soul may not be a one-time occurrence, and there may be many throughout one's life.

Before turning 35, I was learning and teaching the lesser spiritual teachings, the qualities typically associated with being psychic. At that time, teaching was possible while still being a productive and respected member of the traditional world. However, once I started exploring deeper mysteries and having related experiences, this became impossible. I was going through an initiation, a death of the old personality and ego—and a rebirth into a higher, greater Self of the soul. This was a very vulnerable and private time. Like others in similar situations, I was undergoing a deep transformation and needed to be removed from the ordinary world for these changes to occur. Spirit placed me in a cocoon to transform from a caterpillar into a butterfly. This process symbolizes a profound change, an initiation into the next stage of the spiritual journey toward enlightenment.

By undergoing this initiation, I re-enacted an ancient process that took place in the mystery schools of many ancient cultures, such as Greece, Rome, and Egypt. These mystery schools imparted knowledge about the nature of life, death, and reality, assisting participants on their inner journey toward Self-realization. There, participants in these mysteries were kept in isolation during their transformation. Years later, when they re-emerged as spiritual teachers, they were known as the twice-born. At this point in human evolution, complete isolation is often unnecessary during the Dark Night of the Soul. Many of us have experienced this initiation in previous lifetimes, and the process is ingrained in our etheric memory. Therefore, it requires less time and energy to undergo the transformation again. Still, we are pregnant with our inner child, and it is preferable to be quiet until the child comes to term.

However, I'm getting ahead of myself. Let's return to the experiences that led to the Dark Night of the Soul.

Returning from Lake O'Hara, I resumed my former life, busy and productive as ever, until a series of events changed everything.

The phone rang one day. "Hello, I'm Joe Cote, the host of Metro Morning on CBC (Canadian Broadcasting Corporation)," said a warm voice I recognized from the radio. "I've heard about your past life regression work. We would like to record you regressing me, and then we'll air it on the radio."

Metro Morning was the most popular morning radio program in Toronto, so I was overjoyed and said, "Yes, I'd love to meet you, Joe. I enjoy your program."

"Great," he replied. "Could I come with our production crew this week?"

Joe was an excellent regression candidate. He vividly experienced two past lives, complete with names and dates. In one life, he was a riverboat captain in Brazil named Frazer Montgomery. In another, he was a Portuguese fisherman who drowned after his leg became entangled in the ropes thrown over the side of the boat. Joe presented parts of both lives, enhanced with music and sound effects. It was an outstanding production, so much so that the program was aired three times and became the most widely acclaimed show they had ever created.

The publicity was enjoyable, and within a few months, I had guided numerous radio and television hosts through past life regressions and been featured in many Canadian and American newspapers. Being successful in my own eyes and in the eyes of the world, I was unprepared for what came next. Naively, I hadn't realized that corporate clients might not share my enthusiasm for this emerging spiritual notoriety. This is an example of a typical conversation with someone we'll call Tom.

"Tanis, I heard you on the radio regressing the announcer to his so-called previous life," Tom said, not looking pleased.

"You are jeopardizing the credibility of our work here," he continued intently.

"I'm not regressing anyone in our workshops, and only discuss this topic when asked," I said, attempting to moderate the situation.

"That may be true, but you can't continue teaching here because of credibility," Tom replied, concluding what he had come to say.

"But my reviews for the courses have been excellent for five years. Doesn't this make a difference?" I asked, stunned.

"The topic is not open for discussion. I'm sorry it has come to this," Tom said, standing up and making it clear that nothing else could be said.

Initially, when corporate clients fired me for conducting past life regressions, I was in shock. However, in hindsight, I wouldn't have agreed to stop spiritual teaching even if given the choice. Why? Because if we compromise our spiritual integrity once, it could set a pattern of ongoing compromises that might lead to spiritual regression. This was something I was determined to avoid. Still, it was a deep personal wound because many of those who fired me weren't just colleagues, but also friends.

Within six months, more than half of the corporate clients had fired me. I have noticed on several occasions that if we are willing to give up something we value, the Creator does not require a complete sacrifice. Sometimes, it is our attachment to money, fame, success, and relationships that is asked of us, but if we say a willing "Yes" to these sacrifices, Spirit does not make us endure the entire process. It is only when we resist that we are bashed again and again until we finally say, "Not my will but thine, God."

For ten years since that painful day, I didn't contact a single corporate client seeking employment. Instead, I accepted whatever opportunities the Creator provided, and there was always enough. In fact, this period often involved more meaningful work with traditional corporations.

For example, the Atomic Energy Commission of Canada hired me to prepare their senior executives, who managed international nuclear plants, for severe cutbacks. I don't support nuclear energy, and have participated in anti-nuclear demonstrations, and donated money to oppose it. Picketing Atomic Energy one minute and working for them the next might seem hypocritical. However, my goal in life is to help individuals become aware of their actions so they can be responsible co-creators on this planet. My preference is to persuade people through facts, bioscience, and appealing to their conscience to change their view of the world. To do this, I plant seeds to transform the inner person. Fortunately, I have a non-threatening small body and a friendly personality, as these traits are non-threatening to others.

That said, I failed to sway the senior executives of the Atomic Energy Commission when they decided in the meeting to start irradiating fruits and vegetables as a way to boost profits for their company. Feeling I had failed Spirit and the Earth was painful to bear, but an important lesson arose from this pain. Life presents two goals. The first is to achieve what you want, but this may or may not happen. The second goal you can always attain is knowing you've done your best. Furthermore, success and failure are not absolute. Maybe I planted seeds of sustainable energy thinking in some individuals during that workshop, and perhaps, on higher spiritual levels, these changes took root.

In traditional organizations, I've been fortunate to meet many spiritual allies over the years, and one particular encounter stays vivid in my memory. The date was August 17, 1987. The event was the Harmonic Convergence, when a Mayan prophecy predicted an era of peace and spiritual awakening. A few weeks before the convergence, I felt a calling to visit the Serpent Mounds on Rice Lake, an ancient sacred site for First Nations people in Ontario.

Many friends asked me to lead a spiritual ritual there with John Beaver, a man from the First Nations. We met for the first time at the Mounds, where John and I spontaneously created a ritual for the Harmonic Convergence. After we finished, John invited our group back to his cottage on Rice Lake for lunch. While we were eating, we discussed his experiences with spiritual teachers in the East, and our conversation eventually turned to our work.

"What do you do when you're not leading spiritual rituals, John?" I asked him.

"I'm Chairman of the Atomic Energy Commission," he replied, smiling.

This was an extraordinary coincidence. It felt as if Spirit had guided both John and me to the Atomic Energy Commission to make changes that align with Spirit's vision. This experience opened my eyes to the many undercover agents for Spirit working within traditional government and corporate structures. Those who do this work are admirable. It requires unwavering dedication and persistence to operate within these organizations. I lack many of the qualities needed for this, as you will see in the next story.

Although I'd learned over the years what to say and what not to say to corporate clients, at times, I'd pushed beyond these boundaries. In retrospect, my judgment about what to say and to whom was not working well during this period.

After the media attention, I looked for ways to introduce spiritual truths into corporate settings. Maybe my ego was inflated, and Spirit needed to deflate it. Maybe I was ahead of my time, too impulsive, and needed better judgment about when to speak and how much to share. The universe repeatedly delivered the same message.

Let me give you some background. For four years, I had led successful Stress and Burnout seminars at the annual convention of an international accounting firm. In those seminars, the partners willingly lay on the floor to practice guided visualization and progressive relaxation techniques. Other management consultants were often amazed that such a conservative group would participate in something so non-traditional. I was never surprised because I provided enough supportive left-brain documentation to encourage them to take the necessary risks.

Because of this previous success with accountants, I was thrilled to be invited by The International Institute of Chartered Accountants to deliver the keynote on Future Trends at their annual convention. Successful speakers customize their presentations to engage most of their audience without boring the well-informed or alienating those who know less. This lesson has served me well over the years, and as the time for the Future Trends presentation approached, I realized it was essentially a New Age speech. Why? Because I was going to discuss the paradigm shifts the world would soon experience. I shared my concerns with those who had hired me. They were supportive and encouraged me to deliver my prepared presentation.

The day of the presentation arrived along with the worst snowstorm of the year. The taxi was almost an hour late, making me half an hour late for the presentation. In a disheveled, anxious state, I tied the mic around my neck and faced the hundreds of people gathered there. The presentation was a disaster from the start. The audience was both confused and unsympathetic. I stuck with my planned presentation—a poor decision—because I could think of no other option. Today, in that situation, I would probably stop the presentation and switch to an open forum to address the audience's confusion and hostility. However, being more afraid of rejection and failure back then, I stuck to the prepared material. After all, wasn't I telling them "the truth"? The information was accurate, as shown by how quickly my predictions about changing paradigms in the world proved to be true, but my approach to the audience was not.

Failure to reach the audience that day taught me a valuable lesson: What good is being right if we cannot convince others? Is it not better to say 20 percent of what you know if people are only capable of absorbing 20 percent? I alienated and confused my audience by giving them 80 percent of what I knew. No wonder they reacted as they did.

The evaluations were not favorable.

"If you ever bring that woman back again, I'll never attend another conference," summed up the sentiments of half the audience.

Another quarter remarked, "I have no idea what that was all about." Thank heavens the last quarter commented, "That was the most thought-provoking talk I've heard in a long time."

This was not the only time I found myself in trouble that year for promoting metaphysical beliefs. Obviously, I posed a risk to myself and others until I learned what to say and to whom.

Yet, there were many good times during the Dark Night of the Soul. The notoriety that followed the past life regressions with Joe Cote on CBC may have closed doors to corporate work but it opened doors to meet interesting people. Of these, Father Osborg stood out.

Father Osborg was a Liberal Catholic priest living in a remote part of Nova Scotia. He heard the radio program and wrote to express his belief in reincarnation and his desire to meet me. As luck would have it, I was teaching in Halifax in the next few months, so offered to visit him. His return letter was surprising, as it implied that priests in his religious order were allowed to marry.

"My wife and I are looking forward to your visit," he wrote.

After the seminar, I rented a car and drove along the winding Fundy coast to his home overlooking the sea. An elderly couple emerged from an old farmhouse. She was slender and bent with age, but she radiated immense peace. Beside her stood a more robust man with a white beard who extended his hand and said in a firm, German-accented voice, "You must be Miss Helliwell. I'm Father Osborg, and this is my wife, Doris. You are the first guest we have had in 12 years. How long are you staying, and are you psychic? I have some questions for you."

These two were such a contrast, but my heart opened to both of them immediately. He exuded will and power, while Doris carried the traditional female energies of calm, gentleness, and deep acceptance.

Father Bernd Osborg was one of the founders of the Canadian Association for Suicide Prevention. He played a vital role in having suicide, and later capital punishment, removed from our legal code. He also served as the national coordinator for Amnesty International in Canada for three years. In addition to his dedicated social activism, he hosted a twice-weekly classical radio program during the 1980s that reached as far as New Orleans and Alaska. These accomplishments alone were more than enough for one lifetime, but his greatest achievement may have been the daily mass he conducted for the world. Ordained in the Liberal Catholic Church, he celebrated mass every day for 20 years, and aside from Doris and myself, very few people were present. His powerful mass included great teachers from many religions and angels assisting human evolution.

I visited Doris and Father Osborg for many years, and they had a great impact on me. Doris taught peace and unconditional love through her example, while Father Osborg taught the right use of will and power. They were living examples of how one can serve Spirit while living in a remote area and interacting with few people.

They had no children, and one day, Father Osborg sat me down and said, "Doris and I would like to leave you the farm to turn into a retreat center."

Their offer was extremely generous. Their property spanned many acres with stunning views of the Atlantic Ocean. However, I felt overwhelmed by the responsibility of establishing a retreat center in my 30s.

"It's too much for me," I replied. "I'm still too young to know what Spirit wants next with me."

I know my refusal to accept this large property was passing a temptation. It's easy to say "Yes" to free gifts, but it's important to stay

The corporate consultant

Father Osborg

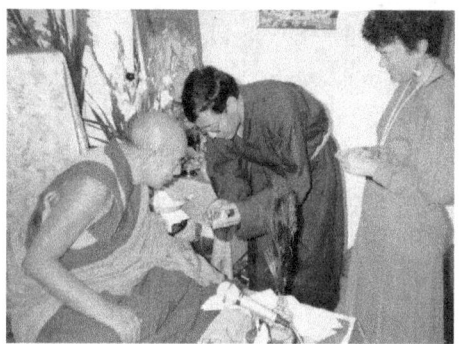

Zasep Tulku Rinpoche giving my crystal to his fellow monk

Spiritual Allies. Left to Right: Christa Faye Burka, Samaya Ryane, Wanja Twan, me,
Jenny Linley

on track with our spiritual purpose. I try to remain alert to various temptations, and it helps to keep in mind Jesus' temptations by Satan in the desert. One of these was to receive worldly power and use spiritual gifts for the wrong reasons.

Over the coming months, something unsettling started to happen. I began to lose my memory. Following on the heels of losing corporate work and facing many failures in the outside world, this blow to my inner self left me feeling numb.

Recalling where I had placed things or what I must do that day was difficult. Sitting by the phone for hours, I would try to remember if I needed to call someone or if someone was going to call me. While driving downtown, even remembering how to get back home was a challenge. I was constantly getting lost. Friends, family, and colleagues began to notice a change in me and commented on it. To them, it seemed as if I was spacing out. In the middle of conversations, my eyes would glaze over, I'd become silent, and my consciousness would depart. Mom would joke when this happened and wave her hand in front of my eyes.

"Tanis," I would hear her call from far away. "Come back!"

After returning, she would ask, "Where did you go?"

That was a difficult question to answer because that place was empty and silent. There were no thoughts or feelings in that space. It simply existed, and I moved through it passively. The veil separating the everyday world from the Void behind it had become very thin, and more and more, I spent time in the Void. In this state, I became numb to both external and internal stimuli, gradually losing my will to return. Mentioning to friends that I was becoming invisible only confused them. Bill didn't believe me either until one dramatic event confirmed it.

One day, we went to see a new film. Tickets were in high demand, so I waited in line with people who had tickets while Bill stood in a separate line to buy tickets. After some time, my line started moving into the theater. Although Bill hadn't returned with the tickets, I, in a neutral state, moved forward in line without hesitation and only became aware of my surroundings once inside the theater. No one stopped me to ask for a ticket. I found this amusing and claimed two seats before going outside to find Bill. He was at the end of a long line.

"What are you doing here?" he asked, surprised to see me.

"I got us two seats inside," I replied, laughing.

"How did you get in without tickets?"

"I told you, I'm invisible."

"I don't believe you can do it again," he said jokingly.

"I'll see you inside," I countered. "The seats are six rows from the front."

I re-entered a neutral state and walked through the cinema doors. Once again, the guards did not ask for the ticket. As the lights dimmed to start the film, Bill rushed in and sat down.

"They cut off the line at the person before me. The only reason I got in was that I said you had two seats inside," he said breathlessly.

That incident did much to improve my credibility about becoming invisible. The reasons behind it were somewhat more difficult to decipher. Part of it was that I was spending more time in the Void to dissolve old thoughtforms in my physical, emotional, and mental bodies. This is desirable on the path of spiritual transformation. However, my total passivity and lack of self-protection were not desirable. When we lose our willpower, as I was doing, we become vulnerable to influence from other entities. A gifted British medium assisted me with this problem.

A friend had given me the name and phone number of Edna Twigg, mentioning that she was an exceptional medium. As luck would have it, two months later, I was traveling through London on the way to teach in Germany, so I called Mrs. Twigg to request an appointment.

"I'm sorry, but my husband passed away a few months ago, and I'm not seeing anyone right now," she said.

"Please accept my condolences, Mrs. Twigg. Of course, you don't want to see anyone," I replied. As I was about to hang up, Mrs. Twigg interrupted, "You're a healer, and you're in trouble. I'll see you."

I hadn't told her anything about my profession or current state of invisibility and lethargy. While I was grateful she would see me, her words made me realize I might be in worse shape than I thought.

The next day, following her directions, I arrived at a modest little bungalow on the other side of London. An average-looking, late middle-aged woman answered the door. There was nothing remarkable about Mrs. Twigg except for her walk and eyes. She walked modestly but confidently with the self-assurance of a woman who knew who she was. And when you looked into her eyes, you could see where that self-assurance originated. Her eyes resembled black holes in space, suggesting she had traversed the Void for many years and had returned with no terror of that path.

"Come in and make yourself comfortable," she said, gesturing for me to enter the living room while she took the cherries I'd brought her to the kitchen.

The floor was covered with hundreds of letters. I sat in the only vacant chair, gazing at the mound of mail, when Mrs. Twigg returned.

"People keep sending me books and letters asking to see me. Look at these," she said, gesturing towards the pile on the floor.

"I can't see everyone. Just last week, the BBC was here interviewing me for a documentary they are doing."

She withdrew her attention from the letters, looked straight at me, and asked, "Now, how can I help you?"

For the last few minutes, I had become increasingly aware of my good fortune to be in such a sought-after position. Intrigued by her, I had neglected to formulate a question.

"I'm not sure what I want. What do you do?" I asked.

"Give me a piece of jewelry that you bought for yourself," she said, sitting down on the arm of my chair.

I handed her a ring. Peering into my eyes, she said, "Your father is here, and he tells me that you were not with him when he died."

Mrs. Twigg could hardly have found a more painful regret. My father had taken three months to die following surgery. On the night of his death, I had been with him and knew by the way he calmly looked at me with resignation that he would pass away that night. I told him how much I loved him, what a good father and husband he had been, and that he could go knowing he had done a good job. Then, I telephoned Mom and informed her that Dad would pass away that night. I asked her to come to the hospital, but she was very tired from working and decided not to come. Never having seen anyone die and lacking the courage to stay with him myself, I went home. Several hours later, the hospital called to say my father had died.

Mrs. Twigg's comment rekindled this remorse. However, she mentioned my father not to hurt me but to build trust in what she would say next.

"There is an entity who committed suicide who is hanging around your aura sapping your energy. Have you been feeling tired with a lack of willpower?"

"Yes," I replied.

"This is extremely dangerous," Mrs. Twigg said. "You must not allow this to happen. You must rid yourself of this entity and protect yourself from it occurring again."

She gave me instructions on how to do this, which involved using my will to better protect myself. I remembered an invocation to Archangel Michael that I learned at the New Age Church of the Christ convention, which has protected me ever since. It is: "Archangel Michael come with your sword of blue flame and seal me in front, behind, on both sides, above and below me from everything not of the light. I ask this in God's most holy name I AM." As I say these words, I visualize myself being sealed in the way the words describe. After doing this, I go through the day or night confident that my body is fully protected.

Having helped with a solution to the invisibility problem, I thought the interview had ended. However, Mrs. Twigg paused and looked at me intently, then continued, "There is a great being who wishes to work with you. I am not at liberty to say who it is, but this being is a stern taskmaster, and you must be very strong to work with him. Even now, you are being prepared. So much will be demanded of you; I'm glad that it isn't me."

"Is it the one I refer to as The Great One?" I asked, knowing on a deeper level that it was not.

"No. It is someone else who will come when you are ready."

I had an image of who she was referring to, but I knew, as did Mrs. Twigg, that I was not to speak of it further.

"Did you know you had a life in Glastonbury?" she asked, jumping to another topic.

"Where?" I asked, intrigued.

"You were connected to the Arthurian story," Mrs. Twigg answered.

I must have looked puzzled, for she continued, "You know, King Arthur and the Knights of the Round Table. You must go to Glastonbury to discover who you are."

Noting that she had said "are" instead of "were," a vision of the individual she was referring to flashed through my mind. It was a knight who was deeply connected to the story of the quest for the Holy Grail. I didn't have time to dwell on this insight because Mrs. Twigg stood up and indicated that her reading was finished. I thanked her, gave her an offering, and left. I did go to Glastonbury, as she suggested, and this started a new field of exploration to speak of later.

Returning to Canada, I felt re-energized and more optimistic than in the past few years. Though unaware of it at the time, Spirit was granting me a brief rest before an even greater descent into the depths. By that fall, I had somewhat accepted the period of invisibility. While still working with some corporate organizations, I was no longer attached to doing so. I had surrendered the outer world to gain the spiritual one…or so I thought. A few surprises awaited me, ready to shake me out of complacency and spiritual inflation. Spirit, not me, knew the areas where I hadn't fully surrendered my attachments.

I knew in theory that on our journey to Self-realization, we must surrender physical, emotional, mental, and spiritual expectations and attachments, and some of these areas may prove more difficult than others. I also understood that these steps aim to create a soul-infused personality so that our personality serves our soul, not the other way around. Fortunate are those who, by the Grace of our Creator, emerge from the Dark Night of the Soul enlightened, but that final goal may or, as I discovered, may not happen.

# 11

# Endings

Life often involves two steps forward and one step back. Spirit had decided it was time for another step back, which would further disconnect me from my old life.

During the Christmas holidays, Bill and I went cross-country skiing in northern Ontario. We had a wonderful time, and on New Year's Eve, we decided to do one more trail on our way to see my family that evening.

It was a perfect winter day: sunny, with blue skies and crisp but not too cold air. We were halfway along an eight-kilometer trail when we came to a steep downhill. Bill pulled off to one side and expressed concern about going down it. My next words and actions were unusual, since he was a more courageous skier than I was.

"I'll go," I said, words I would soon come to regret.

A few seconds later, I lay on the ground, wrapped around a tree. My head was facing downhill, while my twisted left ankle pointed uphill. I looked like the hanged man from the tarot deck. And like the hanged man, the meaning was to surrender and let go of an attachment.

Fortunately, a shelter was a few hundred yards away, and just then, another skier arrived. The two men carried me to the shelter.

"My ankle is broken," I said to Bill. "Don't take off the boot; it's holding the ankle together."

I managed to endure the discomfort for a few more hours while Bill waited for additional help to carry me out. Finally, six strong men arrived, and they were able to link their arms together to lift me.

Just before we began, one of the men, looking concerned, said to me, "It's four kilometers, and there will be a lot of jostling. Are you ready?"

"Yes," I replied. "I know you'll do your best to minimize the discomfort. Thank you for helping."

Then, I shifted my focus away from my physical body and entered the superconscious state that had served me well in the Amazon jungle. In that state, it was possible to observe what was happening without experiencing pain. Nearly two hours later, I returned to my physical body as we reached the highway and our car.

Since it was faster than calling an ambulance, the men placed me in the passenger seat, and Bill drove to the nearest hospital.

"Your ankle is broken in three places," the doctor said as he examined the X-rays. "You will need surgery to screw the bones back together. We can't do the surgery until tomorrow, and probably not until the day after because it's New Year's Eve."

Hearing the doctor's news, the best solution popped into my mind. "This hospital is three hours from anyone who could visit. Bill can drive to my mother's house, and I can go to the hospital there."

"Honestly," the doctor said, "I'm surprised you're not in more discomfort. Would you like some pills for the pain?"

"Thanks for your concern, but I'm fine," I replied, focusing my attention above my physical body. From this superconscious state, controlling the discomfort was doable.

Bill put me back in the car, and three hours later, after stopping at Kentucky Fried Chicken for Bill, we arrived at my mother's house.

"The doctors aren't going to operate on the ankle tonight," I said to Bill. "So I may as well come in for New Year's Eve."

"I don't think that's a good idea," he said with good reason. "But let your mother decide."

He went to get my mother, and she came out to the car. "No," she said, brooking no argument. "You have to go to the hospital right now."

No one believed that I was not experiencing a lot of pain. This was because I kept a mental image of well-being in my mind and sent healing thoughts to the ankle. That said, when I got to the hospital, I asked for the painkiller Tylenol to help with the discomfort.

"The doctor said to give you a shot of morphine if you want," the nurse replied, "but we're not authorized to do anything else."

There's a significant difference between morphine and Tylenol. It was becoming apparent that it would be an uphill struggle to take charge of my own healing in a hospital setting. Deciding against the morphine, I spent the night without any painkillers. The next morning, a surgeon came to check on me. Dr. B was an attractive man, moving not too gracefully into middle age. His intelligent, bloodshot eyes suggested that he hadn't enjoyed a quiet New Year's Eve, and I sensed he was well acquainted with Dionysus.

I requested what I needed to recover as quickly as possible. This was my first time as a patient in a hospital, and considering my requests for different treatments, I must have been a doctor's nightmare.

"Don't put an IV in my arm when I wake up from the anesthesia," I said.

"Very well, you won't have it," he promised.

Regrettably, I failed to request the smallest possible dose of anesthetic because I was unaware of how it would affect me. I woke from surgery in excruciating pain, and each time I received a shot of the opioid Demerol, I vomited. The anesthetic had stripped my aura, making it impossible to control the pain. Combined with bone surgery, this turned the following days into a true ordeal. The last thing I wanted was to eat, but drinking fluids helped flush toxins from my body. I only started eating when Dr. B threatened to feed me intravenously. I trusted my body to guide my healing, but that conflicted with many hospital policies. Instead, I turned to crystals, healing music, and mental imagery.

A few days after the surgery, Dr. B showed me the before-and-after X-rays of the ankle. Shockingly, one of the large bones was still sticking out at a 30-degree angle.

"Why isn't that bone back in place?" I asked, attempting to keep my voice calm.

"That bone isn't needed for walking. It will eventually dissolve back into the body," he replied matter-of-factly.

It was very upsetting that the ankle bone was not attached to the leg, so I decided to get another opinion as soon as possible. Unfortunately, it took three weeks before I could get an appointment with an orthopedic surgeon. During those weeks, friends told me about several malpractice allegations against Dr. B. Evidently, he was a general surgeon, not an orthopedic one, and it was questionable whether he should have tried to treat such a severe break in my ankle. By the time I finally saw the orthopedic surgeon, my emotions fluctuated between despair and fury.

"Why is this happening to me?" I asked Spirit.

"So you learn compassion for another's pain and forgiveness for those who unknowingly treat you unjustly," I heard Spirit answer.

The orthopedic surgeon said that Dr. B had not done a bad job. If he re-broke the ankle, he might get another 10 or 15 percent movement. He left the decision to me.

Dr. B was furious that I'd consulted another doctor and called to defend his surgery. We had completely different ideas of what success meant. For him, success was that I could walk without a limp, but for me, it was having the bone reconnected the way the Creator intended. I liked Dr. B as a person. Beneath his arrogant exterior, he was sensitive, and my heart went out to the pain I was causing him. He was a talented surgeon with genuine healing gifts that he was only partly using. In that way, he reminded me of myself in Atlantis when I was a talented, bored, and half-hearted healer.

I decided not to go through the surgery again, and two months later, returned to the hospital to have the four pins holding my ankle in place removed. Both Dr. B and the anesthetist came to prepare me, and I explained what my body needed.

"I'd appreciate it if you didn't administer a pre-op anesthetic," I said to the anesthetist.

"Why?" the anesthetist asked curiously. "It's standard procedure."

"It makes me ill and strips my aura, so I cannot control the pain after waking up. You do this to calm people, but I am already calm, so it's unnecessary. Also, please give me only the minimum amount of anesthetic to put me under. I need much less than the average person since I practice meditation."

"Do you?" he replied with a smile. "I've read about the deeper levels of consciousness that meditators achieve, and am interested in exploring them. I will try to do what you're asking."

Dr. B watched this interchange with restless interest.

Turning to him, I took his hands, gazed into his eyes, and bared my heart. "Please, approach this surgery with love," I said softly.

"I always do it with love," he replied, looking embarrassed and chippy.

"Of course you do, but please think kindly of my ankle as you do it."

"OK. Let's go! Other people are waiting." Dr. B spoke briskly, but I knew he had assented.

They wheeled me into the operating room, and the staff in scrubs were still painting my leg when the anesthetist put the needle in my hand. I felt no fear and joked with them. I awoke while being wheeled out and walked out of the recovery room less than two hours later with minimal discomfort.

I was grateful that both doctors considered my requests. Breaking my ankle taught me many lessons. It was a valuable experience to see firsthand how our traditional medical system and its professionals operate. Usually, I wouldn't have done this because I prefer naturopathy, aromatherapy, and therapeutic massage for healing. There is, of course, definitely a place for traditional medicine, and I was thankful that Dr. B, rather than a naturopath, performed the surgery on my ankle.

I stayed with my mother for three months to recover because she could take me to physiotherapy, and she lived in a house with few stairs. Three months away from Bill allowed time to reflect on our life paths. They no longer lay in the same direction. Returning to Toronto, I told Bill it was time to separate. We had been together, learned a great deal, and shared many experiences for more than 14 years. A cycle had ended in our lives, and it was time for both of us to move on. Clairvoyantly, I had seen two daughters on his path and had mentioned this to him before. He always tried to talk me out of this vision because he wanted to stay with me. However, neither of us could grow into who we needed to be if we stayed together.

Bill didn't believe me at first, so we ended up living together as platonic friends for over a year. That was necessary to allow the unwinding to happen and give Bill a chance to find a new life partner. Now, he is happily remarried and has two daughters and grandchildren. We shared a wonderful youth traveling the world, buying our first house, and enjoying many friendships. These memories are precious, and there was nothing wrong with our relationship. We can love many people in different ways. I did love Bill, but my top priority was to stay on my spiritual path.

This decision was perhaps the hardest part of the Dark Night of the Soul. Losing corporate work and breaking my ankle were difficult experiences, but Bill had been supportive through those and many other times. Spirit takes no prisoners; it asks us to let go of whatever we're attached to. In this way, Spirit ensures we stay on the awakening pathway to consciousness. We can refuse, but doing so only causes us to regress. I intuitively understood this and knew that Bill could not accompany me on the next steps.

My situation is not unique. Men and women from various backgrounds may feel an inner calling that compels them to prioritize their mission over their children, spouses, or parents. For instance, doctors and nurses working with Doctors Without Borders or other service organizations might leave their families to assist those less fortunate. Others raised in traditional cultures might deeply disappoint and even alienate their parents by not marrying the person their parents chose.

Many individuals, being true to their nature, don't follow the traditional path, and if they did, they would not be fulfilling their soul's purpose. Moreover, simply observing one life often does not clarify why one must choose a particular life path. A person might need to fulfill a commitment made before entering this life or do what they are doing now to prepare for the next one.

# 12

# Soul, Sirius, and Krishnamurti

Shortly after returning to Toronto, I was guided during meditation to go into seclusion for the summer to write a book. Writing a book had never been a goal. In fact, at age 36, I felt I was neither old enough nor wise enough to tackle such a task. When I asked about the book's subject, the disembodied voice said that everything would become clear in May. This was not reassuring. Still, as instructed, I cleared my schedule and sat down on May 1ˢᵗ to start. For the next three months, I wrote every day until I finished the first draft of *Decoding Destiny: Keys to Mankind's Spiritual Evolution*.

People have asked whether *Decoding Destiny* is channeled, and some have even assumed that it must be. Through meditation, I documented what I saw, felt, heard, and knew, but I was always fully conscious and an active participant in the process. I ascended to higher spiritual levels, where my soul resides, to access the Akashic Records or Book of Life. The information in *Decoding Destiny* was not beyond my soul's knowledge because the soul is united with Spirit, which is united with The Source of All. [3]

Writing a book, teaching, or speaking on any topic to influence others carries an ethical responsibility to embody what we advocate. This responsibility is even more crucial when it comes to spiritual matters. If there is a disparity between our theories and our practices, we must close that gap by doing our inner work. To achieve this, we often need to pause, sometimes for an extended period, before introducing new perspectives and ways of being into the world. Five years of editing ensued before I felt that *Decoding Destiny* was ready to be published.

I was finishing a phase of learning and teaching, getting ready for the next chapter of my life, even though I had no idea what that would involve. I spoke less often with The Great One and other Masters. Still, their watchful presence guided and directed me toward increasingly unconventional sources of knowledge. Some of these even pushed the limits of my willingness to believe.

One day, a friend asked me to find the answer to a question that had been bothering her. Ruth was a private person, so I knew it must be important. She drew an image that had recurred over several years and asked what it was.

As soon as we meditated, a great Hawk Being appeared. The Hawk was of the same lineage as Horus, the child of Isis and Osiris, the mother and father gods of the ancient Egyptians. The Hawk said that Ruth was of the same lineage as him. He took us to Arcturus, where, with the permission of the Source of All, beings like him were genetically engineering humans and other races.

Before this meditation, I had never seen this Hawk Being. However, other experiences have shown me that some people might not be fully human. For example, some have come from the angelic, elemental, dragon, and dolphin evolutions. These beings are hybrids who have entered human evolution, but they still carry the genetic and blood traces of their original evolution.

This story of encountering unusual beings doesn't end here. Shortly after meeting the Hawk Being, Alma Bell Brown took me on a journey through our solar system. From a high frequency, I saw an intricate energy grid—which in metaphysical terms is referred to as "the ring-pass-not"—surrounding the Earth. This ring existed etherically in higher frequencies for two reasons. First, to prevent humanity from contaminating other evolving species in the universe with our negativity. Second, to protect humanity and other Earth beings from higher frequencies that we were not yet ready to deal with. This temporary safeguard is now being slowly removed as the Earth and humanity enter a new stage in their evolution.

During the meditation, a black hole appeared in front of me. It expanded, and I felt myself entering the darkness. In an instant, I traveled through a small opening at the center of the black hole and found myself outside of my body, gazing down at the Earth. Intuitively, I knew that after passing through the black hole, I could use my will to travel to another solar system.

"Go home. Go to Sirius," my soul said from within.

As that thought crossed my mind, a gateway opened in space before me. My mind carried me through the entrance and into a tunnel that traveled faster than light to another gateway, which I knew was the door to Sirius. It may sound cliché, but it felt like I was donning Dorothy's ruby slippers from *The Wizard of Oz* and heading home. At the Sirian gate, I requested permission to enter. In an instant, I found myself in a vast area where Beings of various evolutions had gathered in a circle. This was the High Council of Sirius.

Despite there being 12 Great Beings on the Council, I could only see half of them clearly. One was Adam Kadmon, the archetype of humanity. Another belonged to the same race as the Hawk. There was also a Dragon, a Bee, and one reminiscent of Pan. It had an intelligent, goat-like face with red eyes and stood upright on two legs with cloven hooves. Additionally, there was a Being whose presence I recognized but could not see—the one Christians call The Holy Spirit. Overseeing the Council was the Great Lord of Sirius, a phoenix who had risen from his own ashes. He shimmered white, although all colors of the rainbow radiated through this hue.

The Beings turned their attention to me, and the Lord of Sirius addressed me telepathically, "This is interesting that you were able to come here," he said.

His remark wasn't disapproving. He was pointing out that, at my current level of consciousness, it was unusual for me to be present there.

He became more serious and instructed, "Stop breathing."

I thought of my physical body lying far away in Alma's living room, and a flurry of thoughts arose.

The first was, "I might die if I don't breathe."

The second, stronger thought was, "There is no need to breathe."

I ceased breathing.

The next thought emerged: "I can stop my heartbeat and still be alive."

Lord Sirius, through his command, showed me how easy it is to relinquish our bodies and that we are eternal. The Great Beings turned their attention back towards their circle, signaling that the interview had ended. They needed to continue their work without interruption from this novice.

"Thank you," I said, telepathically sending my appreciation to them. As I withdrew down the tunnel, I found myself in space once again. Next, I attempted to reach higher vibrational frequencies, but without a clear goal, I couldn't progress further. This was, in itself, an interesting observation.

"Travel down into the microcosm, and you'll learn all the lessons you would receive by voyaging in the macrocosm," my soul said from within.

Returning instantly to Earth, I traveled through atoms and smaller particles of energy. Everywhere, I sensed a great life force, but I wasn't as skilled at understanding the microcosm as the macrocosm. Eventually, not knowing what else to do, I decided to return to my physical body. Hovering above it, I saw it lying on the couch, with Alma sitting in a nearby chair. Feeling no emotion, I knew it was possible to stay outside my body much longer, perhaps forever. With only a slight preference, I chose to re-enter it. Afterwards, I lay there for quite some time before making a conscious decision to breathe.

"You weren't breathing for a long time," Alma said a few minutes later when I reopened my eyes.

"Yes, I know," I replied, before telling her what I had seen and learned.

Words cannot capture the transformative nature of this experience. Even though I wasn't breathing for many minutes, there was no urge to breathe. I was completely relaxed, peaceful, aware, and entirely unafraid of physical death. I was not my physical body. Living or dying didn't matter. Yet, knowing I still had work to do in this life, I chose to return.

Being with Lord Sirius and the Council of 12 gave me insight into the enormous scale at which the evolution of conscious beings occurs in this and other solar systems. Additionally, I learned the talents of six of the beings. From this experience, I gained more humility, compassion, and a deeper desire to serve the Divine will.

Because the information I receive through experience is so unusual, I often seek validation and clarification from others, whether in esoteric books or in person. As mentioned earlier, it is of utmost importance that we do not provide erroneous information to others that could mislead them on their spiritual path. Moreover, I seek companionship with other spiritual allies who have had similar experiences.

After this transformative experience, I read *Initiation* by Elizabeth Haich. Her book is autobiographical, and Horus, the Hawk-Being, is featured on the cover. Thinking Mrs. Haich might be able to provide insight into these Beings, I wrote to her. She responded by suggesting that I visit. Within a few weeks, I was at her school in Switzerland and scheduling an appointment for the following day.

As I entered the school, a young woman asked me to remove my shoes and stand in line in the large foyer. There must have been 40 people ahead of me, all waiting to speak with a large, elderly, imposing woman—Mrs. Haich. I was not amused. I had just flown from North America and had taken a lengthy train trip to get here. Nevertheless, calming myself, I observed the proceedings. Each person generally received about 20 seconds of her time, which involved them asking a question and Mrs. Haich responding. Her booming German voice made privacy impossible. Finally, it was my turn.

"I'm Tanis Helliwell from Toronto, Canada, and you invited me to come," I started.

I hoped she'd grant me more time if she understood who I was and how far I'd come. Her face remained impassive, so I quickly pressed on before my time ran out.

"I've been seeing and talking to a Hawk Being like the one on the cover of your book, *Initiation*," I said.

"Oh, you have quite the imagination," she chuckled sarcastically before adding, "Horus is an archetype."

With those words, she dismissed me. Confused and deflated, I shuffled to the side of the room, trying to decide what to make of her words. Was I mistaken in my vision? Was she mistaken in hers? Were we both right? Was Horus an archetype, but I can speak with archetypes? Too many questions and too few answers.

A woman sitting behind the desk I was leaning on spoke, "Are you Tanis Helliwell?"

"Yes," I replied, still shaken.

"I'm Mrs. Haich's secretary. I wrote the letter to you," she said with a smile.

"I'm unsure about what to do next," I replied, knowing that she, along with everyone else in the room, had overheard my conversation with Mrs. Haich.

"What you should know is that Mrs. Haich is an elderly woman who dislikes having her authority questioned."

Questioning her authority hadn't been my intention. Instead, I was hoping she would shed light on my vision.

Mrs. Haich's secretary lowered her voice and continued in a confidential tone, "Mrs. Haich is not a seer."

Her words helped me fully trust my vision. At the same time, I did not negate what Mrs. Haich had said and kept her comments in reserve until I could more fully understand them. Now, I see more clearly the difference between archetypes and evolving beings. Perhaps her words, either consciously or unconsciously, were meant to trigger that inquiry.

Archetypes are thoughtforms created by the Great Beings who assist humanity in its evolution. An archetype may reflect an aspect of a Great Being, and it has a kind of half-life. For example, Horus is a conscious being that currently resides in very high realms, which are beyond the reach of most people. As a result, Horus has created an archetype, a replica, to continue guiding humanity. Archetypes grow and change through their interaction with our thoughts, and as humanity progresses, the conscious beings who initially programmed the archetype can modify it.

While searching for something to do during the three weeks before my flight back to Canada, I discovered that Krishnamurti was teaching nearby in Saanen, Switzerland. Having watched videotaped discussions with him and the British physicist David Bohm, I appreciated the chance to see him in person.

I took the train to Saanen and followed the crowds to a large tent where Krishnamurti was teaching. Hundreds of people had gathered inside, and I sat down on a chair in the middle. Krishnamurti entered dressed in white, and his physical frailty struck me. He was nearly 90 years old, and this was only a year and a half before he left his body. There was a radiance and peace about him, and his words carried no hint of frailty.

Krishnamurti would pose a question, and others would answer it. By listening to the questions and answers, you became an active participant in the process. Then, he would refine the question, send it in different directions, and guide you to more clearly see his perspective, perhaps a more truthful, profound view, of the spiritual world and its laws.

Initially, I remained anchored in the physical reality. However, it wasn't long before the atmosphere in the room and his questions led my perception to expand, revealing other beings surrounding Krishnamurti. These beings flowed in and out of Krishnamurti's permeable aura, and his words were shaped by their personalities. I was taken aback to see an Indian chief in a headdress among them. Another presence was an elderly oriental man with a Fu Manchu beard. Part of me relished witnessing the spectacle, while another part sought to interpret what I was witnessing.

"Are these his past lives, or are they other beings speaking through him?" I wondered. "And if he is so spiritually advanced, why does he need other beings to provide him with information?"

Continuing to watch, I became increasingly aware that Krishnamurti was allowing his physical body to be used for this purpose and that he had only a tentative hold on bodily life. He was a selfless server who permitted these beings to have a vehicle for expression. I'm not sure if this was a recent development or if he had taught in this manner for many years. I also realized that he and these beings were not separate; he embodied both himself and them simultaneously. This paradox helped me dissolve my preconceptions about how we progress in consciousness. For instance, what remains "I" and what becomes "We" when we attain enlightenment?

These experiences with Mrs. Haich and Krishnamurti raised more questions than they answered. There was much more to know about Spirit than I understood at that time. Questions and their answers reside within us; however, they don't always come in matched sets. Instead of settling for a less accurate answer, it's important to allow time for a more precise one to arise.

As we progress spiritually, we must let go of lesser truths to embrace higher ones, and often an uncomfortable phase of uncertainty is needed to move from the lesser to the greater truth. We must never underestimate the importance of pausing. This is as important a pathway as any on our awakening journey. For example, just today, nearly 40 years later, I received confirmation of my experience in 1986. I found out that those present during Krishnamurti's passing said his last words were, "I am not sure the body can take any more."

# 13

# Kundalini Awakens

After returning to Canada, nothing unusual happened for half a year—a brief pause before the next storm. In December, I was in Yellowknife, Northwest Territories, leading a Managing Stress seminar. On the day I arrived, a hot, itchy rash appeared on my hands and quickly developed into large blisters. The blisters grew larger, and the rash spread to various parts of my body. The heat and itching caused significant discomfort, so the night was spent lying in a tub of water, reading Job from the Bible in the motel room.

If you are not familiar with Job, let me summarize his story. Job was a good man who was loved by God. He had a wife and children, was well-liked, and prosperous. The devil asked God if he thought Job would ever turn away from him.

God said, "No way. Go ahead and do your worst."

In a short time, Job's children died, he faced financial ruin, and his friends abandoned him. As if that weren't enough, his body was covered in oozing sores…hence my interest in Job's story.

Job asked God, "Why is this happening to me when I have followed you?"

God's reply indicated that Job could not understand the reasons behind his trials. Job accepted his trials as God requested, and everything, along with more, was restored to him. Having experienced the positive path where he received all that he valued, Job now needed to face the negative path of losing these attachments to develop humility and deepen his compassion for others through suffering. The lesson for us is that, like Job, we must accept suffering even when we do not understand the reasons. It's easy to have faith and trust Spirit when everything is going well in our lives, but it's not as easy when it's not. We need to remain steadfast on the journey to consciousness, no matter what happens to us.

There were some parallels between Job's life and mine, which gave me hope that the blisters would heal and that the experience would improve me as a person. At that time, I did not realize that these "fire attacks," would last for many years and lead to people and practices I would have never sought out otherwise.

By the time I flew back to Toronto, my hands were swollen almost twice their normal size and covered in oozing blisters.

Bill met me at the airport and, after taking one look at my hands, declared, "We're going to the hospital."

"They'll want to give me cortisone, but I don't want that," I replied.

"No, they won't," he replied while driving to the nearest hospital.

When we arrived at the hospital, the doctor said, "Please undress so I can see the extent of the problem."

I did as instructed, and after taking a deep breath, he said, "I've never seen such a bad allergic reaction. I want to give you a shot of cortisone."

"No. No cortisone," I replied, looking at Bill. "However, please tell me how this was caused, what foods I can or cannot eat, and what to bathe in to relieve the itch and burning."

"I'm not sure how it happened, but bathing in colloidal oatmeal might help. I recommend taking the cortisone," the doctor said.

Refusing the cortisone once more, we departed from the hospital. The following days were spent soaking in oatmeal, eating almost nothing, and drinking plenty of water. Relief came only from taking scalding hot baths. The intense heat of the water was almost pleasurable on the blisters. Cold water did nothing to alleviate the condition. After a few days, I began to improve and felt better within a week. I hoped the fire attack was a one-time occurrence, but that was not to be.

After Christmas, I flew to Hawaii to lead a nine-day retreat called The Circle of Creation. The retreat center wasn't ready, so I spent the first day preparing it. My hands started to itch and heat up, and unfortunately, I was about to experience another fire attack. By the time the participants arrived the next day, blisters had already begun to form on my swollen hands and body.

Dora Kuntz, one of the founders of the healing technique Touch for Health, was conducting a healing workshop on the property. I approached her to ask if her group and mine could meet one night to exchange techniques and experiences. She kept glancing at my hands as I spoke.

"Do you know that you are on fire?" she asked.

"Yes," I said.

"You might end up being a victim of spontaneous combustion," Dora continued.

"I know that's a possibility but think it unlikely," I smiled, attempting to reassure both of us.

"Let me try to help you," she offered.

I extended my hands. Dora couldn't get any closer than eight inches due to the heat radiating from them. I appreciated her concern, but my condition continued to worsen. Many healers, including Reiki Masters, naturopaths, chiropractors, psychiatrists, and teachers from The Course of Miracles, attended my retreat and all kindly tried to help, but the situation didn't improve. Most of the time when I wasn't teaching was spent lying in a bath. People became accustomed to sitting on the toilet seat and chatting while I soaked.

Needing help, I asked for it. This marked a departure from my usual self-sufficiency. The myth of the perfect spiritual teacher was gone. Still, I didn't act irresponsibly. Each day, I led the group in a guided visualization, chanting session, or mask-making activity. Afterward, I became a group member, just like everyone else. This was a valuable learning experience for all of us. The lines between teacher and student disappeared. This shift from one role to another became a natural and beautiful gift for everyone involved. We trusted that we didn't need role titles to know what was needed by whom at what time.

Near the end of the retreat, we had a day dedicated to fasting and silence. I went for a walk on the beach. This was the first time outside since the fire attack started, as I didn't want to worsen the situation with sun exposure. I arrived at a quiet part of the beach with a few shade trees and sat on a black volcanic rock outcrop to meditate and ask for healing. I was exhausted from a week of little sleep, minimal food, and physical discomfort from the burns and blisters.

"Take off your clothes and lie naked on the rock," my higher Self said.

I did as instructed, but with reservations. The lava rocks were razor-sharp and they could easily pierce and infect the blisters.

"Pleasure yourself four times, while giving your energy back to the earth, water, fire, and air," my higher Self said.

I was reluctant, to put it mildly, to do this on a public beach, but past experiences have taught me to trust such inner guidance. Long-standing concerns about what people would think arose, but I followed the instructions. There was an inner sense of rightness about giving my energy to the elements that created and sustained this body on Earth. At that time, having been celibate for nearly a year, part of the issue seemed to be a buildup of undischarged energy. After finishing the exercise, I felt better almost immediately.

The next morning, I shared these actions with the group. It was best to explain the purpose of the ritual in case anyone had seen me, even though it might jeopardize my credibility. Still, trusting them, myself, and Spirit was important. Everyone was happy to see that the burns were improving.

Following the retreat, I flew to California to visit Richard Moss, an author and spiritual teacher. Although Richard's path was quite different from mine at that time, we both appreciated each other's abilities and commitment to serving humanity.

I had intended to leave on the third day, but Richard pressed me to stay, saying, "There is a wonderful man I'd like you to meet. His name is Franklin Merrell-Wolff. He lives not far from here and has a few people over on Sunday mornings for teachings."

I had never heard of Dr. Wolff before, but agreed to go. We joined a small group in his living room. Dr. Wolff, who was in his mid-90s, spoke very little. He played a tape of one of his recorded talks, and Richard led a discussion about it. When the discussion ended, Dr. Wolff met with people individually and signed copies of his book, *Pathways into Space*, an autobiography detailing his journey to awakening.

His mere presence put me in a superconscious state where I could hardly coordinate walking and talking. Dr. Wolff was the first person whose very presence caused this. This experience, more than any words, testified to the truth of his claim to be enlightened. There are levels of enlightenment, and, like Krishnamurti, both men had transcended the individual ego and united with the Divine.

After leaving Dr. Wolff's, I drove to Los Angeles, where my mother was staying with Aunt Dorothy and Uncle Wilton. On the way, I visited some friends and, mentioning the second-degree burns on my body, asked if they knew anyone who could help.

"There's a well-known spiritual teacher, Omraam Mikhael Aivanhov, visiting LA. He might be able to help you if you can get in to see him," my friends said, giving me the contact information.

I had never heard of him, but after I got to L.A., I wrote to request an appointment.

Four days passed, and Dorothy and Wilton took Mom and me to San Diego, where they decided on a spontaneous overnight stay. I felt nervous about their decision because I intuitively knew Omraam Mikhael Aivanhov had agreed to see me. When we returned to Los Angeles, there was a message on the answering machine saying that the appointment had been that day. I quickly called the number, and a woman answered.

"Hello, I'm Tanis Helliwell, and I just received your message about the appointment with Mr. Aivanhov," I began.

"You missed your appointment," the woman replied, her voice both incredulous and accusatory.

"Please accept my apologies. I was out of town and have only returned now. Would it be possible to have another one?"

She was on the verge of saying "No" when a male voice in the background told her to give me another appointment. I guessed that voice belonged to Mr. Aivanhov.

The next day, Dorothy drove Mom and me to the meeting. The woman, whose voice I recognized from the previous day's phone call, answered the door and let us in. Mom and Dorothy were taken to a room lined wall to wall with books by the mysterious Mr. Aivanhov. The woman led me to another room where she gave detailed instructions on where to sit and how to behave. She kept referring to Omraam

Mikhael Aivanhov as "The Master." She spoke about him with such reverence that my curiosity was sparked.A majestic man entered the room dressed in white trousers and shirt, over which he wore a flowing oriental blue robe. He had a white beard and hair, and although he was not tall, he walked erect and purposefully, conveying a strong sense of self-possession. He moved over to the couch where I sat and, carefully arranging his robe, took a seat beside me. This was not where he was supposed to sit according to his assistant's information. As instructed, I waited for him to speak.

"I don't speak English very well; do you speak French?" he asked.

"Je ne parle pas bien le francais, mais je vais essayer," I replied in halting French.

Since his English and my French were equally awkward, our conversation became a blend of the two languages and we did quite well understanding each other.

"What would you like to ask me?" he inquired, getting straight to the point.

"I'm having problems with burns on my body," I replied.

"Show me!" he commanded.

In the physical reality, there was nothing for him to see as my skin miraculously healed without scarring after these outbreaks. However, I extended my hands to show him.

"Anywhere else?" he questioned.

"Yes, on my legs, stomach, and arms," I replied.

"Show me," he commanded once more.

After a brief pause, I rolled up my sleeves, lifted my skirt, and unbuttoned my blouse.

"Ah," he said, waving his hand gracefully as only French speakers can. "This is very unusual and very sacred. This is the kundalini fire rising in your body. Do you have a partner to do tantric exercises with?"

"No," I replied. "I've been celibate for a year."

"You must work with a man. You have a gift. I'm going to suggest something I advise all my students against because it can be very dangerous for most people." With those words, he guided me in tantric exercises.

"I want you to stay and teach me English," he requested after his tantric instructions.

This man wasn't accustomed to people refusing him, but it felt right to go home and put the house up for sale. Bill and I were still living in the same house, and this needed to end.

"Thank you for asking, but I need to go home to complete a part of my life," I replied politely, leaving no room for negotiation.

My refusal opened a door for Master Aivanhov. I sensed that by declining rather than accepting his invitation, I had passed a test. He paused for a moment, examining and weighing me.

"Do you know who you are and who I am?" he asked.

He was referring to who we really were, not the Tanis Helliwell and Omraam Mikhael Aivanhov sitting in the room.

"No, I don't," I replied, preferring not to hazard a guess. He was about to say something of great importance.

Master Aivanhov stood up and left the room, calling out behind him, "Wait!"

A few minutes later, he returned holding a book. He handed it to me and told me to read the passage he indicated. The passage was about the enlightened gurus in the Hindu tradition called Rishis, who lived thousands of years ago and created the Vedas. He waited patiently until I finished and lowered the book.

"This is who we are. Do you understand?" he asked.

Overwhelmed by the information and the whole experience, I was more than a bit hesitant to accept his hypothesis that we were both Rishis. He noticed this reluctance.

"I have never told anyone what I have told you," he said, glancing at his watch. "I usually spend no more than 20 minutes with individuals. We've been together for an hour and a half because of who you are."

Knowing our discussion was over, I thanked him and left the room, feeling unsure and shaken about what to believe. Dorothy and Mom were waiting in the book room, and there was a dramatic change in the woman who had spoken to me earlier.

"I have been with the Master for five years, and he sees people for only 10 or, at most, 20 minutes."

Her unspoken words were, "Who are you, anyway?"

"I was very fortunate," I volunteered, and asked to buy the book on the serpent power that Master Aivanhov had recommended. I sensed that he had mentioned how long he typically spends with people to make me trust the other things he'd said. It was as if he knew his assistant would make a point of mentioning the time because it was such an unusual occurrence.

Later, I found out that Omraam Mikhael Aivanhov was originally from Bulgaria and had studied in India. His main center was in France, but he had hundreds, possibly thousands, of followers around the world. Not knowing this, I acted completely naturally and spoke to him as I am speaking with you. This might have even been a welcome change for him. I don't mean this disrespectfully, but great teachers are still human beings. It must be refreshing to be addressed casually. When Master Aivanhov left Los Angeles, he returned to his ashram in France, where he went into silence. He passed away not long after his return. In one way, that surprised me because, although he was in his 80s when I saw him, he had immense vitality and physical power.

My inner critic stayed active but started questioning if some of what he said might be valid. The question was: how much?

The next morning, Dorothy drove me to the airport to fly back to Toronto. I boarded the plane, and we taxied out and sat on the runway. After an hour, we taxied back again and disembarked. The flight was scheduled to go through Chicago to Toronto, but due to fog, no flights could land in Chicago. Two hours later, the flight was rescheduled to fly directly to Toronto.

Finally, I was on the flight to Toronto, waiting for takeoff, when a last-minute passenger hurried onto the plane and took the vacant seat beside me.

"I've been booked on the wrong airline. I never fly Air Canada," he immediately started moaning, which was actually amusing given the circumstances.

He sat still, wrapped in his coat, with his briefcase on his lap, as if he might leave at any moment. We started talking, and within 15 minutes, he said something that took me aback.

"Your energy is so strong," he said. "I find it hard to sit next to you. I might have to move."

There were no free seats, so where he thought he'd move to would have been a problem. He then told me many things that were identical to what Master Aivanhov had said the day before. My seatmate concluded by saying, "I'm a happily married man, and I've never cheated on my wife, but I must see you again."

This conversation was very upsetting for many reasons. First, it was shocking to have a stranger tell me what Master Aivanhov had told me in confidence. Second, I had no intention of having an affair with a married man. I excused myself and went to the bathroom to calm down and listen to my inner guidance. It clearly told me that this man, Ted, was honest and trustworthy.

When I returned to my seat, his first words were, "What did your meditation say?"

"That you are honest and trustworthy," I replied.

We kept talking throughout the five-hour flight, and gradually I relaxed, realizing it wasn't necessary to decide immediately about seeing Ted again. We could go our separate ways once we landed in Toronto. So engrossed in conversation, we didn't even notice we were landing until the flight attendant interrupted us.

"Buckle up," she said. "We're about to land in Montreal."

"Montreal? We were supposed to be landing in Toronto," I replied anxiously.

"Didn't you hear the announcement?" she replied. "They're fog-bound in Toronto, so we have to land in Montreal for the night."

Ted smiled at me and said, "It's fated."

He was right. Both of us were on different planes than we had originally intended…and now this. After disembarking, we took a taxi to a hotel and, unsure about the correct protocol in this situation, checked into one room. Humor, goodwill, mutual attraction, and respect allowed us to proceed.

The next day, we boarded a flight back to Toronto. Ted was very amusing and likable, but I had no intention of continuing a relationship with a married man.

Shortly after takeoff, the pilot's voice came over the intercom: "I apologize for any inconvenience, but Toronto is fog-bound, so we will be continuing our flight to Thunder Bay."

Ted and I exchanged amused glances, chuckled, and in unison exclaimed, "Thunder Bay!"

We had to spend another night in Thunder Bay. Clearly, we had been brought together to practice tantric sexual-spiritual exercises, and that time had not yet come to an end. Just two days earlier, Omraam Mikhael Aivanhov had told me that I needed a partner to practice tantra. This amazing synchronicity reinforced my belief in other things that Master Aivanhov had mentioned.

Ted and I were in a relationship for a year and a half. It was both painful and pleasurable for us. I believe his marriage was initially neglected by Ted because of our relationship, but I hope it ultimately grew stronger. From my perspective, I learned what it's like to have an affair with someone who is married. This increased my understanding of what happens when people engage in such relationships, but it also confirmed that I wouldn't choose that for myself. While committed to our shared purpose, I am monogamous by nature.

With the end of celibacy, my fire attacks became less frequent and less intense, but they still continued. Seeking permanent solutions led to attending a series of workshops with Harley Swiftdeer Reagan. The Native American tradition interests me. This interest has led to studying with many medicine teachers. Although I feel a heart connection, the simple messages of many Native American teachers (excluding Sun Bear and Dyhani Ywahoo) are less mentally engaging. I am more drawn to the mysteries and sacred laws that underpin rituals.

Swiftdeer claimed that he taught the sacred laws of the Twisted Hair tradition, and this appealed to me. Before continuing, I want to emphasize that Swiftdeer was a rogue, and there is considerable controversy surrounding his claims of being part of the Cherokee nation. He held black belts in judo and karate, and his early training was in martial arts. He was a warrior of power, while I am a warrior of love, so our paths differed.

I do not condone pretenders claiming First Nations heritage, but regardless of where he learned or created some of his information, he was an excellent teacher, possessed many spiritual gifts, and demonstrated integrity in workshops I attended. Many lessons from him have benefited both me and others. One of these is to refuse to be manipulated by the guilt-inducing, angry, self-pitying, bullying, and other such teaching tyrants in your life. Working with him catalyzed my power and will, both of which I needed to develop.

The first workshop I attended with Swiftdeer was on healing. I was impressed by his knowledge and the rituals he led, so decided to take his Quodoushka workshop. Quodoushka, in the Cherokee tradition, teaches how to employ kundalini energy for healing, sexuality, physical well-being, and spirituality. Eastern traditions emphasize channeling kundalini into spiritual awakening, and I was exploring this and other uses for this energy.

I did not have a partner with whom to work in Swiftdeer's workshop and, as I am both private and careful with whom I share my sexual energy, this aspect of the workshop made me highly uneasy. While nude we spoke about our sexual experiences from our first encounter to the present. Some people had satisfying sexual experiences and were at the workshop to explore sexual techniques and other uses for their energy. Others had been victims of incest, rape, or had some dysfunction and were hoping to be cured.

One overweight man, whom I found physically unattractive, was in his 50s and had experienced only two sexual encounters in his life. His story was so sad, and he was in such pain while telling it that when the women were asked to choose partners, I chose him. We were instructed to help our partners open their chakras through touch, visualization, and voice. I opened myself to love my partner and spoke to him about his beauty.

Swiftdeer sat nearby the entire time, and when the exercise finished, he told the group he had never seen a more natural phoenix fire woman. A phoenix fire woman or man is someone who can work with kundalini energy. In Cherokee tradition, there are eight roles that both men and women can play for themselves and for others. These roles include mother, daughter, virgin, explorer, career woman, traditional wife, priestess, and tyrant. If you can embody all these roles at the appropriate times, you are a phoenix fire woman. The male counterparts are the same. Swiftdeer's words reinforced what Omraam Mikhael Aivanhov had said, but I felt uncomfortable with him speaking publicly about me.

According to Swiftdeer's teachings, there are four levels of orgasm, with different chakras activating at each level. In the lower levels, only the lower chakras open, while in the higher levels, all chakras become activated. From his description, I realized that my ecstatic experiences, feeling plugged into an electric circuit with my entire body vibrating, were fourth-level orgasms. These experiences weren't necessarily linked to being with someone or engaging in any sexual activity, as they are unrelated to genitals for me.

Swiftdeer taught a fire-breathing technique—similar to holotropic breathing—to induce this fourth-level orgasm. My body naturally engages in this breathing during such experiences, and it was intriguing to discover that many practices I had discovered naturally were also Quodoushka techniques. However, not everyone reaches bliss through fire-breathing. If our chakras are blocked, we might feel nauseous, see demons, cry, become angry, or experience other reactions. Many people at the workshop experienced these effects when they practiced the fire breath. I tried to help those who struggled, and most were grateful, but one woman was not.

"Get away from me, you bitch," she spat through clenched teeth.

Many women in our society feel threatened by other women's sexuality. It's disheartening when women don't support each other in celebrating our feminine beauty. Women can be especially resentful toward those who embody traits of Aphrodite, like Marilyn Monroe. These women are often exploited by men and rejected by other women. I have always downplayed my sexuality by wearing baggy clothes, minimal makeup, and avoiding flirtation. Therefore, this woman's words struck a painful chord. Although her comment came from her own pain, it made me withdraw as if slapped.

Then, the realization dawned. My sexuality was connected to fears of rejection. This fear came from boils and styes around my eyes while entering puberty, which made me feel unattractive to boys. My fears of rejection by women came from my mother. When she discovered I had hosted a spin-the-bottle party for kissing boys while she was at work, she was furious and hit me with a tea towel. That's the only time I remember her hitting me. Although she didn't physically hurt me, her disapproval of my innocent sexual explorations as a pre-teen was painful. Mom's anger might also have stemmed from her feelings of being a bad mother because I was acting this way, but this thought never entered my mind at the time. When you're 13 and just entering puberty, you see everything from your own perspective. I thank the woman in Swiftdeer's workshop for helping me uncover the root of my fear of rejection and shame related to my sexuality. As often happens, by exploring why words or situations trigger psychological pain, you can identify its source and free yourself from these uncomfortable feelings.

Studying Quodoushka helped me understand many aspects of my energy. For instance, I found that my physical energy was considerably lower than my spiritual energy. This imbalance caused my physical body to struggle with the volume of spiritual energy, resulting in fire attacks. The fire attacks served as valuable teachers that led to seeking assistance from Omraam Mikhael Aivanhov, Harley Swiftdeer, and Ted, my tantric partner.

What I didn't expect was that these fire attacks could actually help others. For me, they were a personal experience, even though I kept working while enduring them. One day, I received a call from the Discovery Channel in the USA requesting an interview for their show, Unexplained Phenomenon. Someone had told them about these fire attacks, and I was apparently one of the few survivors of spontaneous combustion. Not wanting notoriety for such a private matter, I declined. Soon after, Larry Arnold, who had written a book called *Ablaze: The Mysterious Fires of Spontaneous Combustion*, called. Urging me to reconsider, Larry explained that my experience might help others. In the end, I agreed, which led to a second documentary featuring others who had witnessed my fire attacks being interviewed as well.

The fire attacks gradually decreased in frequency and intensity over time, and now they occur only as a gentle reminder when my physical body lacks balance. These fire attacks are less troublesome now because of my age and because I am more grounded in my physical body. Many people concentrate on opening only their chakras from the heart up and do not work with their lower chakras. That was not my path. I wanted to open all my chakras.

During this challenging period, I connected with my darker, unconscious, and more primal earthly nature. The blocks in my lower chakras were transformed and burned away by the kundalini fire, which also serves as a fire of purification. As these lower channels and chakras cleared and opened, the energy rose unobstructed to my heart. Here, it met the descending spiritual energies that had been available to me for many years. In other words, my body became more balanced between the spiritual and earthly elements. As this transformation occurred, the intensity of the fire attacks decreased. The kundalini energy didn't vanish; instead, it traveled through a broader channel, became more grounded, and transformed into an energy to help others.

Talking about sexual experiences wasn't easy earlier in my life, especially references to married men, sexual workshops, and revealing conversations with Master Aivanhov, a well-known spiritual teacher. Still, this story wouldn't be complete without including that information. Many people in our Western society feel uncomfortable discussing their sexuality. I know I did because sex was a taboo topic never mentioned in my family. I've discovered that any subject we feel uneasy talking about—like sex, money, or love—benefits from exploring. These topics often represent conditioned responses, and on our spiritual path, we need to release our aversions as much as our attachments.

# 14

# Summer with the Leprechauns

Meanwhile, the house that Bill and I shared was for sale, but no one was buying it. Bill might have been unconsciously holding onto the house because he was afraid to let go of our relationship. Therefore, leaving for the summer to give Bill time to pursue his new relationship and to move forward with my life seemed like a good idea.

One of my patterns is taking time off between two stages. This happened after graduating from university by traveling across Europe for a year to mark my entry into adulthood. Then came a 20-month break traveling around South America and Southeast Asia between working as a high school teacher and starting a business. Now, a complete break from the outside world was calling.

An Irish friend was going to Ireland and offered to find me a cottage in a remote place to meditate for the summer without being disturbed. When she returned, she said she hadn't been successful until the night before her flight back to Canada. That evening, she was having dinner with a friend in Dublin, and, with little hope, she mentioned to him that she was looking for a cottage. He said he had the perfect cottage on Achill Island.

The name Achill Island was perfect because the goal of the retreat was to eliminate my character flaws, the Achilles' heels. If you're not familiar with the story, Achilles was immortal except for his heel. It was a wound there that ultimately killed him. In Ireland, my aim was to undergo a symbolic death by examining and removing negative traits and, through this process, to become enlightened.

In late June, I flew to Dublin with a return ticket booked for the end of August. Right away, I went to meet Mr. Douglas, who was renting the cottage.

"I'm sorry but you can only have Crumpaun cottage for one month," he announced. "The place has been sold."

This was a clear sign that an ideal summer of meditation was not meant to be. Still, when one door closes, another opens, and that change in plans must serve a purpose. Thanking Mr. Douglas for allowing me to stay for a month, I boarded a public bus to Achill Island on the west coast of Ireland.

After four hours of driving, the terrain became rugged and barren. The land was slashed by cuttings and stacks of peat. Brown was the dominant color of the landscape, and a heavy gray sky loomed over everything. Occasionally, we caught glimpses of the sea, where swells crashed against the shore. It was a raw, powerful landscape. The hazy sun hung low in the sky when the bus driver stopped the bus.

"It's about a 20-minute walk up that lane," the driver explained, pointing up a winding path.

Picking up the pack filled with sheets and clothes, I set off in the direction he indicated. Twenty minutes later, at the top of the lane, I arrived at a white cottage with a blue door that matched Mr. Douglas's description of Crumpaun cottage. The door was ajar, inviting me in. A turf fire burned in the grate, but when I called out, no one answered. Mr. Douglas had said that he would inform his neighbor, Mrs. Toolis, of my arrival and that she would open the cottage. The fire must have been her welcome. [4]

Melting into warm feelings of gratitude, I caught sight of other beings in the room out of the corner of my eye. A family of leprechauns—a male, a female, and two children—stared at me. My first thought was disappointment. What kind of retreat was this going to be in a cottage occupied by leprechauns? The hope of spending a summer meditating in isolation quickly evaporated. There was no time to pursue this line of thought as the male leprechaun addressed me.

"If you plan to stay here for the summer, we need to come to an agreement," he said, getting straight to the point.

"What type of agreement?" I asked.

"We don't want you to move anything in the cottage, and you must give me a gift, which I'll specify at the end of the summer. In return, I'll protect you from the elementals on this lane who don't like humans. You'll need my protection."

"It's a deal," I responded without hesitation.

It had been an exhausting day, and after reading his thoughts about the gift, the exchange felt fair. The family disappeared, and it was time to explore the cottage. There was a living room, a bedroom, a bathroom, and a stand-up kitchen with a two-burner cooker. Adequate. While unpacking, I made a cup of tea, ate the cheese and crackers from the flight, and slid between cold sheets. Moments later, I re-emerged, put on long johns and a wool sweater, filled the hot water bottle in the kitchen, and flopped back into bed. Summer in Ireland bore no resemblance to summer in Toronto. It was damp and cold, and throughout the summer, I always slept fully clothed with a hot water bottle for company.

The sun streaming through the window woke me. Outside, the misty haze was trying to lift, while inside, my breath was visible. Quickly slipping on shoes, I hurried to the kitchen to boil the kettle. With a cup of hot tea in hand, I wrapped myself in a blanket and stepped outside to survey the surroundings.

The cottage sat atop a hill. To the right, a small village was visible in the distance, while flowering hedges lined the right side. Straight ahead, a vast expanse of sea crashed against a sandy beach. In front of the cottage stood a white picket fence matching the whitewashed building. The fence offered some privacy from the narrow lane passing by the door. Between the cottage and the fence, about 30 feet of lawn stretched out, decorated with white-headed daisies, dandelions, tiny pink flowers, and clover.

Feelings of gratitude for such good fortune washed over me, as did hunger. Taking the blanket and teacup inside, I dressed and started down the lane toward the village. Wild yellow irises intertwined with hedges of red, yellow, and white flowers lined the shoulder. Everything smelled fertile and alive. Strolling along, I passed a few other houses, but none were as rustic as Crumpaun cottage. Some were new constructions, while others were old farmhouses. Sheep and cattle roamed in the surrounding fields. Overall, there was a sense of peace and harmony with the land.

The lane ended at a pub on the only street in the village. The village had two pubs, a butcher shop, a handicraft store, and a general store that also served as a post office. Entering the general store, I strolled through the two aisles checking the limits of my diet for the next month. Not bad. Some vegetables, Irish soda bread, plenty of canned goods, and European wine for occasional rewards. I bought as much as it was possible to physically carry back up the path. While at the checkout counter, the owner started a conversation.

"Are you a holiday maker?" he asked, attempting to downplay his curiosity.

"I've rented the Douglas cottage for the summer," I said.

"The Douglas cottage," he replied, surprised. "Did you not know it's haunted?"

"Haunted by what?" I replied, as if this were news to me.

"By the little people. In fact," he continued, "the whole lane is haunted. There was a caravan parked in that lane, and it would shake back and forth all by itself with no one inside and no breeze."

Thanking him for the information, I bid him farewell and began walking back up the haunted lane. The sky was turning gray, a cool breeze had picked up, and rain was on the way. I quickened my pace, clenched my teeth, and wondered if enlightenment was possible in such an environment.

"At least it's not necessary to interact with people," I told myself, trying to find the silver lining. "It will be a summer of meditating without interruption and only going to the village for food. Staying in silence for days on end will be nice."

These thoughts were comforting, until I was unpacking the groceries and looked out the window to see a woman coming up the walk. She was dressed in muddy wellies, a well-worn coat missing more than one button, a kerchief tied over her hair, and she was carrying a long staff. When she reached the door, she raised the latch and poked her head inside.

"I'm Mrs. Toolis. Mr. Douglas said you'd be comin' so I lit the turf last night," she said with a toothless grin.

"I've been out with the coos and thought I'd stop by to see how you'd be makin' out."

Torn between the desire for a silent retreat and acceptance of whatever Spirit wanted, I invited her in for a cup of tea. She went to the cold fire, tidied it up, and began lighting a new one. Once the tea was ready, we sat down and waited in silence for the turf to catch. Every five minutes or so, Mrs. Toolis would lean over the hearth to adjust a piece of turf or fan the glowing embers. After half an hour, a nice fire was burning, and we returned to enjoying our second cup of tea.

"Where are you from?" she inquired.

"Canada," I answered.

"I've family in Boston," she said.

"Yes, there are a lot of Irish people in the Boston area," I responded. Then we returned to silence for the next five minutes and watched the fire.

"How long will you be here?" she asked.

"Only a month. The cottage has been sold," I replied.

"Ah," she acknowledged. And we fell silent for another five minutes and watched the fire.

"You'll need to get some turf in. You'll need a fire goin' all summer. The cottage is damp and hasn't been used for a year," she said, poking the fire.

"Where can you buy some?" I asked, fully aware of how cold the cottage was.

"I'll see to it," she replied, returning to silence. Five minutes later, she got to her feet.

"I have to be goin'," she said. "Thank you for the tea."

The following morning, Mrs. Toolis appeared at the door.

"Thought I'd stop by to see how you're makin' out," she said, smiling.

Inviting her in for tea, she went over to start the fire as she had the previous evening. I was overjoyed to see her after spending a frustrating two hours trying to master the subtleties of setting up a turf fire. Cold and unsuccessful, I was huddled in blankets on the couch when she arrived. A half-hour later, she had a fire blazing in the hearth. Within days, Mrs. Toolis began dropping by in the evenings on her way home from the coos. This became our morning and evening ritual for the summer, and soon, I looked forward to her visits.

Tea and cookies by the turf fire with Mrs. Toolis became just as important as meditating. Although the retreat was not what I had originally envisioned, small moments, like Mrs. Toolis' visits and shopping for food in the village, brightened what could have been a very heavy summer.

Within a few weeks, it became clear that the goal of enlightenment was unattainable. Naively, I had thought that giving up attachments, like my warm-hearted, good-humored partner Bill and our house, would lead to enlightenment. Spiritual books mention this, and my soul believed it too. What I had not considered was that only the Creator, not me, could decide when enlightenment would occur.

Clearly, I was attached to enlightenment and needed to let go of this attachment. Additionally, it was necessary to deepen my compassion and unlearn society's lessons. I needed to uncover the shadows in my unconscious, transform them, and integrate them into my conscious life. I hoped by doing this to develop greater compassion for others. Deep down, I knew that once enlightened, I might have chosen to leave embodiment for higher spiritual realms. But this would not fulfill the purpose of this incarnation. Therefore, that door was closed.

Surrendering the goal of enlightenment, the focus shifted to the deeper recesses of my unconscious. To do this, I weaned myself off as much stimulation as possible to avoid distractions or attachments. This involved re-editing *Decoding Destiny* for a few hours each day, meditating, journaling, and taking long walks in the rain along the streets or by the sea.

Once a week, I treated myself to dinner at a village restaurant and attended mass with Mrs. Toolis and her family on Saturday evenings. Sometimes, we would visit the local pub for a pint after mass and listen to a local balladeer perform. The Irish are wonderfully practical and hold mass on Saturday evenings to avoid ruining a sleep-in on Sunday. This is how my life appeared to an outsider, but another life was constantly stirring underneath, emerging after dark most evenings.

Darkness arrives late in the summer in Ireland. It's often around 10 or 11 before the energy fully shifts, although since dusk, energies from unseen realms increasingly demanded attention. Midnight to three in the morning appeared to be the peak times for exploring the shadowy recesses of my unconscious fears and attachments. Although I had delved into these for many years, now it was like being a deep-sea diver entering the dark underworld where light never penetrated. My consciousness served as a torch, illuminating and revealing thoughtforms that, until then, I hadn't realized existed. Some were ugly, while others were beautiful.

Some nights during these midnight meditations, I used various rituals to eliminate social conditioning. I confronted the thoughtforms of the seven deadly sins, and analyzed how I had created and fed them. I searched for the positive seed from which they initially grew and consumed the negative aspect of the thoughtform to transform it back into the positive seed. Another way to eliminate a thoughtform is to call upon beings of light to help dissolve it. This method is safer for most people, but consuming what I had created felt like the right technique for me.

Facing our greed, lust, anger, sloth, gluttony, laziness, and envy while examining where these exist in our lives presents a challenging scenario. Actively choosing to dissolve what we have created and resisting the urge to feed these thoughtforms demands a significant amount of willpower. When immediate rewards are scarce, it's tough to deny ourselves food, sleep, sex, or any form of gratification. Trusting in the Creator's plan and being willing to surrender to this plan gave me the strength to persevere.

I view this as a Garden of Gethsemane experience. If you remember the biblical story, it was night, and the disciples were sleeping when Jesus, meditating alone, asked God three times for the cup to pass from him. It didn't, and finally, he surrendered to God's plan. All who walk the path of the Dark Night of the Soul undergo Garden of Gethsemane experiences where loneliness prevails. We may feel that no one understands what we are going through. It may seem like a contradiction, but it's a time to continue persistent self-examination while simultaneously developing greater compassion for others. Everything I learned that summer sharpened this paradox.

Next came examining relationships with my father, mother, brother, Bill, and others to identify ways I wasn't fully loving them. These journeys initially brought me despair and self-criticism, but eventually, it was possible to let go of self-pity and embrace forgiveness for both them and myself.

Sometimes at midnight, my soul said to get dressed and go out. The nights were often rainy and always dark, which made this idea unappealing. However, doing as requested, I walked for miles along the lanes or by the sea, practicing the skills my soul was teaching. At times, I even attempted to de-materialize to pass through row hedges—but without success.

At other times, I sat in a cemetery with discarnate beings, some of whom were friendly while others tried to harm me. This gave me practice in self-defense while also helping these tortured souls move to higher planes where they could get help. Some were attached to the earthly plane due to grief, greed, violence, and anger. Nighttime vigils in graveyards were difficult, but they helped me overcome many fears and develop courage in those situations.

Sometimes, guides from higher realms provided instruction. On a few occasions, we traveled to an ancient stone dolmen tomb where I spent hours surrendering various aspects of my ego. Once, after stabbing my fingers on a rusty barbed wire fence to leave a blood offering, I lay down on the wet ground in different positions of the Celtic Cross to understand their meanings. Wandering in the hills on a rainy, foggy night, it was difficult to see where I was walking, let alone find the path home. Faith and trust in the guides, along with my surrender to the conditions, were continually tested.

Another time, the guides said to leave my glasses behind and walk several miles back to the cottage. Following their instructions, I wondered if the glasses would still be there the next day, and if not, how I would see for the rest of the summer. The next morning, I returned to where I had left the glasses and found them. Experiences like this strengthened my faith in inner guidance, no matter how bizarre the request. On nights like this, I might come back at 3 or 5 a.m., or sometimes at sunrise. The neighbors never knew about my nighttime outings, and I was always home in time for morning tea with Mrs. Toolis.

These nighttime practices in the cemetery and dolmen aligned with those of Hindu adepts who worship Kali, the Hindu goddess of destruction and death. Kali destroys evil demons, which symbolize negative thoughts. The souls in the cemetery were victims of these negative thoughts of famine, anger, and violence. By spending time with ghosts in a place of death, I gained courage while also helping them. When we confront our fears, no matter how we do it, we overcome them. The importance of doing this, cannot be overemphasized as it is an essential technique on the pathway to consciousness.

Alongside these day and night lives, a third life emerged that summer. The male leprechaun turned out to be a fascinating companion. During our initial days together, he engaged me in conversation. This conversation was telepathic in the same way beings from other dimensions communicate with me. (5)

"I'm studying humans," the leprechaun said. "It's wonderful to communicate with a human who can see me. It helps that you have had past lives with elementals. I use the word "elemental," which isn't our exact term, but words are powerful, so I won't share our true name. We prefer "elemental" to "faerie.""

"I've lived with elementals," I thought to myself. "I wonder what that means?"

Hearing me, he continued, "I know your real name, even one that you don't know at this moment, but I won't misuse it. I read in your vibration that your true essence is not human."

"If you know my name, what's yours?" I asked, making sure we were on equal footing.

"You can call me Lloyd," the leprechaun said with a smile.

"You mentioned a moment ago that I lived in the elemental world. Have I ever incarnated as an elemental?" I asked.

"No," Lloyd said. "But you have spent time in our world before returning to the human realm. Everything you have been, are now, or will be is recorded in your vibration. I can read this and know you are friendly to elementals."

"If I answer your questions about the human world, could you teach me more about the elemental world?"

X-country skiing just before the accident

Me in front of the Leprechaun's cottage

Mom and I launching Decoding Destiny

Just love those leprechauns

"Yes, I was hoping for that," Lloyd replied.

"And can I also speak with the female and child leprechauns?"

"No," he replied. "They are immature. In the human world, you become emptier as you evolve. It's the opposite in the elemental world. As we advance, we become more substantial and solid. I'm solid enough, and you're empty enough for us to communicate, but the female and young 'uns are not solid enough."

I could see the children playing in the corner of the room. They kept disappearing and reappearing.

"What are they doing?" I asked.

"They pop in and out of the Void, the space between matter," he answered. "Our young 'uns play like that and practice traveling to any place and any time. You can do the same, too, if you travel through the Void. In fact, you could even do this better than us if you believe it's possible."

"The Void," I contemplated to myself. "I wonder how elementals die?"

"When elementals die, we give up the will to live. We dissolve, dematerialize, and flow back into the Void from which we came," Lloyd stated, reading my thoughts.

"Do elementals ever incarnate in human evolution?" was the next thought.

"Evolved elementals have done this. Because you possess the free will to act, only humans can become fully realized creators on this planet. Thus, elementals have incarnated through human evolution to learn free will and cultivate love, enabling them to return and assist in elemental evolution. The individual you refer to as Vincent Van Gogh was one of these."

"And he shot himself and lived a miserable life," I reflected to myself.

Picking up my thoughts, Lloyd continued. "It's not easy for elementals to incarnate in human life because we don't share the same values as humans. We are beings of joy and don't limit who we share our energy with, so in your world, we are seen as unloving and immoral. By the way, we are far superior to you in dance, music, and art. In your human world, painting and sculpture are static art forms. In our world, these arts are multidimensional and constantly in motion. This is what Van Gogh was trying to show humans how to do. Our races don't always understand each other, but some humans and elementals have collaborated and formed friendships, so there is a precedent for you and me."

"What types of elementals exist and what are their functions?" I probed.

"We have guilds. Elementals are born into a guild and never consider changing their roles like humans do. Guilds consist of musicians, artists, craftspeople, healers, scholars, and storytellers. We even have a few prophetesses, and you are similar to them. We evolve by becoming experts in our calling. I'm a scholar, and my special study is humans."

"Why do you study humans?"

"It's a relatively new area of study. We are learning how you think and act to understand how to use free will like humans. And, to be honest, so we can protect ourselves."

"What do you eat?" I asked, as it was fascinating to discover more about Lloyd and elementals.

"We don't eat anything that is a living being," he replied, looking at me with disapproval. "Grains, fruit, honey, and milk are acceptable because the plants that produce them are alive. We don't kill them. Elementals find it obscene to watch humans eating flesh or even lettuce since it is a living being. By the way, I wouldn't mind if you gave me some toast and honey."

I did as Lloyd requested and often prepared food for him and his family. Although the food did not disappear, he said he absorbed its essence. On one occasion, I ate my piece of toast and, after half an hour, took a bite of his toast because I was still hungry.

"I've already extracted the living essence from the bread," Lloyd said, shocked by my action. "You are eating my waste."

We had many fascinating conversations over the summer, and he taught me a lot about the elemental world. Additionally, he offered protection from the aggressive, angry elementals living along the lane whenever I went out at night. Even today, I can call him anytime, and he always responds. Lloyd has assured me that he will always do so.

That summer, I also met the body elemental that builds and maintains my body from life to life. Most people don't know their body elemental. If they did, they could develop a good working relationship and heal themselves. The body elemental is, by another name, Spirit in form. By co-creating with it, you accelerate your spiritual evolution.[6]

My month was nearly over when Robert, Mr. Douglas's son, arrived with two friends on motorcycles. Robert asked if they could camp in the garden, and I happily agreed and invited them for lunch. They stayed for three rainy days, and one evening, Robert came in by himself to dry off by the fire. As we were talking and roasting apples, the leprechaun sat down beside me.

"Tell Robert that you have the cottage for the rest of the summer," Lloyd urged.

I resisted doing any such thing, but the leprechaun persisted, "Tell Robert you have the cottage for the summer."

After five minutes of badgering, I finally gave in to his request. "Robert," I said, "there's a leprechaun sitting next to me."

Robert was intrigued and asked, "That's amazing! May I ask him a few questions?"

"Yes," I replied.

"What does he think of my family?" Robert asked.

"We're really happy with them and sad to see you go," Lloyd replied.

"C'mon. Tell him you have the cottage for the rest of the summer," the leprechaun nudged me."

"Robert, the leprechaun says that it's possible to have the cottage for the rest of the summer," I said.

"That's impossible," Robert said. "You need to leave because the new owners have to vacate their rented cottage at the end of July. The cottage belongs to the German writer Heinrich Böll, who is arriving on August 1st. Otherwise, you could have stayed here."

We spoke a little while longer before Robert left. The next morning, I was washing dishes when Robert arrived at the door, a newspaper in hand. He looked shaken and cautious. He opened the paper to the front page and turned it toward me.

"Heinrich Böll dead," the headlines read.

"Neither I nor the leprechauns killed Heinrich Böll, Robert," I said, addressing his unspoken fear. "Elementals can foresee the future. They knew there would be no obstacle to my staying in the cottage and told you so."

Robert left for Dublin that day. He must have told his father the story because the following week a letter arrived from Mr. Douglas saying I could stay in the cottage for another month.

Lloyd was happy to have me for another month and had a request.

"I want you to write about everything I've taught you about elementals in 10 years," he said, lounging on the couch.

"How will I remember everything in 10 years," I said, hoping to not write another book.

"I'll be there, darlin', so you'll remember everything," Lloyd answered, grinning from ear to ear.

True to his word, Lloyd and his friends have often joined me since then. I just have to think of him, and he's there. The book became *Summer with Leprechauns*, and, as Lloyd requested, it was written 10 years later. Living and learning about elementals from Lloyd was the first time I had developed a relationship with a non-human being. The spirit guides and Masters I'd communicated with until then were all human. Lloyd was an unexpected and delightful departure from my focus on human evolution. He opened the door to embracing many other non-human beings. Through this repeated pattern, I learned that one of my main soul purposes was to build bridges between worlds. This has been a key pathway to consciousness for me.

During that summer, I lived three lives. The daytime life was that of an ordinary guest in Ireland, being visited by Mrs. Toolis, her family, and others in the village. However, the other two lives—the nighttime adventures and chats with Lloyd, the leprechaun—were secret because the locals wouldn't have understood.

Perhaps you can relate to this in your own life. Have you also held back from discussing your meditation practice or other activities because you were certain others wouldn't understand? If so, it might be helpful to reconsider whether that assumption is still valid or needs updating. I believe that, at the time, secrecy was justified, but it no longer is about these topics. Why? Because the world has changed. Many things that were once unacceptable to discuss or do decades ago can now be openly talked about.

While in Ireland, our house was sold, and Bill decided to marry the friend he had been dating. Everything was both ending and beginning nicely, but it was still a shock to return home and have only three days to pack and find a place to live. There was an apartment building being renovated at the top of my old street, and luckily the owner said I could rent one of the unrenovated units.

I moved into this new home, but then couldn't think of anything else to do. This aimless feeling had happened before after returning from two long trips, so it was nothing new. However, during those times, new goals quickly appeared. It was just a matter of being patient and waiting for them to come up. This time was different. I didn't have any sense of future goals or a desire for them.

I wondered if Zasep Tulku Rinpoche could offer guidance on what to do next. I didn't realize how deep my despair was until I spoke with him.

"I don't have any more goals," I said.

"It's very good to give up attachment to goals," Rinpoche replied.

"But there's nothing I want to do in life anymore," I continued, starting to cry. Three months of self-pity poured out.

He looked concerned. Perhaps he was wondering if I was contemplating suicide. Realizing the absurdity of the situation, I began laughing.

"I'm not going to kill myself. Don't worry," I joked. "It's just that I have nothing nudging me saying, "Do this.""

"You need to find something you enjoy even a little and pursue that," Rinpoche said.

"Is there free choice about what that is? Are there no further karmic debts to repay?" I asked him.

"Yes. You have the freedom to choose whatever you want to do," he replied, confirming my intuition.

I moved on to another topic, saying, "It's difficult to sit and meditate. The only thing that works is staying conscious in the moment and examining all thoughts and feelings, which helps me maintain right motivation for my actions."

"That's exactly what you should do," Rinpoche said. "Just keep doing that and also practice breathing techniques."

A new chapter began. Now, I rarely spoke to the Masters who had guided me for the past four years. I had free will to choose a path, but these Masters observed to see if my choices aligned with the Divine plan. It was like being a creator on probation. The lessons from the positive, gaining path and the negative, eliminating path were balanced. Now, I consciously decided when to explore the light or shadow realms, and like the mature Persephone, could easily shift my time between them. Still, I lacked a place to apply these gifts and searched for a new direction, something to create. From this search, the Magical Mystery Tours to the sacred sites of the world were born.

# 15

# Sacred Sites and Magical Mystery Tours

Traveling to sacred sites around the world is a powerful and enriching way to awaken consciousness. Schools and centers for studying the inner mysteries and spiritual initiations were often located at these sites. These sites still carry a powerful charge through sacred geometrical and astronomical alignments, the use of magnetic energy lines, and the employment of appropriate building materials. Ancient peoples used these elements to catalyze profound inner changes in those participating in the mysteries. This can still occur today.

These sites can transform individuals at a cellular level once they complete the necessary preparatory work. Such preparation enables a person to become a key that can unlock the door to deeper realities. The correct procedure is essential for achieving this. My gift lies in knowing the procedure that was originally used at these sites and understanding how it can be adapted to benefit people alive today.

## England and Ireland

Over the years, I have experienced many deep inner journeys at the sacred sites of England and Ireland. One of the most meaningful occurred after visiting Edna Twigg in London. Mrs. Twigg encouraged me to go to Glastonbury to explore a connection to the Arthurian legend, and I followed her suggestion. Stonehenge was on the way.

Stonehenge is the most famous stone circle in Britain. It was constructed several thousand years ago by a pre-Celtic culture about which little is known. Scientists have found that Stonehenge served as a solar and lunar observatory. The alignment of the stones created by prehistoric people demonstrates an astounding mathematical precision even today.

Several years earlier, I'd visited Stonehenge and been awed by both the size of the stones and the majesty of the circle. This time, arriving by bus with other tourists, was different. As we approached the site, a ghostly male figure in a gray robe from an earlier era emerged through the stones and spoke to me.

"This isn't where the real initiations took place. Leave here and go to Avebury," he said.

"Who are you?" I inquired.

"I am the guardian of this place. You don't need to come here. Go to Avebury," he repeated.

Although this guardian did not exist in the physical world, our conversation was as easy as speaking with you. This way of perceiving through inner eyes and ears has been incredibly useful in understanding the true purpose of sacred sites around the world. The memory of what happened at the site is recorded in the ether, and it's possible to tune into the vibration surrounding the site to uncover the information.

Sacred sites hold incredible amounts of earth energy that can be utilized for healing both the Earth and individuals. A few years later, on our Magical Mystery Tour of England, we had private access for our group at Stonehenge. We performed a healing ritual at the stone circle by revitalizing and realigning the stones to their original purpose while also making their use relevant for today. But on this occasion, I took the guardian's advice and went to Avebury.

At that time, Avebury had not yet been discovered by tourists, so the town consisted of a single street with about 20 houses and a few shops. After settling into one of the only bed and breakfasts, I took a walk to explore the site and quickly realized that the guardian of Stonehenge was correct. Avebury was the place where the inner initiations took place in Britain, while Stonehenge served as the outer physical manifestation of these inner mysteries.

Avebury was a spiritual fertility site. Its immense configuration of stones is arranged in many interesting alignments. A female circle of stones, whose energy is dedicated to women, and a male circle for men are located there. Some stones reflect the various stages in humanity's development from the distant past to the present and into the future.

The stones stretch for miles on both sides of the lane linking Avebury with Silbury Hill, which is the oldest prehistoric structure in Britain and the largest earth mound in Europe. Originally, a similar set of stones lined the second lane from town; however, locals used these stones to build their homes, churches, and other structures.

After a brief introduction to Avebury, I headed down the lane to explore West Kennett Long Barrow. Archaeologists believe that long barrows in Britain served primarily as burial sites for high-ranking local individuals in the 4th and 5th centuries BCE. However, these long barrows also serve a spiritual purpose. Entering the dark entrance of the long barrow and, crouching under the low ceiling, I made my way through the darkness to the far end. There, sitting against the cold stone wall, I meditated on its deeper purpose. An image immediately sprang into view.

"What is your reason for disturbing this place?" a strong, middle-aged man with a commanding presence asked telepathically. He wore a mixture of furs and skins and carried a spear from a much earlier era.

"Please accept my apology," I said. "I'm from your future and am trying to understand the purpose of this long barrow."

He assessed my words before continuing. "I am the guardian of this site and this region. Our people have lived here for many ages, but there came a time when we faced the threat of invasion from warring tribes who desired our land. We constructed these long barrows to protect ourselves in the spiritual realm, just as others defended us physically."

"How did these sites provide spiritual protection for you?" I asked with curiosity.

"The finest among our people, at the peak of their power, gave their essence and energy to the sites. This long barrow was my responsibility."

"How did you accomplish this?" I asked the guardian.

"I was carried into this long barrow while in a trance. The priests performed rituals of protection, and journeying out of my body, I left my spiritual essence at this site to safeguard it from invaders. I am consecrated to do this and attack the spiritual bodies of those who desecrate this site and our land."

The guardian's words confirmed similarities between his purpose and the pharaohs' tombs in Egypt, which are protected etherically from grave robbers. Unfortunately, that is no longer the case. Returning four years later with a group, something prevented me from going inside. When the others came out, they described the interior in such detail that a question arose: "How were you able to see in the dark?"

"It's bright in there," one man answered, puzzled by my question. "The skylight brings in plenty of light."

Shaken, I climbed onto the outside of the long barrow and stood on the roof. The entire roof had been removed, and a glass skylight had been installed. It was shocking that archaeologists had defaced this sacred site so people could see it more clearly. They were the invaders that the guardians needed to protect themselves from now. However, during my first visit to Avebury, this future defacement had not yet happened.

After leaving the guardian on my first visit, I noticed a circle of holes on a nearby hill and headed there. There were no standing stones at this site; the original pattern was created by wooden posts. Markers indicated where these posts once stood. This crowned hill featured circles within circles of posts surrounding a center without posts. In an expanded spiritual state, I entered the outer circle and sought to understand the purpose of the rings. Then, walking the circle in a specific order, visiting some posts and avoiding others, the spiritual meaning of that circle revealed itself.

Each marker represented a different skill or gift. Initiates would meditate in various positions, discovering their unique paths through this practice. Sometimes, they would begin with one path and switch to another as they moved into the inner rings. At the center was an area of pure consciousness. While meditating on my personal path, I learned—or perhaps it is more accurate to say that it was confirmed—that my primary path was of the unknown, and the secondary path was that of love.

Silbury Hill, built around 2400 BCE, is the dominant feature at Avebury, so it was the next place to visit. From the summit, you get a

360-degree view. West Kennett Long Barrow is in one direction, while the lane back to town, lined with stones, is in the other.

Archaeologists are puzzled about why Silbury was constructed, but both common sense and spiritual observation reveal that Silbury Hill is a pathway to consciousness in many ways. It resembles the pregnant body of the Earth Mother. The hill, her womb, connects with two lanes of stones that represent the fallopian tubes. These lanes lead to the equivalent of two ovaries, which are the male and female stone circles at the center of Avebury.

There is a secondary purpose for Silbury Hill: it is a massive human-made structure conveying a message to other intelligent life forms.

It states, "Look, conscious beings are living here!" This explains why the entire area is a hotspot for UFOs and crop circles.

These explorations took many hours, and as darkness fell, I, exhausted, began walking back along the lane toward town. The darker the night became, the more my awareness grew that the stones lining the lane were watching me—and not in a friendly way. There was an electrical exchange between the stones on either side of the lane. One stone carried a negative charge while its opposite partner had a positive one. Walking between them disrupted their energy pattern. Although I carefully asked for permission, it was very time-consuming, and soon night fell. Suddenly, in the field to my left, more hostile stones than those along the lane started moving toward me. I was horrified.

How could this be happening? Three options quickly came to mind: run quickly up the lane, ignore what I was seeing, or stand still and try to understand why the stones seemed hostile.

Choosing the last option, I telepathically addressed the moving stones. "Who are you?" I asked.

Ignoring the question, they moved closer. "Stop. I apologize for disturbing you," I said.

Their pace slowed, and the beings inside the stones hesitated about whether to speak with me. They still posed a threat of violence. Mentally, I erected external barriers while softening my heart in sympathy toward them. Then, I prepared myself for whatever action was next.

"We're trapped within these stones," one of the beings communicated telepathically.

"How did this happen?" I asked.

"Early in this planet's history, before it became heavy and dense, we chose to manifest physically here. The Great Beings, who were helping with the planet's evolution, advised us not to manifest in this substance because it would become too heavy over time. We decided not to heed their warning, and now we find ourselves trapped."

"Is there anything I can do to free you from the stone?" I asked with concern.

"No, you must not interfere. Our destiny lies in another direction," the entity within the stone asserted.

I sent healing and loving thoughts their way. Although they were still not friendly, they tolerated me, freeing me from fear. I continued walking along the lane back to the bed and breakfast. Heather, the landlady, greeted me as I entered the house.

"Where have you been?" she asked. "I've been worried about you."

"I've been walking up the lane," I replied, trying to sound casual.

"Not even the locals walk that lane at night," she said, amused. "Visiting mediums who come to Avebury only last five minutes before leaving. Others love it."

We exchanged a smile that acknowledged our mutual understanding before I said goodnight and went to bed. It was a brief night's sleep, as the male circle had instructed me to be there by 6 o'clock the next morning.

Gateways to other realities exist within the male and female stone circles at Avebury. Tourists see only fields of megalithic stones because they lack the proper keys, intention, or vibration, so the doors stay closed. However, those who seek the inner mysteries with the correct vibration and motivation can open these doors to other realities. During the summer and winter solstices, full moons, and specific times of day, the veil between physical reality and these other worlds becomes thinner and easier to pass through. The best times to access these energies in the male circle are at 6 a.m. and 6 p.m. daily, while the optimal periods in the female circle are at 12 a.m. and 12 p.m.

When these stone circles were originally constructed and operated as sacred sites, women were only allowed in the male circle under special circumstances. Likewise, men were excluded from the female circle except at special times. It's enjoyable being a woman and not a man, but I work well with what is typically thought of as male or yang energy in our culture, and the male circle invited me to enter.

Arriving at the entrance to the male circle just before 6 a.m., I entered with great respect and waited for guidance. The stones guided my steps in a zigzag pattern between them, reminiscent of Zeus's and Thor's thunderbolts. The energy and active force were empowering.

Sacred sites are often built on the Earth's acupuncture points. Ley lines, or dragon lines, are energy pathways that connect these points, energizing and maintaining the Earth's health. Walking the zigzag pattern, I tuned the male circle to stabilize and energize these points along the ley line, helping to heal the Earth. After fulfilling the male circle's request, I left and waited until noon to join the female circle of stones.

The entrance to the female circle is between two guardian stones. At noon, they granted permission to enter. I walked slowly toward the Mother stone at the center of the circle. One side is attuned to the nurturing, manifesting aspects of the Earth Mother. The other side aligns with her de-manifesting, ego-challenging aspect. I approached her nurturing side first, as it faces the circle's entrance, but was soon guided by the Earth Mother stone to move around to her darker Kali side. On this darker path, the Earth Mother teaches us to de-manifest what we have created and return it to the Void, where the energy is released and made available for re-manifestation.

The Mother stone instructed me to lie down beside her. Doing so, I entered a deep, nearly unconscious state, surfacing occasionally before sinking back down. The Earth Mother stone assessed and adjusted me at a cellular level to hold a stronger vibration. After what seemed like a long time—actually about 45 minutes—she told me to go to a round stone on the circle's edge. This stone felt like a grandmother with nurturing energy.

"She's quite a handful, isn't she?" the Grandmother stone joked about the Mother stone.

Resting beside the Grandmother stone gave me time to reflect on what had just happened. My gaze drifted to a woman sitting on the earth ring at the far end of the circle.

"See that woman," the Grandmother stone addressed me. "Go over to her and say these words."

She then repeated what to say. I stood up and walked over to the woman, who had her head down and was writing in a notebook.

"Excuse me," I said, "are you writing about the stones?"

"Yes," she responded in an icy tone that clearly conveyed, "Leave me alone and don't disturb me."

"Have you thought about sitting by that stone?" I gestured toward the Grandmother stone.

She put down her notebook, looked up at me, and said, "When I first got here, I sat by that stone for three days. Where did you get that information?"

"The stone told me," I replied.

"Can you talk to these stones?" she inquired in a warmer tone.

"Yes," I acknowledged.

The woman's body relaxed and her voice conveyed despair.

"I'm a psychologist from the States. Several years ago, I visited Avebury and made a solemn promise to write about the true purpose of these stones. I am dying and have returned to fulfill this vow. I've read everything about Avebury, but am stuck and can't move any further," she said.

"I haven't read anything about Avebury," I replied. "We could explore together. I can share what the stones reveal, and you can see if this aligns with your research. You'll learn to connect with the stones so you can receive direct insights yourself."

"I'd love that," she said happily.

We spent the afternoon exploring the various circles, and I shared what the stones told me about their purpose. Some of it aligned with her research, while much was new to her. Perhaps the most fascinating instance of our information matching was at a stone on the outer ring that surrounds both the male and female circles. Each stone in the outer ring symbolizes a different stage of planetary and solar initiations. Upon reaching one of the stones, I said to my companion, "This is Lucifer's stone, and this one," pointing to the stone on the right, "is for his consort. Lucifer is the gateway between the planetary and solar initiations."

"This is incredible," she responded. "In books, this stone is called the Devil's stone."

By the end of the day, she was attuning to the stones and trusting the stones to teach her.

A few years later, after leading the Magical Mystery Tour of England, further confirmation reinforced these incredible Avebury experiences. I had read several books on the Arthurian legend, but the one that resonated the most was *The Secret Tradition in Arthurian Legend* by Gareth Knight. I wrote to Gareth Knight and received an invitation to dine with him after our tour ended. A large citrine egg expressed a desire to join us for the meeting, so I decided to take it at the last minute.

At the pre-arranged time, I arrived at the Chinese restaurant to be greeted by a warm, soft-spoken man. He mentioned that Gareth Knight was his pen name and introduced himself as Basil Wilby. Like many influential people, his persona was different from his higher Self. It seemed as if his persona acted as a cover for the strength beneath the surface. You can see this same phenomenon with Tibetan monks, who often display a child-like, laughing persona but still deliver powerful spiritual teachings.

Basil and I enjoyed a meal getting to know each other. We subtly probed each other to gauge how deep we could dive while still being understood. In a short amount of time, we reached a point where we both respected and liked each other.

"What did you think of my new book *The Rose Cross and the Goddess?*" Basil asked.

It's quite risky to even slightly criticize an author's work. For some authors, it's worse than criticizing their children. As a result, I felt anxious about responding.

"I liked a lot of things about it, Basil, but felt you were holding something back," I replied.

His face lit up as he answered, "You're right."

"Why did you do that?" I inquired with curiosity.

"I've been writing for over 20 years and have eight published books translated into five languages. Many people believe in and trust what I say, and I don't want to push their faith to the breaking point. Recently, strange things have been happening to me that no one would believe."

"Try me," I invited.

His persona faded, and his eyes studied me intently to decide if it was okay to share something.

"Sometimes when I'm driving my car, King Arthur sits beside me and talks to me. This is not my imagination; he is really there." He paused, then continued, "And the last time I was in Avebury during the full moon, the Mother circle wouldn't let me enter. You probably won't believe this, but the stones actually moved."

"I believe you," I replied, "because I saw the stones in Avebury move as well. On the Magical Mystery Tour I just led, one of the participants was not allowed to enter the Mother circle to be with the rest of us. When she tried, a forcefield barred her way."

"I hope you'll consider writing about your experiences," I said. "This information needs to be shared, and you could do it with the credibility you've built over the years."

He smiled slightly, weighing what I was saying, and replied, "You may be right. But now might not be the time."

At that moment, I felt a strong urge to give him the citrine egg I had brought. I reached into my purse, took it out, and placed it in his hand. He was overjoyed with the gift.

"You've given me the key to open the door in a process I'm currently going through. I can't discuss it now, but I'll tell you in three years," Basil said.

I was happy to give him something he needed, even if I didn't know what the citrine egg represented for him. But this wasn't the point. Often, we might feel compelled to do something without understanding why, but it's important to listen to Spirit's nudge and act accordingly. Basil and I both appreciated confirming each other's experiences at Avebury. We were spiritual allies for each other. Additionally, his book about King Arthur and the legend of the Quest for the Holy Grail helped me understand my connection to that myth. This was the journey Mrs. Twigg had guided me toward several years earlier, leading me to Glastonbury.

Some accounts suggest that Glastonbury is the location of King Arthur's Camelot, and it's possible that a real Arthur ruled in the 6th century CE after the Romans left. The story of the Knights of the Round Table and the Quest for the Holy Grail has shaped the Arthurian legend. This quest refers to the cup used by Jesus Christ during the Last Supper. According to one tradition, Joseph of Arimathea brought this cup to Glastonbury. In any case, the search for the Grail became a symbol across Europe during the 12th and 13th centuries, representing the quest for enlightenment.

The Quest for the Holy Grail is a story that calls to me. My life story, in many ways, is a mirror of Perceval's, one of the knights who found the Grail. Many of the steps Perceval takes may be familiar to you, too, as his life is a spiritual story of one pathway to enlightenment.

The name Perceval symbolizes piercing the veil that separates physical reality from higher dimensions. Perceval is raised in obscurity by his mother, who keeps him unaware of his origins so he won't leave her and meet the same fate as his father, a great knight. Despite this, Perceval chooses to become a knight and travels to King Arthur's court. He is unfamiliar with proper knightly conduct and, although talented, makes many mistakes and is rejected by the court. Sent away for training as a knight, he becomes involved with a woman and fathers two children. However, dissatisfied with his domestic life, he leaves them to pursue a spiritual quest for the Grail. In the first part of his story, Perceval demonstrates how we must develop our gifts and succeed in the material world. When we realize that this will never fulfill us, we must leave the material world to embark on our spiritual journey—the quest for enlightenment.

Perceval quickly finds the Grail Castle and sees the Grail, which symbolizes a high spiritual state. However, because he fails to ask the wounded, impotent Fisher King—the guardian of the Grail—the question that would heal him, Perceval loses his elevated spiritual state. He neglects to do this for two reasons: societal conditioning that discourages asking personal questions and his lack of sufficient compassion. Although he has both spiritual and physical gifts aiding his success, he has only followed the positive path where everything he desires comes to him effortlessly.

Now, Perceval must walk the ego-denying, challenging path of the Dark Night of the Soul to shed his social conditioning and develop compassion for others' suffering. This occurs through his own pain. The Grail disappears, and he spends the next five years wandering through the Wasteland, fighting battle after battle. These are the struggles that we all must face to overcome our ego's desires and attachments. The Wasteland represents the state of emptiness each of us encounters during our own Dark Night of the Soul.

Perceval finally fights a black knight who defeats him. He surrenders and is willing to die, but the black knight shows mercy and spares him. In the story, we learn that the black knight is Perceval's unknown half-brother. He symbolizes our unconscious and our darker nature that we fear knowing. When the conscious (Perceval) and unconscious (Black Knight) parts of our personality unite, we are ready to advance on our spiritual journey. Together, Perceval and his half-brother discover the Grail Castle and heal the Fisher King, who, on one level, represents our Father God who possesses everything but our love. By giving God our love and our entire selves, we restore the Wasteland to fertility.

When Perceval first saw the Grail, he was too immature to fully understand its message. Only when wisdom, love, and power are in balance can we find the Grail and use it to help others. Walking Perceval's path means valuing and integrating all chakras, from our most physical at the root to our most spiritual at the crown. It involves balancing the lessons of both positive and negative experiences to become a true creator in service to humanity.

Perceval's journey has also been mine, and I am thankful to Mrs. Twigg for guiding me to understand these mythic aspects of my spiritual path. This myth has endured for centuries because its message is universal, pointing to what many of us face on the road to consciousness. This is the main role of myth: myths are signposts guiding us toward understanding our inner journey. It's especially reassuring to know, if you too have wandered in the Wasteland of the Dark Night of the Soul, that these stories confirm that this, too, shall pass. It encourages me, as I hope it encourages you, to trust that with persistence and the right motivation, we will ultimately, like Perceval, reach our goal.

I have led three Magical Mystery Tours to Britain, Ireland, and Scotland, and two of these tours featured special events on Pentecost. In the Bible, Pentecost is the day when the disciples are in the upper room (meaning in a high spiritual state) after Jesus's death. The flame of the Holy Spirit descends on them, transforming them into apostles, and the authority given by the Spirit enables them to teach about Jesus's life.

One Pentecost in Glastonbury, our group participated in an early sunrise meditation atop the Tor. The Tor, the hill overlooking Glastonbury, is sacred to the Earth Goddess and was a pilgrimage site long before the advent of Christianity.

Among our group were Phyllis Furumoto, the Reiki Grandmaster, and several Reiki masters from Europe. Phyllis had previously asked me if, after our meditation, she could make one of her students a Reiki Master. Our group was invited to participate in the experience, but we were told to close our eyes because we were not meant to witness the ritual. After the initiation was finished, I felt drawn to ask Phyllis and the other masters for their blessing. I had long honored the Reiki tradition and wanted to express these feelings outwardly. Phyllis and the other masters formed a circle around me, requested I close my eyes, and granted me their blessing.

One of the hearing-impaired participants, who had not closed her eyes during either the Reiki master initiation or my blessing, announced loudly, "Congratulations. Now you're a Reiki Master."

"I'm not a Reiki Master! That was just a blessing," I declared quickly. I didn't want any erroneous rumors to spread about me being a Reiki Master.

A week later, Inger, one of the Reiki Masters, asked me, "Have you ever thought about becoming a Reiki Master?"

"Wanja Twan wanted to make me a master a few years ago," I answered. "I told Wanja I would only accept if Phyllis approved of me being an honorary, but not a practicing, Reiki Master. Although I feel linked to many masters, it is not my path to teach Reiki."

"What did Phyllis say?" Inger asked.

"She said no," I replied, "and that is fine."

Two months later, a letter arrived from Inger saying that Phyllis had asked her to tell me she had made me a Reiki Master on the Tor. Phyllis explained that I was already a Master and had been given the Reiki Master initiation to acknowledge that. The gift felt comfortable and like an honor, similar to when Alma Bell Brown made me a minister. Both Alma and Phyllis offered these gifts gently, without tying me to a specific path, and for that, I am grateful.

Because Pentecost is so meaningful in my life, I want to share a second experience from Ireland during another Magical Mystery Tour. While in Ireland, we stayed at Bellinter House, operated by the Sisters of Our Lady of Sion, whose mission is to promote peace in a fractured world. Bellinter House is located in the sacred Boyne Valley, which in old Celtic times was the home of the High King of Tara. Interestingly, William Delamere, my ancestor on my mother's side, founded a Franciscan Friary in Multyfarnham near Bellinter House in 1268.

It was more than a little synchronistic that my ancestor and the Sisters of Our Lady of Sion were both engaged in interdenominational work dedicated to peace. It is always important to pay attention to patterns that repeat in our present lives from past lives. Had I been a Sister of Our Lady of Sion in a previous life? Had I been a Franciscan friar? How were these themes interconnected? When we see a synchronistic pattern emerge in our lives, Spirit gives us a clue to examine the underlying spiritual significance. It's important not to dismiss synchronicities as mere coincidences. Witnessing and acting on synchronicities is an active practice we can engage in to become more conscious.

While at Bellinter House, I conducted a weekend retreat called The Festival of Light. The theme was to promote peace among Catholics, Protestants, and people of all faiths. Participants from both the north and south of Ireland joined our tour group. The event culminated on Pentecost, the day the senior sister approached me.

"Could you lead our Pentecostal service this evening?" Sister Beth asked.

"I'd be happy to, but it might be a bit unorthodox," I replied, smiling and giving her a chance to reconsider her request.

"It would be good to shake up some of the sisters and get them thinking in new ways," Beth laughed.

As Beth was speaking, an image of one of the sisters, Mary, who did not approve of me, came to mind. In the food lineup, huffing with disapproval, she always gave me a smaller helping than others.

I arranged the chairs in a spiral in the chapel. The spiral led to the altar, which was adorned with symbols from nature—stones, flowers, water, and candles representing the four elements. When the celebrants entered, they received an unlit candle and chose a spot along the spiral path. The heavy oak doors were closed, and we lit the candles on the altar to start the ritual. Suddenly, the doors blew open. Since these doors faced an enclosed hall, no wind could have caused this. Even a strong gust wouldn't have been able to move the heavy oak doors. The group fell silent, sensing a higher power was present. Someone closed the doors, and we continued the ritual. For a second time, the doors blew open.

"It's the Holy Spirit!" Mary, the most skeptical of the sisters, exclaimed in awe.

We in the chapel felt that, like the apostles during Pentecost, we were being consecrated by the Holy Spirit to serve and help humanity. I started the service for the third time, and this time was allowed to continue. Each person shared their unique gift and dedicated it to helping the world.

After the service concluded, Mary approached me. "When I came in and saw how you arranged the chairs, I almost left," she said. "I didn't think you were doing what was right, but I was wrong. Tonight was the most moving night of my life. Thank you."

The next morning, Mary, beaming with a big smile, put a substantial serving of food on my plate.

It's important to trace our blood ancestry because our life essence is recorded in it. By observing the strengths and weaknesses of our parents, grandparents, and ancestors, we can gain insight into our own traits. Often, as people age and approach death, they feel a strong urge to return to their roots or reconnect with relatives they haven't seen in 50 years. This call deserves to be honored. By traveling to Ireland and England myself and later guiding others there on Magical Mystery Tours, I answered that call. [7]

Additionally, we may feel drawn to travel to a country for spiritual initiation(s). Initiations occur when we release old fears and attachments that bind us to the physical world, allowing our vibration to rise to a higher level of consciousness. We begin to view our lives and the material world with greater detachment. Our values change, and with each initiation, our desire to connect with the Divine grows deeper. Experiences in Avebury, becoming a Reiki Master in Glastonbury, and being embraced by the Holy Spirit during the chapel ceremony in Ireland were powerful initiations. While I have shared some publicly, many initiations remain private, and it is important for individuals to recognize and honor them.

But our life essence is not solely connected to our immediate genetic ancestors. We may have belonged to many different races in past lives, and this, too, is part of the life essence we carry in our blood. Tracing our ancestry in both ways—from our physical ancestors and from our past lives—is necessary. By doing this, we discover our soul and the potentialities we have brought into this life.

# Egypt

The quest to discover what was encoded in my blood from past lives led to Egypt. After completing the first Magical Mystery Tour of England and Ireland, I flew to Vancouver for the Expo. The Expo was a world fair featuring exhibits from around the world, including the Egyptian pavilion of Ramses II. Having visited the King Tut exhibition several years earlier, I was familiar with Egyptian artifacts and looked forward to a similar display. Instead, an unexpected pathway to expanded consciousness opened.

Entering the Ramses II pavilion, I immediately entered a superconscious state. The kundalini vibration coursed through my body, and if anyone had spoken to me, it would have been difficult to answer. Backing up against a wall, I prayed that no one would touch me.

Then, I popped out of my physical body and hovered near the ceiling, looking down at the people walking through the exhibit. The artifacts were catalyzing this energy, but why? In my astral body, I approached a plaque explaining the exhibit and read it.

"All these artifacts were discovered in Tanis, the capital of Lower Egypt in the Nile Delta during the time of Ramses II," the plaque read.

The name Tanis has often pointed the way to understanding my life purpose. Until that moment in the Ramses II pavilion, however, there had been only one signpost. As a child, my parents said that Tanis in Cree meant "my daughter," and later, a Cree medicine man said it actually meant "daughter to the people." Feeling drawn to both study with and befriend First Nations people, this name seemed fitting. Now the name led to Egypt to visit Tanis and learn more about a connection to the ancient Egyptian civilization and Ramses II.

Joe Jochman, a New Age scholar who specialized in the mystical significance of Egypt's ancient sites, was leading a tour of Egypt, and I signed up. Unfortunately, the ancient site of Tanis was not included in his tour, so I had to fly to Egypt several days early to visit it. Easier said than done. Tanis was off the usual tourist route, making it difficult to find public transportation. Additionally, no one could understand why anyone would want to go there since there was supposedly nothing to see. Finally, in frustration, I rented a taxi and set out early one morning for Tanis.

Tanis was located in the delta, once the fertile and lush region of Egypt. There was no desert to protect the remains, so very few buildings still stand. Because of this, the site offers little to attract tourists. Others warned me that, while it was being excavated, the site was not open, but why not take a chance? We arrived just as the archaeologists left for lunch and, after giving a small baksheesh to the guard, gained entry.

Wandering around the site as if watching a movie, I saw many lives in Atlantis. After Atlantis sank, I went to Egypt to preserve and carry forward the remnants of Atlantean high culture and civilization. Tanis was my last Egyptian life, witnessing the decline of the Egyptian culture I had dedicated several lives over thousands of years to develop.

The next life was in Crete, where the Minoan civilization was already established.

Most of the buildings at Tanis remain buried beneath the sand, but the cobras painted on the temple walls caught my attention. Since ancient times, snakes have been associated with goddess worship. They symbolize death and rebirth because they can shed their skin. They also stand for healing and spiritual transformation. The upright poses of the cobras indicated the awakening of kundalini energy and helped reveal that Tanis was a place for initiation in later Egyptian dynasties. It was here that initiates focused on opening and using their crown chakras.

I saw that Egyptian priests viewed their country as a gigantic human body. They built temples along the Nile at energy points that matched the body's chakras. Egyptian initiates traveled from the solar plexus chakra at Karnak, where they received their first training, down to Abu Simbel, which represents the lowest chakra in Egypt. Ramses II built a temple in Abu Simbel because it was the perfect spot in Egypt to channel physical power.

Leaving Abu Simbel, initiates began a journey through the temple sites that represented the other chakras until they reached the crown chakra in Tanis. This process would take years, and some individuals never completed it, choosing instead to stay in various temples along the way. Those who did reach Tanis still had not finished their journey. They returned to the third eye chakra, the Sphinx, on the Giza Plateau, which functions as the gateway between this world's reality and that of the unseen world.

Witnessing this process and Tanis's role in it, there was a sense of closure. There was nothing more the site could teach me; the experiences there merely skimmed the surface of deeper connections to past life links with Egypt. I didn't have to wait long for these connections to surface.

Returning to Cairo, I joined Joe Jochman's tour. We stayed at a luxurious hotel called the Mena House, which resembled something out of the Arabian Nights. The hotel was located near the pyramids. On the very first night, as my roommate Suzanne and I were getting ready for bed, Spirit urged me to visit the pyramids.

"Where are you going?" asked Suzanne when she saw me preparing to leave the room.

"I feel called to go to the pyramids right now," I replied, not wanting to say more.

"Can I accompany you?" asked Suzanne, getting out of bed and starting to dress.

"I will probably be away for several hours and would like to remain silent," I replied, making sure she understood the conditions.

"Yes, fine," she said, smiling.

"Also, someone is waiting for me at the Pyramid of Giza, and I will leave with him. You will have to go back to the hotel on your own."

Surprisingly, she agreed, and we left the Mena House to start along the path leading to the pyramids.

Seeing the pyramids shimmering under a moonlit sky transported me to another time. This was more than just a vision of a past life. Time and space shifted, and I was physically alive in a different body from that past. It was daytime, and the sun was blazing as I walked along the same path in a procession. People lined both sides of the well-worn path, watching me. I was a small woman with nearly Asian features wearing a white ceremonial dress. Her name was Tari.

Tari was one of the daughters of the gods, which is what the descendants of the Atlanteans who colonized Egypt were believed to be. As Tari, I taught and helped the local people, who were the natives of that land during that period. These individuals were not particularly intelligent, and I sought to raise their consciousness and plant seeds of morality and high culture within them. They loved me dearly, even though some of my kin regarded these efforts with good-humored amusement. Many of them couldn't understand why I chose to spend time with the locals when they were far more stimulating company. These Atlantean descendants overlooked the fact that our race was dying out and that the local people would eventually succeed us. I was passing on all that was best in Atlantean culture to the local inhabitants so it could be preserved.

A tall, silent man accompanied me in this work. He may have been a eunuch, and he resembled neither my race nor the indigenous people. He was descended from a much older race that had been in Egypt long before our arrival. He served as a kind of guard, although it was unnecessary, as no one attempted to harm me. We shared a strong, unspoken bond, since our purpose in helping these people was the same. This man, Abdel Hakim, was our guide on my current trip to Egypt. Seeing this reinforced how the people we meet in this life are also known in past lives. I also knew that when Tari died, she was buried in a temple built for her on the Giza plateau.

Suddenly, as if a page turned in a book, I found myself transported to another time and in another body, that of a tall woman with darker skin and more Negroid features. Her name was Nefertari. I descended from an ancient race south of Egypt, a land controlled by the Nubians during that era. Our ancestors had the ability to manifest physical objects by channeling the power of their lower chakras. This ancestral power to create in the physical world through their lower chakras is reflected in Neolithic goddess figures, where the Mother Goddess is shown with large hips and belly. As Nefertari, I still carried some of that power within me and chose to use it to help Ramses II, who was my husband. We were equal partners in this endeavor. He built the Abu Simbel temple as a generating station to harness that energy for Egypt's defense.

The pharaohs were the highest initiates in Egypt, and if they could not pass the initiations, they were not permitted to be pharaoh. Pharaohs were priest-kings, considered the most spiritually and physically fit to rule. Ramses, who began his reign in 1279 BC, ruled for almost 70 years just before the decline of Egypt's high culture. Both Ramses II and Nefertari recognized that Egypt was destined to decline but sought to prolong the period so that more knowledge could be disseminated and more hybrids between the blood of the sons of the gods, the Atlanteans, and the local people could be born.

I had never heard of Tari before this experience, but was familiar with Nefertari. It was interesting to notice a resistance to seeing myself as a famous person, which may stem from a resistance to having an inflated ego. However, this is what I experienced. The fact that Ramses II established his capital in Tanis, my namesake, confirmed this experience for me. By building a temple in Abu Simbel, the root chakra, and then making his capital in Tanis, the crown chakra, Ramses aimed to harness the entire kundalini energy of the land.

Nefertari lived at a later period than Tari. In both lives, I was walking toward the Great Pyramid of Giza to undergo an initiation, knowing that initiators would be waiting there for me. Tari and Nefertari had no fear of the initiation process because they had gone through initiations in many previous lives. Tari and Nefertari remembered all their lives, both on Earth and even before. These two Egyptian lives kept switching back and forth by slightly shifting focus between them. I was also in my current life and existed at the same time in all three lives.

Approaching the pyramids as Tari and Nefertari, I saw four priests wearing masks representing the four sons of Horus, waiting at the entrance. Each son of Horus guards a different direction and protects vital organs of the human body. Each organ system must be balanced before a person can undertake the initiation into the inner mysteries. These four priests were the initiators overseeing the ritual of death and rebirth I was about to experience. Even while remaining Tari and Nefertari, I knew there would be a similar kind of initiation that night in my current life.

Walking in this superconscious state, I arrived at the entrance to the Great Pyramid. Suddenly, a massive man stepped out of the shadows. "I have been waiting for you," he said. "Come with me."

After I nodded in agreement, he turned and walked into the desert, confident I would follow.

Suzanne, who had been silently accompanying me until now, finally broke her silence. "Are you sure you know what you're doing?" she asked. "I'm going back to the hotel."

From a superconscious state, I heard myself say, "It's alright. I'll return before morning. Thank you for accompanying me this far."

It was fitting that Suzanne was there, as she had been my handmaiden during Nefertari's life. However, whatever was about to happen now was for me alone. I followed the strange man into the night, knowing he was the guide for this unfolding inner journey. Still in a superconscious state, my body moved automatically, much like it had on the trek several years ago in the Amazon jungle. Finally, we reached the Sphinx, and after a few words to the guard, we were granted passage through the gate. He led me to the paws of the Sphinx.

"You stay here and I will come back for you later," he said in heavily accented English.

Spending the entire night between the paws of the Sphinx revealed many things, many of which do not align with traditional archaeology. The Sphinx is older than the pyramids and was built by the Atlanteans more than 10,000 years ago. The medium, Edgar Cayce, claimed there was a secret chamber between the paws of the Sphinx that would reveal the lost records of Atlantis. This information can be accessed in humanity's Akashic records. These records are not physical but etheric. In a superconscious state, this information can be read as easily as reading a book in the physical world.

That night, these records revealed that the Sphinx is the unicell of the Earth, containing the memory of all that has happened, is happening, and will happen on our planet. This is why the final destination for initiates was not at the crown chakra of Tanis, but at the Sphinx, which opens the pineal gland to higher consciousness. In addition to this revelation, the cells in my physical body were attuned at the Sphinx to hold greater amounts of energy than before.

Near the end of the night, when the first rooster crowed in the nearby village, it was time to leave the Sphinx and find the guards. They were enjoying a cup of coffee and a cigarette and invited me to join them. They spoke no English, and I spoke no Egyptian, but we sat together in silence, savoring the last stars of the night. Finally, clasping my hands in a prayer position over my heart, I bowed in a Muslim fashion to show gratitude. Then, excusing myself, I walked back to the hotel where Suzanne was just waking up.

The tour lasted for another two weeks. During that time, I kept my experiences private and didn't mention anything to our guide, Abdel Hakim. The day before our tour ended, we returned to the Giza Plateau to visit the pyramids. This was the right time to speak with him.

"Hakim, have you heard of a temple for a priestess named Tari?"

"Yes," he replied.

"Could you please take me to see it?"

Hakim focused his intense green eyes on me and said gently, "You are Tari. You were my priestess then, and you are my priestess now."

With those words, he gestured in the direction and said, "Go by yourself. You won't need me to say anything. You'll know everything on your own."

Before leaving, I shared with Hakim the experience of our life together, and he said he had seen the same thing. It was a joy to find someone who shared this knowing. The temple is small and seldom visited and likely of little interest to anyone but me. However, it features an unusual frieze illustrating the five stages of initiation for humans. This small temple served as a preparatory initiation site where individuals would meditate on how to pass the various initiations.

Some countries and places feel more familiar to us than others. This can be because our ancestors came from there, or we have significant past lives in those locations. It's important to honor the call to visit the country that resonates with you. First Nations people stress the importance of living on their ancestral land, as it holds memories for them. I share this belief. Accessing your past life memories is easier when you're in the country, especially in the specific place where you once lived in a past life.

You may ask, "Why is it important to remember our past lives?" Doing so sheds light on our purpose in this life, but not only that. Our soul holds the memories of all we have been and are. Remembering the roles we've played, the gifts we've had, and the errors we've made helps us better understand the path back to Spirit.

For over 20 years, I led annual tours to sacred sites, including locations in Egypt, Peru, Bolivia, India, the American Southwest, New Zealand, France, Greece, Ireland, Britain, and Japan. Each of these countries called to me, reawakening something within my body's cellular memory. Additionally, one of the purposes was to give others the chance to awaken their memories as well. But the most important reason was that the Earth called us to visit sacred sites situated on her acupuncture points to help heal her and assist her in shifting to a higher, more conscious frequency.

Although I continued leading tours and walking pilgrimages, after this initial experience in Egypt, a significant cycle of learning and teaching in the world was coming to an end. The need to pause current activities and create space for the next phase was growing. There was no work I wanted to start, no courses, whether traditional or spiritual, new or old, that I wished to teach. I needed time to reevaluate my life and choose a new path for the future. We can only teach and support others through what we have learned; therefore, it would have been a disservice to both others and myself to resist the emptiness that lay ahead. This, at least, was how I viewed my spiritual growth and contribution to the world at that moment. Spirit often guides us in unexpected ways, and that was indeed what happened.

# 16

# A Big Life Change

Several years earlier, Father Osborg had introduced me to a doctor living in Nova Scotia who, like him, was involved with Amnesty International. Rod was tall and attractive, with dark hair streaked with red and gray. He had Celtic heritage, something I've always found appealing in men. We felt a strong attraction to each other; however, he was married with three children, so we did not pursue a relationship at that time. He and his wife had now separated, and we became increasingly close. After dating for a year and a half, we decided to live together. Considering the children, I agreed to move to Nova Scotia for a year. Afterward, if I didn't feel at home, he would come to Toronto for a year. Committing to Rod was mainly a personal choice rather than a spiritual one. Still, lines often blur when deciding what is personal and what is spiritual, and I had a vision of three distinct past lives with Rod.

After moving to Nova Scotia, I felt like a nobody doing nothing. Although I had experienced the Void before, the depth and length of the Nothingness that first year was greater than ever before. Writing about this is difficult because, on the surface, very little happened. There were no grand visions or spiritual breakthroughs. It had been hard to meditate and communicate with spiritual Masters for some time before moving to Nova Scotia, and this did not improve. As a result, my main source of spiritual support—which I could usually rely on during difficult or confusing times—was unavailable. Also, getting out of bed in the morning was tough without my previous roles of counseling, workshops, or writing to keep me busy. Still, on a deeper level, it felt right to let all outward forms of expression and old roles fall away.

In the past, during periods of Nothingness, it would have been possible to visit with good friends to lighten the load. Now, that was impossible, and since Rod had not maintained friendships from his marriage, there were no friends available. It was not an easy time for Rod either, as he had given up medicine, and none of the projects he had pursued had materialized. This was devastating, both emotionally and financially, as Rod sank deeper into debt trying to support his ex-wife and three kids with no income. We navigated through the emptiness together at a time when both of us had little positivity in our lives.

Unexpected lessons arose from living with Rod and in a small town in Nova Scotia. One area of growth was in my weakest area: being a traditional wife and stepmother, and supporting my partner through adversity while putting my own needs second. This proved to be challenging. Before living with Rod, I viewed my work as a manifestation of the Creator's work on Earth, which, by my definition at the time, was more important than the everyday responsibilities of being a wife and stepmother.

Now my time was consumed by watching one of the kids play hockey, golfing with the others, buying videos and food the kids liked, and attending soccer games with teams Rod was involved with. This was a world I'd only read about. Although this was my weakest area as a woman, I appreciated the importance of engaging in it with love for Rod, the kids, and myself. I began to gauge my progress by how much I enjoyed doing these things for them without my inner child shrieking, "What about me?"

What made this situation even more difficult was that I spent the year withdrawing from stimulation. Since age 18, I had either lived in Toronto, enjoying plays and ethnic restaurants, or traveled to exciting and interesting places around the world. In the small town where Rod and I lived, such entertainment was hard to find. At first, I didn't recognize my addiction to cultural and social stimulation, much like how some people are addicted to coffee, drugs, alcohol, or cigarettes. The signs of addiction were classic. They were feeling annoyed and depressed when I couldn't engage in enjoyable activities. I also spent a lot of time figuring out how to satisfy my addiction. Eventually, I tried to negotiate and, on my worst days, manipulate myself into feeding this addiction.

Recognizing my addiction to the excitement of big cities, travel, and ego satisfaction, I understood the need to overcome that dependency.

My new environment was perfect for this; it was like going cold turkey. My previous roles as a management consultant, counselor, or spiritual teacher were no longer valid. Whenever I tried to bring these aspects of my identity into conversations with new people, I alienated them. Only by talking about children, soccer, or the pub where Rod and I were co-owners was I able to make others feel relatively comfortable. Conversations about spiritual topics were definitely off-limits. Additionally, none of my old friends visited, so my former self-image was never reinforced.

Gradually, this old persona diminished, and I became more comfortable with my new role as a stepmother and traditional woman. Since my mother had never played with my brother or me, I had no role model for nurturing and playing with younger children. Rod also was not good at hands-on parenting of young children because, until now, his main role had been his career as a doctor. Fortunately, they had a wonderful mother, Jill, who welcomed me as a support for the kids, and I found a comfortable role as an older, wiser companion to them. I learned that there are two ways to be a mother: the first is the traditional mother, who generally wants children and loves the baby and child stages; the second is the companion, who enjoys her children when they mature, and she can be a friend. Jill was a traditional mother, whereas my mother—a great friend once I became an adult—was my role model as a companion. I had always loved teenagers, and now learning to love younger children became a gift.

I started to approach small tasks with the same love and attention I once gave to what I thought was more important. Over time, I reached a point where my ego no longer felt the need to assert itself. I accepted my new role without feeling it defined everything about who I was. The tension in our relationship eased as Rod and I both found a more harmonious way to live together in our new roles.

After a year in Nova Scotia, I began to emerge from the Dark Night of the Soul, not out of fear, resistance, or addiction to stimulation, but because its time had ended. I had explored the unfamiliar and shadowed parts of my personality and let go of what no longer felt right. Intuitively, I knew that my main purpose in this life was to use my spiritual gifts to help others. But how? I was devoid of desires, which was a good thing—yet, being at a standstill, I had no idea what Spirit wanted me to do next in the world. Rod couldn't help with this, nor could I help myself. Maybe other spiritual people could inspire this change. This desire led me to a Y.M.C.A. camp in New York State to participate in a series of monthly courses with Jean Houston. The series focused on the biographies of famous individuals who have changed our world.

I was drawn to Jean's courses for many reasons. After a year of spiritual isolation, I felt a deep need to be with others who were also interested in spiritual topics. Moreover, both of us taught the inner mysteries and guided people on tours to sacred sites. Jean was a woman with keen insight into what was happening in our world, and she had earned a well-deserved reputation as a teacher of teachers. One of her notable sayings was, "Don't pathologize, mythologize your life." She had applied this axiom in her own life, and perhaps she could assist with mine. Jean was a powerful woman who excelled at manifesting her potential in the world. Although I had been hesitant to fully embrace my power, it was the next lesson I needed to learn. Love, wisdom, and power must be balanced for us to fully manifest Spirit's wishes. I was born with wisdom, had nurtured love throughout my life thus far, but my willpower was lagging.

Power had been my weakest area for several reasons. I was afraid to step into the spotlight because, if I was wrong, I might mislead others. Also, what if my ego grew too large and overwhelmed my soul? This fear was rational, as it has happened to many spiritual teachers. Furthermore, I had been murdered in many lifetimes for being a mystic and for openly using these gifts. However, my biggest fear was that others would sense my differences and either dislike me or put me on a pedestal. Both reactions would be isolating.

I had been with Jean for nearly a year when she asked us to examine the recurring patterns or fractals we've created in our lives. My two strongest patterns conflicted with each other. In one case, the spiritual gifts I wanted to help others develop became clear. This represented a positive fractal where people appreciated these gifts. In the opposite fractal, I experienced failure and rejection when I tried to share them. This last image stemmed from forgetting my lines on stage as a child, being rejected by corporate clients for spiritual work, and even from past life rejections.

There were about 60 people in our class. Jean always used a microphone to speak and regularly passed around another microphone for group members to share their experiences during the exercises. Although I was comfortable speaking in small groups, I had never spoken in front of the entire class. This time, I decided to face my fear.

When Jean asked if anyone wanted to share their experiences, I stood up and, trembling, took the microphone. I mentioned that not only had these two patterns existed throughout my current life, but they had also recurred in my past lives. I handed the microphone back, thinking my revelation was complete. That's when Peggy Rubin, an actor and Jean's co-leader, suggested to Jean that I stand in front of the group.

Mixed feelings overwhelmed me as both positive and negative patterns surfaced at the same time. At that moment, Jean said something that dramatically changed how I saw myself.

"If you don't like the pattern, change it," Jean said. "This or other incarnations aren't the issue; it's the other stories. You get so caught up in a narrative that you play it out and frame it."

Turning to the group, Jean continued, "Now this is a lady who can see. One of the challenges of being able to see between the worlds, to explore the deeper realms, both the inner and outer realms together, is that the body, brain, and nervous system tend to close down other ways of seeing for oneself. It's a protective mechanism so that she doesn't necessarily observe the magnificent patterns of co-creation that are yearning for her."

I was glued to the spot, my heart fluttering, as Jean spoke, her words unmasking me.

Turning to me, Jean asked, "What is your dream, Tanis? How can we see you that will charge you with new patterns?"

Her commanding words propelled me into the same soul's truth that I had experienced many years ago when Zasep Tulku Rinpoche mentally seized and questioned me.

"My great dream is to teach people how to see the things I see," I said. "To help others explore the depths, heights, the elemental world, other worlds, the future, and the past. At the same time, I don't want to be isolated because of these gifts. I want to be accepted, respected, encouraged, and challenged to fully realize these gifts and help others develop their spiritual gifts."

At that moment, Richard, a professional actor and director in our group, spoke up, "Are you willing to do this anyway—even if we don't help?"

"Yes, at this point, I'm going to pursue this with or without your help," I replied. "It's clearly a deep thing for me."

"Yes, clearly!" Jean responded. "Tanis, I want you to visualize being seen. Share about the energy waves you're picking up from the group."

Richard stepped forward and held the microphone while the three professional actors guided me through this ritual. Peggy knelt on my left, holding my hand. She embodied the archetypal energy of a mother, full of love and compassion. Jean, on my right, represented wisdom and power. Richard, standing behind me, brought both masculine energy and completed the triad to help me release the old story of fear about being seen in my authentic Self. The universe, these three professionals, and the group supported success. Little Tanis felt terrified, but my higher Self recognized that Jean was right. It was time to create a new story.

Participants sent out positive energy in various ways over the next few minutes, encouraging me to share what I was receiving. I was now truly a mystic out of a closet. Once finished, I thanked them and sat down, feeling complete, accepted, and grateful. What happened next was life-changing.

Jean began the closing exercise for the night. We were to reenact the initiation story of Persephone. In that ancient Greek myth, an unwilling Persephone is taken by Hades into the Underworld, where she discovers her true power to become the queen of the Underworld. Like Persephone, I had been an innocent girl-woman when I, too, was abducted by a Hades-like man and taken to the Underworld. Since then, I have visited that Underworld many times, but have never fully embraced my true power as Persephone had. The time had come.

In the ritual, each member of our group received a small candle enclosed in a glass holder. We were then instructed to line up in a single file to silently walk through the spiral maze of the labyrinth. At the center of the labyrinth was an altar with water, frankincense, and myrrh, which we were to use to bless ourselves. I took my place in line and noticed the woman who had fallen in behind me. She was a weekend guest who, the previous evening, had performed a solo show for us. This weekend seemed to be filled with actors accompanying me.

The line started to move, and soon, I entered the maze. While walking, I contemplated what had transpired that evening and prayed to Spirit to release my old self-defeating pattern and empower my higher Self's vision. Before long, I reached the entrance to the center of the labyrinth, where the altar lay. Someone was at the altar, so I stopped to await my turn.

Suddenly, smoke and flames shot from the top of my head. The other participants rushed over and struck me on the head, trying to extinguish the fire. Since we were in the middle of a sacred initiation ritual, this was done in silence. Sensing the deeper significance of what was happening, I remained calm and at peace. This was a modern equivalent of empowering Jesus' disciples in the Upper Room when the flame of the Holy Spirit descended on their heads. From that moment, the disciples became apostles, messengers of the Word of the Creator, empowered to share Jesus' teachings with others. This was the third time the Pentecostal fire had blessed me.

The others returned to their places in line, and the altar was cleared. I stepped forward, picked up the water, and anointed not only myself but also the woman who had been walking behind me. Then, silently, I made my way back through the labyrinth. The woman, followed me through the maze, exited behind me, and signaled for me to go to a corner of the room.

"The flame jumped off my candle and landed on your head," she whispered anxiously. "I'm so sorry. My biggest fear is lighting my own hair on fire. Now I've done it to you. The flame actually jumped onto the top of your head."

"Don't worry," I assured her. "You've done me a service. The flame landed on my crown chakra. I've had issues with fire before, and now the fire has come through my body and out my head. This is a gift. Thank you."

At that moment, another woman approached and handed me a mirror. There was a large, circular bald patch on the top of my head where my hair had been burned away in a modified version of the tonsure worn by medieval monks. The Holy Spirit had delivered a powerful message.

"You only need to ask, and this and more will be given to you," Spirit had said.

The fire served as a physical confirmation of what had already occurred earlier. In the dark room, alone with my thoughts, I reflected on the entirety of the evening's events. In a moment of revelation, I envisioned myself as a woman, an Essene, living in Qumran during the time of Jesus. John the Baptist was part of our community, and while Mary and Joseph did not reside within our Essene community, they were connected to us in some way. We Essenes lived a private life because the established religious order would persecute us if our mystical, spiritual beliefs became known.

Suddenly, the scene shifted. In this vision, I was standing back from a large crowd gathered on a hillside, listening to Jesus speak. I felt content to be alone, as it let me observe what was happening. I recognized Jesus as a highly evolved being and was internally considering whether to embrace the task of sharing his message with others. I had free will and felt no pressure other than a strong sense of rightness. Although I wasn't part of his inner circle, I resolved to take on the task.

I was not a successful messenger in that life. I failed to convey the true meaning and mystical importance of Jesus' words. This caused me to lose heart over the years. Moreover, it was a dangerous job since I traveled alone from one town to another, fearing for my life. As the vision unfolded, I saw myself weary in middle age. Upon reaching the outskirts of another new town, I chose to enter as a childless, poor widow instead of as a follower of Jesus. This decision was driven out of fear of being alone in old age and the prospect of a painful death. At the same time, I realized I had not fulfilled my life's purpose and would need to do so in another life. This is one of the karmic debts I brought into my present existence.

Being called three times by the Pentecostal fire into service to Spirit profoundly changed me. The first time occurred during the years when I experienced intense fire attacks that left large blisters on my body. The

Abdel Hakim, Egyptian guide in this and
a past life.

Jean Houston, teacher of teachers

Left to right: Joe (Missy), Rod, McBeath, Chris, my brother Mark holding son Eric, Mom, me, Jenny

second time happened in the chapel in Ireland when the heavy oak doors swung open after I called on Spirit. Now, a third, unequivocal message insisted I heed the call.

Outwardly, I kept living with Rod and doing my best to be a good stepmother during the next three years. Inwardly, my commitment to serve the Divine took root and grew. I had promised Rod that I would live in Nova Scotia for one year, and he had promised to move wherever I wanted if my living there didn't work out. After spending four years in the small Nova Scotian town, it was obvious that it was too traditional an environment to nurture my authentic Self and what Spirit was calling me to do. Rod left for weeks at a time to fill in for doctors on holidays, so his work was not happening in Nova Scotia either. Initially, Rod said he wouldn't leave. However, when he saw me leaving, he agreed to join me if we went to Vancouver, which would be a fresh start in an unknown place for both of us. He stayed for a year before deciding to return to Nova Scotia. I remained in Vancouver.

Returning to Nova Scotia would mean breaking my promise to Spirit— something I had previously done and wanted to avoid repeating. I was thankful to Rod for many reasons. He had introduced three stepchildren into my life, who are still, 30 years later, a cherished part of it. Living in a small town with a conventional man had pushed me into areas I had previously steered clear of. During that time, I worked through my shadows—at least the ones that had emerged—and I now valued the many gifts that small-town life offered.

Still, I realized that staying in Nova Scotia and continuing my relationship with Rod would no longer foster growth but instead lead to stagnation. Relationships are either growing or diminishing. Although Rod and I loved each other, certain issues had arisen for both of us during our time together that were unresolvable. Neither of us could compromise on our essential natures. At 47, I listened to my soul's call and moved forward on my own into an unknown future.

I bought a condo in Vancouver and was ready to take action to embrace my new life. On the surface, my life couldn't have been better. David Suzuki and his wife, Tara Cullis, invited me to lead their annual board meeting and staff retreat for the David Suzuki Foundation, which is dedicated to protecting the environment of our precious Earth. We became friends, and I visited their cottage in the summer while beginning to write *Summer with the Leprechauns*. Meanwhile, my corporate work thrived. I started teaching courses called *Take Your Soul to Work* and was soon invited to give keynote speeches at international conferences. This led to the publication of a book with the same title, by Random House in 1999. My spiritual work also grew. I began leading walking pilgrimages, along with guiding people on tours of sacred sites.

For several years, while my outer life thrived, I struggled internally. I mourned the end of my relationship with Rod. To be clear, I recognized that, given the circumstances, ending it was the right choice. However, a mix of conflicting emotions arose, including anger and deep sadness that we hadn't fulfilled our purpose together. In contrast, when my relationship with Bill ended, it felt like we had succeeded; with Rod, it felt like we had failed to break a karmic pattern.

As with all pain, we have an opportunity to learn from our suffering. I developed more compassion for those who loved someone deeply only to realize that their love was partially an illusion. We might love one aspect of a person while ignoring other aspects that don't match our idea of the ideal relationship. When we are eventually forced, through repeated experiences, to face the truth, we may blame ourselves for ignoring what was there all along. This can lower our self-esteem and shake our confidence in our judgment. I struggled with these feelings of inadequacy and refrained from starting a new relationship for many years. I wanted to prevent repeating past mistakes or bringing unhealed parts of myself into a new relationship. Over time, I healed.

In retrospect, I recognize that time with Rod, my stepchildren, and small-town Nova Scotia were meant to open my heart to love more. Without this, I doubt I would have been able to progress to the next step in my spiritual transformation. Earlier in my life, I had developed my superconscious gifts; however, love is ultimately the key to spiritual transformation. Love draws us to help others and sustains us through difficult times.

# The Fruit

*Allow the day to pass, watching it*
*sunrise to sunset and into the dark,*
*being one with the Sun and Earth*
*in clockless time.*
*How many days do we live this in a life?*
*Children forget to be and learn to do,*
*returning in old age as senility and death beckon.*
*Unwilling, we are forced to our knees by time,*
*relentlessly pushed to submit to 'what is.'*
*Much better to enjoy now while we still can choose*
*to savor the depths and heights of a day—any day—*
*Perfect.*

# 17

# The Assignment

This next stage in life, a time of maturity, Spirit arranged many ways to share all I had learned. These ways, mostly unforeseen, took me into areas I probably wouldn't have chosen. The common theme became service to others, where the response "Yes" received a lot of practice. This response led to spiritual growth for both myself and others. This period was the fruit of my life for which the preceding years were training.

In late 1999, just before the end of the millennium, several individuals asked me to mentor them in depth. I didn't want to practice psychotherapy again, and they weren't seeking therapy. They wanted a mentor to assist them with their spiritual transformation. Not knowing how to respond to their request, I said, "Yes," and asked them to share what they needed. From our conversations, it was clear that the in-depth program they sought would help others. Together, we crafted a mission statement, which remains unchanged to this day.

"The International Institute for Transformation (IIT) believes that human beings are called to become conscious creators who work with the spiritual laws that govern our world. Global and organizational transformation happens through the transformation of individuals. We are committed to supporting individuals to achieve self-mastery in their lives, work, and world and to create ongoing communities for transformation."

But how to fulfill this mission statement was unclear until December 31st. While meditating, El Morya appeared to my inner vision as a tall, middle-aged Persian or Indian man of medium build with a beard. Sometimes, I see him with a turban and glimpse the possibility that he was one of the three wise men who came from the East at the birth of Jesus. Except for the time in Nova Scotia, El Morya had been answering my questions during meditation for several years. However, I had never felt the full force of his will before. This time was different.

"You must weave the threads of your life together for integration and unity as the next step in creating The International Institute for Transformation," he said in a voice giving an assignment.

"Can you be more specific?" I asked, feeling unsettled.

"You possess all the information. There are no surprises, only the revelation of your complete task."

"I can't even see the first step, much less the complete task," I replied, overwhelmed.

"You are switching to the blue ray to work with me now," El Morya said. "Over the past decade, I have gradually collaborated with you more. Now, there will be further active involvement."

"The blue ray! That's the ray of will and power, isn't it?"

"Yes," he replied. "You've developed your wisdom and love. Now you need to strengthen your will to become a complete creator. Furthermore, will is essential to establish The International Institute for Transformation, which is intended to be a prototype for the Aquarian Age."

El Morya had a stern, commanding presence. Until that moment, he had been gentle. Now, there was immense power behind his words—a power that demanded obedience. I don't mean to imply a lack of free will, but refusing him would come at a significant cost to my soul and spiritual development.

"You won't see the fruits of your labor for 20 years," he said, and as he spoke, a glimpse of the path ahead appeared.

"You are receiving the flow, the feeling of how to do this," El Morya said gently. "It's soft with the breath of the Holy Spirit. Combine all you know about the spiritual world with everything you've learned about manifesting goals through working with organizations. This is what individuals need in order to become full creators. Each course must be integrated physically, emotionally, mentally, and spiritually."

He waited for me to assimilate his words before continuing, "You have always been in my ashram," he said.

"Could you explain what you mean?" I asked, intuitively knowing the answer, but seeking confirmation.

"Because you, too, are an El," he replied, fading.

His comment confirmed my inner knowing, but there was no time to ponder its meaning. That evening, on New Year's Eve, my friend Jenny and I walked a labyrinth in an old church. We spent three hours chanting and meditating as we welcomed the Aquarian Age. During that time, I began to feel increasingly unwell. The next three days were spent alternating between the bathroom and bed. A terrible headache, something I rarely experience, gripped me along with spinal aches, an unfamiliar sensation. Past lives merged with the current one and new knowledge was downloaded, although "knowledge" isn't quite the right term. It was more like the etheric body, which holds all soul memories, was transferring this information into my physical body. The consciousness within the cells was ascending in frequency. The headaches, back pain, and fever were burning away the remnants of old thoughtforms that could have inhibited this upgrading process.

The first week-long retreat, Transform Yourself, took place just over a week later. This transformative course was designed to help individuals eliminate their old thought patterns. However, realizing that this wasn't enough time for lasting change, I developed a three-month Transform Yourself-2 program that could be done either on your own or in groups. This program was optional for those who attended the retreat, but at least half of the participants enrolled. This comprehensive self-study course was a key step toward building a dedicated community of people who studied together for many years. Additionally, this evolving process developed into a Master's program in spiritual transformation, allowing me to share insights and practices discovered over decades.

Before this, I enjoyed the freedom to teach courses and lead retreats that lasted, at most, a week. I had never wanted an organization but here it was. It was like never wanting children and finding yourself pregnant. Committing to ongoing mentoring and creating in-depth courses that would last several years was challenging, but honoring El Morya's request was essential. Still, my commitment was continually tested.

On one hand, I experienced self-doubt. Considering that each person's path is unique, would my journey of spiritual transformation benefit others? Would the processes, including workbooks, exercises, MP3s, and videos, effectively assist most people? A second issue arose. Although our corporate advisors suggested the structure of IIT and how to promote courses, it ultimately remained my responsibility. Following their advice, I rented a three-room office in downtown Vancouver and hired three staff members. By 2002, IIT had lost $160,000. Quite a sum in those days. Fortunately, through ongoing work as a management consultant and leading tours, it was possible to cover this financial loss, but the situation was not sustainable.

It was painfully evident that a corporate structure was ineffective for IIT. After a year, the salesperson and manager still hadn't sold a single course. However, when I spoke with someone on the phone, they most often registered. It was revealing to learn that unless people had undergone their own spiritual transformation, they couldn't attract others. Still, not wanting to spend time promoting courses made this a difficult period. For two decades, as a corporate consultant helping others build healthy organizations, I was struggling with my own organization. This was a humbling and confusing experience when I was doing the best I could to help it succeed.

I had no doubt that IIT was meant to continue, but how? After two years, in the midst of shutting down the office to relocate everything to my home, Merle Dulmadge, one of the most dedicated participants in our courses, called me.

"Tanis, El Morya appeared in meditation. He said we were to relocate IIT to Calgary and for me to take over the office," she stated.

"Your offer is incredibly generous, Merle," I replied, "but there's not enough money to pay what you earn as a management consultant. So, it's not a good idea for you."

"El Morya told me to do this. Ask him," she insisted.

I hung up the phone and meditated. El Morya appeared almost immediately. "Accept Merle's offer," he said. "She is an angel hybrid working with Archangel Michael in service to humanity. Els build the form, and angels imbue the form with essence. Her purpose aligns with yours, and together, you will create the necessary structure."

El Morya continued, "IIT is an organic organization rooted in conscious co-creation with others. You're to develop an evolving prototype for the type of organization needed in the Aquarian Age. However, these are still early days. You must build a bridge between the Piscean Age, where corporations thrived, and the Aquarian Age, which is grounded in community. Do not measure success by the number of people taking the courses or by the revenue generated. These are outdated standards."

"What standards should we use, then?"

"The organization must be dynamic and flexible. Some individuals will only attend one course, while others may purchase a book, and still others might join your walking pilgrimage or tour. You are planting seeds for transformation. However, some will commit more deeply and study in-depth for many years. People are at various levels of spiritual development, and you are here to assist those at different stages."

"How can I tell if we're doing the right things?" I asked, seeking clarification.

"Your heart and intuition will be the guide. Release ego needs and fears to hear your soul's voice," El Morya replied.

"Is there anything else to help overcome self-doubt?"

"Yes," he replied. "Even if you do not achieve success in the material world, know that success will be recorded in the etheric plane…as long as you remain committed to the goal of creating an organization that facilitates spiritual transformation."

With his final words, El Morya disappeared. I sat quietly, reflecting on his words and instructions before calling Merle to begin a new, unexpected journey together.

I am eternally grateful to Merle for co-creating with me for seven years during our difficult startup period to establish The International Institute for Transformation. Co-creation without ego involves working together to find the best way to do something, listening to what Spirit wants, and then implementing it. We attempted to do this, and we also sought to co-create with others.

Our students recommended various courses, and we experimented to see which ones would take root. For instance, Women's Mysteries was a tremendous success, while only one man registered for the Men's Mysteries course. Subsequently, we organized a summer camp for children and teens facing spiritual difficulties and transformations. The parents and children loved it, but it nearly bankrupted us. Since many professional organizational consultants and psychotherapists had studied with us for years in the in-depth program, we hoped that they could also facilitate some of the programs. They offered to lead some of our week-long introductory retreats, but unfortunately, few people registered. Although I wanted to shift the focus away from myself, it didn't seem that Spirit wanted this.

Fortunately, many of our experiments were successful. Most people who took our introductory Transform Yourself and other courses later enrolled in the ongoing self-study or group study. I never led these ongoing courses, so communities could form independently of me. It was heartwarming to hear how much participants enjoyed their groups and felt connected to our IIT community.

The deeply committed individuals in our spiritual transformation Master's program were known as focalizers. This term describes those who direct spiritual light to Earth for others. The goal of spiritual transformation is to surrender our ego's personal desires in order to serve Divine will. Our program helped focalizers achieve this objective. For the first several years, we studied *Decoding Destiny*, that had been published more than a decade earlier. I had never taught from my own book and had been integrating its high spiritual teachings until now. Feeling ready, I created application exercises based on the book to help focalizers understand the broad and far-reaching information.

Committing to be the mentor they had asked for, I developed a program to assist focalizers in every aspect of their spiritual development. Every year, I did a soul reading for each person, which became their assignment for that year. With their permission, I assessed whether they were aligned with what their soul wanted from them. This might confirm what they were already doing or help them align better with their soul's recommendations. Additionally, they volunteered in areas of their choosing, such as hospices. The purpose was for them to learn the importance of serving others with no expectation for themselves. During their in-depth course, each focalizer also presented to the group a spiritual topic related to their area of expertise. In doing so, we practiced co-creation. The Ascended Masters on higher planes co-create, and it was beneficial for us to start practicing. Their final assignment for graduation was to write their spiritual autobiography.

At first, I thought it would take focalizers about four years to complete our in-depth transformation program, and many did graduate then. But, to my surprise, many focalizers were still studying with me 25 years later. Of course, spiritual transformation never really ends. Their confidence in what we were doing in our community helped me grow spiritually, so I could better support them.

While struggling to build a foundation for IIT, my corporate workshops thrived. *Take Your Soul to Work* became a Canadian bestseller, and many invitations to give keynote speeches across Canada and the U.S. ensued. Another book, *Summer with the Leprechauns*, also found success and was translated into several languages. This led to teaching about elementals throughout Europe, which resulted in Europeans enrolling in our International Institute for Transformation's courses.

Although Merle, working from home in Calgary, had significantly reduced our expenses, IIT rarely broke even. My corporate work, tours to sacred sites, and other spiritual workshops continued to subsidize it. Additionally, at times, generous donors came to our aid, allowing us to carry on. El Morya continued to support and guide me and knowing this gave me strength to continue.

We didn't attract beginners on their spiritual journey…regardless of how we spoke of our courses. We magnetize to us those who resonate with our interests and vibration. There are also karmic links. Most people interested in our courses were successful in the material world and had already engaged in psychological self-work. Now, they were ready to experience what is esoterically called the second initiation, which involves transforming their negative thoughts and emotions into positive ones. This process requires moving beyond judgment, blame, pride, lust, greed,

Founding our International Institute for Transformation

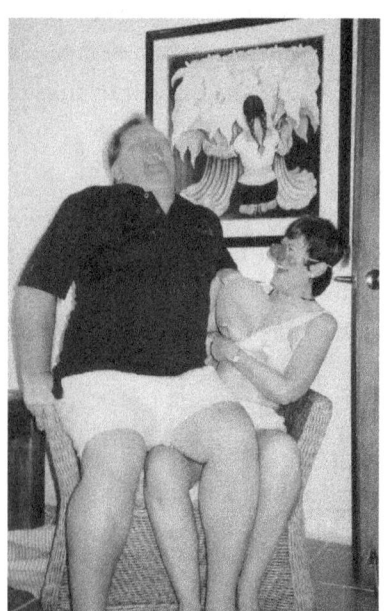

Clowning with Darwyn, an IIT focalizer

Merle Dulmadge, my right hand with IIT

anger, and self-pity to become more forgiving, compassionate, tolerant, flexible, and good-humored. Our course, Transform Yourself, supported this development.

Individuals who emulated these positive emotions were drawn to our Master's program, which focused on deepening non-attachment to ego desires and surrendering to the guidance of Spirit. Ultimately, this involves dedicating oneself to serving the world in whatever form the Divine Creator may request. This process is known as the third initiation. My role with IIT was to support those engaged in the second and third initiations. There are no strict boundaries between these initiations, so someone can be 80 percent through the second initiation while also being 20 percent into the third.

Our vibrations fluctuate based on our thoughts, feelings, and actions each day; however, we usually settle into a certain resting state. My goal was to help people identify what was holding them back and to provide practical steps and support to remove these obstacles and raise their consciousness. We can only help others spiritually to the extent of our own transformation. Therefore, I am grateful to the many who trusted and encouraged me to explore my own process, which helped me better support them. Helping others catalyzed my own spiritual transformation and raised my vibration—which was desirable—but it also caused concerning physical symptoms.

"My heart is trembling and having palpitations," I said to El Morya one day.

"Your physical heart is transforming so you can support others more effectively," he said. "This is a delicate process—a spiritual surgery—and you need to rest."

"What do you mean when you say my heart is transforming?"

"Previously, what you refer to as your "fire attacks" expanded your central channel and burned away the residue of outdated thoughtforms. This process took place in your physical, astral (emotional), and causal (mental) bodies. Now, the kundalini fire is opening your heart in all three bodies, serving as a beacon of light for the world. Energy from all three bodies will begin to flow through it to others."

"Are you saying that my heart isn't merely physical?" I asked.

"That's correct," El Morya replied. "The heart is the cup that overflows, as mentioned in Psalm 23 of the Bible. This cup, the heart, is what the knights sought in the Quest for the Holy Grail. The heart must be fully open in surrender—although perhaps dedication to the Divine is a better term than surrender—in order to achieve enlightenment."

"That's very interesting. However, I'm concerned I might have a heart attack," his response had done little to reassure me.

"You're not going to have a heart attack," El Morya replied. "Put that thought aside. However, you need to rest. Others aren't pushing you; you're pushing yourself."

"Am I undergoing another initiation?" I asked.

"You are," El Morya replied. "In the third initiation, as demonstrated by Jesus in the Garden of Gethsemane, an individual feels alone, as if no one else understands what he or she is experiencing, as if others are asleep. However, the third initiation is essentially a private matter. You have completed most of the third initiation in your life so far. Once you commit to serving the Divine for the benefit of others rather than yourself, you begin the fourth initiation, which is public. During this initiation, others may falsely accuse you, you may endure physical suffering, and you may be abandoned by those close to you. These public trials are meant to strengthen your commitment to the Divine. They continue the lessons of the third initiation. You pass these spiritual tests by staying uncomplaining, forgiving, and seeing them through…whatever it takes."

"I understand what you mean by the different tests. I'm familiar with many of them. However, Jesus and his disciples died during the fourth initiation. Am I going to die?" I asked, feeling concerned.

"Of course, you are going to die," El Morya replied firmly. "At your stage of evolution, as well as for most of humanity, you will physically die. However, you are living in a very different time from Jesus. Jesus' purpose was to demonstrate that the inner spiritual journey of initiation culminates in the death of the ego, the false self. This was what his crucifixion spiritually represents. The fourth initiation still culminates in the death of the ego, but now individuals may experience this process over several lifetimes or through multiple crises within a single lifetime. You can think of this as a series of mini-crucifixions."

"I feel as though I haven't completed the third initiation yet," I said.

"As stated," he replied, "the fourth is a continuation of the third, where one's tests are more public than in the third, which is more private."

"The participants in our Master's spiritual transformation program are attracted to the idea of world service. However, there often appears to be a gap between the theory and practice of service in their lives. Could this suggest the difference between the third and fourth initiation?"

El Morya smiled and replied, "You've identified one of the key differences: the third initiation is mainly about personal transformation, while the fourth emphasizes serving the group, community, and the world. During the fourth initiation, one must let go of all ego attachments so that one's sole aim is to serve the Divine at all times and in whatever form is requested."

"Sometimes, it feels like I've lived all of this in past lives. Is that true?" I asked.

"You have undergone these initiations in previous lives, and your intuition and spiritual abilities come from those experiences. However, for several reasons, it is necessary to go through these initiations again," El Morya replied.

Reflecting on what El Morya was saying, I began evaluating my current life in areas where total commitment was lacking. He interrupted my thoughts.

"Don't waste time evaluating your progress or lack thereof. Instead, strengthen both devotion to Spirit and willpower to move forward. To pass the fourth initiation, you must hold nothing back from Spirit, the Divine, the omnipresent ALL. Meditate more. Walk in nature and allow yourself to rest. Anxiety and worry generate stress that lowers your vibration, while gratitude and joy elevate it."

"Even if I'm not participating in the fifth initiation, is that what Jesus demonstrated when he ascended after the crucifixion?" I asked.

"Jesus of Nazareth," El Morya responded, "had already undergone the fifth and even higher initiations before he began teaching. When one's heart is purified of all attachments, one is baptized in a stream of spiritual light and overcomes all darkness, Maya, and illusion. One then surrenders one's separate existence and becomes one with God. Jesus reenacted these steps after the crucifixion to guide others," El Morya replied.

I was absorbing El Morya's words when he continued, "The presence of the Holy Spirit is the unifying force of The International Institute for Transformation. It is the fire of the Holy Spirit that consumes the dross during the transformation meditations you've created for the Transform Yourself course. A small flame of this energy arises during the second initiation, while a greater flame appears during the third initiation as the Holy Spirit cleanses the chakras. However, no one can fully feel the force of the Holy Spirit before the fifth initiation."

"I've taught that St. Germain is assisting with the Aquarian Age, burning off the negative thoughtforms in our Transform Yourself meditations. Is it incorrect for not stating it was the Holy Spirit?" I asked, concerned, as it is a serious spiritual error to teach something inaccurate.

"The Holy Spirit works through all Masters," El Morya replied. "The Holy Spirit is an aspect of the omnipresent One. Master St. Germain collaborates with the Holy Spirit to assist with the Aquarian Age."

With his final words, El Morya disappeared from my inner vision, leaving me filled with knowledge, inspiration, and deepened commitment to the spiritual journey. Discussing the five stages of spiritual initiation on the path to enlightenment shed light on the next steps. Still, regardless of our current stage, willpower and faith in the process are essential to move forward. Knowing that Spirit never gives us tests we are not prepared to pass has always been a source of strength for me, even when facing tough challenges.

In our lives, we might have felt that Spirit was urging us to undertake something overwhelming. Maybe it was leaving a secure job to start our own business or completely changing our career path. It could also have meant becoming a foster parent or adopting a challenging child. It might have involved volunteering our services, even if it meant spending less time with our family.

If this request comes from our soul and we listen to it, doing our best despite the challenges, we grow spiritually. It was reassuring to realize that this remains true even if we are not ultimately successful in our new endeavor, because Spirit does not judge success that way. Spirit is only concerned with whether we have given our all.

# 18

# Trials on the Path

Life continued mostly the same until 2004, when a mix of positive and challenging transformative experiences occurred. In January, after Mom moved into my brother's house, she gave me spiritual books she had received. Among them were many books by the yogi Paramahansa Yogananda. Reading them, I knew Yogananda wanted me to follow his recommended practice for awakening, called Kriya Yoga.

I contacted Yogananda's office at Self-Realization Fellowship in California and learned there was a six-month to one-year study period before one could be initiated into Kriya. But there was a shortcut! A friend had received the initiation many years earlier and told me what to do. Sadly, as was revealed later, her instructions bore little resemblance to Kriya Yoga as taught by Yogananda. So much for shortcuts!

Although Yogananda left his body in 1952, I sensed him overseeing my progress from higher realms. At the same time, El Morya was gradually withdrawing, although I intuitively knew he was also observing from afar. Without their guidance, I attempted to discern what Spirit/ the Divine/ God wanted day to day, moment to moment. This is a crucial step in each person's spiritual journey, as Spirit observes how well one fares when standing alone. This process often brings forth a series of difficulties, since an individual, like a sword, is forged in the fire of transformation and struck upon the anvil multiple times. The finest swords, those that withstand great pressure, are crafted through this very process.

Many strikes landed that year. The first came from The Banff Centre, my primary corporate client for over 20 years. For several months, Andre, the head of management programs, had hinted that he was considering hiring someone else to teach the Personal Leadership Development course, a course that I had developed. Given that the reviews were excellent and my course was one of their top money-makers, there was no factual reason for this decision. However, Spirit has its own reasons.

The evening before St. Patrick's Day in March, I meditated and spoke to Spirit, saying, "I'm tired of trying to persuade Andre to let me teach my course. Make it clear what you want."

At 9 a.m., the phone rang. "We are hiring someone else to teach Personal Leadership Development," Andre stated.

Accepting his verdict, I told Spirit firmly, "I've been searching for five years for a one-room cabin by the water to write and meditate. I want this today."

I contacted real estate agents I had spoken with over the years to see if they knew of any cabins like that. They all said no... until the last call.

"This morning, a house on the waterfront just outside Powell River has become available," said Kathy, the realtor. "Someone is flying in to see it tomorrow, so you'd better come today if you're interested."

Hanging up the phone, I quickly drove to catch two ferries to Powell River. Meeting Kathy at the entrance to the property, she said, "It's not exactly what you were looking for. It's not a cabin; it's a house, but it has a lovely garden and a great waterfront location."

Driving in, we noticed an assortment of leprechaun statues lining the way. Turning to Kathy, I said, "It's St. Patrick's Day, and I've written a book about leprechauns. It's a sign to buy this house."

The garden was beautiful, featuring rose bushes and trees, but the old house was in dire need of renovation. However, knowing that Spirit wanted it, I signed the offer to purchase and left.

Then, while driving back to the ferry, a clear, inner voice said firmly, "Go back!"

Following the command, I turned the car around. Several minutes later, pulling into the driveway, I saw a woman, clearly the owner, gardening. Although this wasn't the usual procedure, my heart urged me to introduce myself. Stepping out of the car, I walked forward to meet her. She looked up from her task and removed her gardening gloves.

"Hello," I said, smiling and extending my hand. "I really love your home and garden, and have made an offer to purchase it."

We continued talking for a few minutes, and she felt like family. There were several better offers on the property, but Janet liked me. Four months later, my condo in Vancouver was rented, and I was camped in a home renovation project in Powell River. Friends in Vancouver were horrified about my move to a pulp and paper town where I knew no one, but I had followed Spirit's signs and acted accordingly. Even when it didn't make sense on the surface, Spirit had closed one door and opened another on the same day. We must pay attention to such signs.

During this stressful time, strike two struck. My mother died, or perhaps it's more accurate to say she chose to leave her body. Mom and I usually spoke on Sundays; however, one Saturday, I decided to call her. We chatted about Mom going away with seniors to a lodge the following week. In every way, Mom was lucid, optimistic, and content. We shared some good laughs about the people Mom was meeting at her senior's center.

"I greet people by their names when they arrive. Everyone enjoys being called by their names," said Mom, expressing one reason why so many people liked her.

Listening to my brother Mark as he brought her lunch, I said, "I'll call you next week before you go to the lodge, Mom."

"You don't need to call, dear," she replied. "We had a good talk today."

That was the last time we spoke. Mark left the room and came back 30 minutes later to find Mom sitting up, but she was gone. After she had finished her favorite lunch—a grilled cheese sandwich—her heart had stopped.

It was a cause for celebration that Mom had left so quickly and without pain. Still, we had been very close since I became an adult. After Dad died, Mom participated in seven sacred site tours, attended my spiritual workshops, and took part in Buddhist talks and Native American pipe ceremonies. She showed love to everyone she met. Mom worked with my brother in their paint and wallpaper store until her mid-70s, and then, until her mid-80s, she volunteered. During the day, she delivered Meals on Wheels to seniors, and at night, she answered calls at a distress center.

Although happy about her peaceful passing, her absence left a pain in my heart. Moving away from friends and home in Vancouver and losing my biggest client, The Banff Centre, also made me feel rootless. It was a challenging time filled with multiple losses; nevertheless, a deep sense of rightness remained within me.

Strike number three was on its way! At that time, I was still hedging my bets that if Powell River didn't work out, I could return to the Vancouver condo. Knowing I still had an attachment, Spirit decided to sever that cord as well. Within a few months, the furnished condo had been rented three times, and the last renter had moved out. A friend then found a fourth, more dependable person to rent it.

"I've found a wonderful guy, Francois Milly," Samaya said. "He's a window dresser at Hudson's Bay, and his boss says he's very reliable."

"Super," I said. "Go ahead and rent it. I'll come in a week to meet him."

A week later, I returned to the condo to find that Francois had broken into my locked cupboard and stolen the artwork, credit cards, and banking information. Afraid he might become violent, I changed the locks and called the police. They arrived several days, not hours, later, near midnight.

To preserve Francois's fingerprints, I hadn't touched several of his items and was shocked when the officers picked them up. "Don't you want his fingerprints?" I asked.

"He's an identity thief, lady," one officer replied. "He stole the other guy's identity, and now he's taken yours. We'll never catch him."

Losing my identity was a kind of rape. Francois, or whatever his name was, had withdrawn large amounts of money from my bank accounts and made purchases on the credit cards. The insurance company denied my claim because, according to them, Francois was my tenant. It took months of negotiations to have their decision reversed. No longer feeling safe in the condo, I decided to sell it and move full-time to Powell River.

Corporate work no longer appealed, but adhering to my old axiom of accepting what Spirit provided, I continued to say, "Yes." Additionally, speaking about bringing spirituality into the workplace, as discussed in my book, *Take Your Soul to Work*, was still enjoyable and felt important.

In retrospect, it's possible I waffled about saying goodbye to corporate work. Why? Because, having lost so much in such a short time, I sought a place where I still felt valued. Spirit, finding another of my attachments, sank its teeth in.

One day, while en route to deliver a keynote speech, I got off the plane and found hundreds of people shouting, "Tanis Helliwell is a devil worshipper!" The CBC—Canada's national broadcasting station—was filming the protest and swung the cameras from the crowd to me.

"What do you say about this accusation?" a well-dressed male reporter inquired, thrusting the microphone in my face.

"It's absurd," I retorted, horrified by what was happening.

The leader of the demonstration lunged forward, pushing his face into the camera. "It's right here in her book, *Decoding Destiny,* where she discusses the redemption of Lucifer."

"Do you have a comment?" the reporter asked, swinging the microphone back to me.

"I'm here to talk about spirituality in the workplace based on my book, *Take Your Soul to Work,*" I replied, shaken. "I'm not a devil worshipper."

Squeezing past the crowd, I hurried through the airport and jumped into a taxi. My heart raced as we drove to the venue where I was scheduled to speak. At the hotel entrance, more people held anti-Tanis placards and shouted. It was evident that the ordeal had not yet ended. As we pulled up, the organizer who had hired me opened the car door. He did not seem pleased.

"The auditorium is filled with people waiting for you to speak, and they had to get past those demonstrators," he said. "What did you do?"

He didn't give me a chance to answer before adding, "I just called the David Suzuki Foundation and spoke to Jim Fulton, the executive director."

"What did Jim say?" I asked.

"He gave you a great recommendation, or we would have canceled your talk," replied the organizer, guiding me through the demonstrators and into the hall. All eyes turned in my direction. Some looked curious, others smiled, and a few glared and frowned. I was quite shaken, so it wasn't my best speech. However, there were no further interruptions. After finishing and when the audience dispersed, it was a relief to see that the demonstrators had also left. I called Jim to thank him. By this time, I had led three annual board retreats for the David Suzuki Foundation, and Jim jokingly referred to me as their "spiritual advisor."

"So not everyone liked what you said?" Jim joked, diffusing my distress. He had run many gamuts in his own life, so he understood firsthand how anger and disapproval felt.

The mini-crucifixions with Banff and the corporate client made me wary about pursuing any corporate work, prompting me to decline new invitations. Therefore, when the prestigious management consulting firm McKinsey asked me to lead their annual partners' retreat, I responded, "No."

They responded, "State your price."

"$25,000," I said, confident they would back off.

"Done," they replied.

Searching for a different way to deter them, unconventional words surfaced: "I would need complete freedom. Maybe you'll need to create the masks you wear and then show them to the others."

"Great! That sounds wonderful," they exclaimed.

This wasn't going as hoped. They wouldn't accept "No".

"Where are you having the retreat?" I asked, thinking of declining because of the location.

"The Banff Centre," was the reply.

"Fine," I agreed, finally convinced that Spirit had orchestrated my acceptance.

On the day the McKinsey retreat began, I was dining with them when Andre—the same Andre who had fired me—approached our table.

"Could you please introduce me to the partners?" he asked in an obsequious tone.

"Of course, happy to, Andre," I replied, genuinely pleased to do so.

How the tables had turned, with him undervaluing me and now asking for a favor. What an interesting world it is to observe that we are neither significant nor insignificant. Life is a dream being dreamt by God. We are minor players in the drama of life. We shouldn't become attached to our roles or how others perceive us at any moment. All will change in a flash, if Spirit wills it.

It's common to go through times in our lives when we face challenges that seem unfair. We might even struggle to understand why these hardships happen. Maybe we lose a job we loved. Perhaps our children blame us for their problems and no longer want to see us. It could also be that friends turn against us for reasons we don't understand. These and many other difficulties can lead us to blame God for what we see as injustice.

I've learned, often painfully over the years, that these challenges—whether private or public—are not given by Spirit to cause suffering. They are either karma from this life or past ones that needs to be repaid, or they are meant to help us release attachments to being loved and respected. Also—and this might be even harder to understand—we cannot judge what is fair in this illusory world, nor can we know the Divine's full reasons for anything. Instead, it's crucial to trust Spirit and fully embrace whatever happens.

# 19

# Writing Books

Silence and retreat beckoned in Powell River at my home, Diamond Heart. When coal is subjected to immense pressure over eons, it transforms into a diamond. It was a hope that the difficulties I faced, not only in this life but in others, would turn my heart into a diamond.

There are several recurring themes in my life. One of these is that periods of emptiness, which we can call the Void, are followed by bursts of active creativity. People, even dear friends, might not notice a difference in me outwardly. This difference exists in my inner world, where stillness and silence prevail. I cannot force myself out of the Void and must surrender to its timing. This inner space is not devoid of movement; rather, any movement or learning occurs beneath the level of consciousness. Just as cosmic consciousness dissolves the caterpillar's body to create a beautiful butterfly, it transforms me through these creatively empty periods.

During these quiet times, reading spiritual books, enjoying nature, and resting at Diamond Heart brought joy. Sometimes, feeling lonely and bored, I would go to Vancouver to see plays and meet friends. When that didn't satisfy the urge for culture, I visited fascinating cities like Prague, Venice, and St. Petersburg with friends and enjoyed week-long hikes in Europe with my stepdaughter, Jenny.

In the following years, as corporate work wound down, leading tours and walking pilgrimages nurtured my love of travel. However, my primary focus remained creating courses for The International Institute for Transformation. Helping individuals overcome the main issues they faced on their spiritual transformation journey was always the main goal. Our courses—Freedom from Fear, Love Yourself Well, Ancestor and Family Healing, Spiritual Ancestors, Self-Healing with the Body Elemental, and

Answer Your Soul's Call—were designed to achieve this. At the same time, I deeply felt that to complete their spiritual transformation, individuals needed to embrace their collective human destiny and become conscious guardians of this beautiful planet. As a result, two of our most popular courses were Nature Spirits and Earth Our Home.

Creating and teaching these courses was a heartfelt labor of love and another form of spiritual practice. It's fascinating how we often don't realize, in the moment, the reasons behind our desires to undertake certain actions. To create these in-depth programs, it was necessary to explore my fears, ancestors, and even feelings of a lack of love. Helping others facilitated my own healing and transformation. Additionally, a second life theme became clear: I enjoyed writing.

Many books were gestating within me, and Diamond Heart provided the peaceful, natural environment needed for writing. This was a gift. In 1988, when Spirit asked me to write *Decoding Destiny: Keys to Mankind's Spiritual Evolution* there was no thought about ever writing another book. Then, when Lloyd, my leprechaun friend, asked for a book about elementals, the answer was once again "Yes." This became *Summer with the Leprechauns* in 1997. I thought at the time that this would be my last book.

However, after moving to Vancouver, I became friends with Samaya Ryane, who published a monthly magazine called Shared Vision. She asked me to write a monthly column about spirituality at work, titled *Take Your Soul to Work*. Being thanked for these columns over the years showed that many people appreciated this information. This was the first time I had chosen to write a book—without any prompting from others—and *Take Your Soul to Work* was published in 1999.

These three books couldn't be more different. There was no trace of my personality in *Decoding Destiny*, which was a spiritual guide about our multidimensional solar system and universe. In contrast, *Summer with the Leprechauns* resembled an amusing novel where my personality was very evident. Lastly, *Take Your Soul to Work* was written by a corporate consultant aiming to help others succeed in the world. Each book had a distinct tone and voice, allowing me to use many aspects of myself. Our soul has many subpersonalities and we are happiest when we can fulfill them. Writing allowed me to do this.

Three books vied for prominence between 2004 and 2008. The first was the rewrite of *Decoding Destiny*. Why? There were several reasons. The main one was that, from the public protest surrounding *Decoding Destiny*, I recognized the need to clarify the subject matter. Also, teaching from *Decoding Destiny* at our spiritual transformation retreats led to the creation of application exercises that would help others. Moreover, re-editing a book seemed much easier than starting from scratch—or so I thought. This proved not to be true. As I advanced on the spiritual path, the book kept getting better as the information moved from theory to deeply experienced reality in the cells of my body. It was an amazing discovery to find that lasting spiritual transformation requires that our knowledge needs to move into our body in order to affirm its truth.

Re-editing *Decoding* Your *Destiny* took years, and the book was finally published in 2011. No publisher wanted it, so without another option, I self-published the English and German translations. Our publishing branch became Wayshower Enterprises because the purpose of the books was to illuminate the way, the path, to Spirit. Becoming a publisher was another unexpected growth opportunity. You might relate to experiences in your own life that, at first, you would have preferred to avoid, but in retrospect, you realize as growth opportunities. This was my experience with self-publishing.

The second book calling was a collection of poems. I had never considered myself a poet, yet after weeks in silent retreat, poems flowed out of me. Whether they were good or bad didn't matter. They expressed my inner feelings about the many forms of love: nature, God, friends, and partners. There were months, maybe half a year, without any poems. Then, after longer retreats, poems would write themselves in just a few days. However, there were no poems about romantic love until a Green Man entered my life in the summer of 2007.

It felt strange, after 13 years of seldom dating, to become sexually active again. The eros poems from that time clearly show the impact this man had on me. Although our relationship lasted only seven months, it was greatly healing for both of us. We were quite different; he was a homebody without a passport, and me a world traveler. Our similarity lay in a deep love of nature, hiking, and gardening. He was grieving the recent loss of his wife, which made me reluctant to start a relationship. However, Spirit gave many signs, and after he said the magic words, "I will not hurt you," I agreed. My body sprang from winter into spring again, and we journeyed through all stages of love in a short time—from young love to old, wise ones urging retreat. Still, something was healed in both him and me that had been wounded. After many years and much gestation, the poetry book was published as *Embraced by Love* in 2008.

The third book, declaring, "Pick me," was about a horrific tour I'd led in Ireland a few years earlier. Writing *Pilgrimage with the Leprechauns* was to find a way out of the darkness into which the tour had dumped me. If you adored Ireland, had visited countless times, and already led many successful tours shouldn't leading a tour there be a piece of cake? No such luck. From the first day, when the bus driver, tour guide, and I discovered that the tour company had given each of us completely different itineraries, we fell into a downward spiral. Half of the sacred sites I'd requested had been eliminated, and the tour guide was unfamiliar with the other half. No one, least of all the participants, was happy.

To write a book, you need to feel inspired. There has to be energy for the project. Without this, the writing process can be painful, and the final product might not be successful. The book about the tour to Ireland nearly wrote itself. In just two weeks during the spring of 2006, two-thirds of the first draft was completed. Next, came flying to Ireland to revisit Lloyd's cottage on Achill Island to verify the details and the accuracy of my account. To be frank, I also wanted to return to the scene of the tour trauma to free myself from the negative feelings. Being in mystical Ireland filled my heart with good memories again, and visiting locals I'd known over the years restored happy feelings about the country.

When we have a painful experience, it's essential to find ways to purify and neutralize that feeling before it becomes embedded in our bodies. Some people replay traumatic experiences in their thoughts and when recounting their stories to others. By framing their trauma solely in negative terms and failing to grow from it, they continue to re-injure themselves. Now, many years later, when sharing the story of the Ireland tour, I am amused about how many things went wrong and recognize what the Irish call "the Craic" as the leprechauns' and Spirit's way of playing with us.

If you're not an author yourself, you might not realize that a first draft is never the final book. That would be too simple. Instead, the next step is to edit, edit, and edit again. Then, when you've reached a point where you can't go any further and you're pulling your hair out, you hire a professional editor. This process can take months or even years.

Over the next few years, *Pilgrimage with the Leprechauns* underwent numerous edits until I believed it was ready for publication. My agent, Bob Silverstein, was a wonderful man who loved *Summer with the Leprechauns,* and Bob urged me to lighten the tone of the new book. The manuscript's original title, *Hijacked by the Leprechauns,* hints at what he meant. His feedback helped me realize that a deeper level of self-healing was necessary.

Sometimes, healing has many layers; after addressing one layer, you think you're finished, only to discover another layer underneath. It's important to have friends who point this out. Taking Bob's comment seriously, I re-edited the book one last time. In the end, both of us were pleased with the final version. Unfortunately, Bob couldn't find a publisher, so once again, Wayshower Enterprises came to the rescue, and *Pilgrimage with the Leprechauns* was published in 2010.

Meanwhile, there were ongoing issues with the American publisher of *Summer with the Leprechauns.* Paul had not paid any of the agreed royalties for the English book and had now sold the book to a German publisher without notifying or reimbursing me. Discovering the sale was a small miracle. I was teaching a workshop on elementals in England and staying with some new friends, Alice and Rod.

"We've invited a friend to dinner, and he is translating your book into German," Alice said one morning at breakfast.

"That's impossible," I replied. "My book hasn't been sold in German."

That evening, when their friend Fred arrived, I asked him, "Is it true that you're translating my book into German?"

"Yes," Fred replied, "Neue Erde acquired your book from your American publisher."

For over 10 years, my publisher hadn't paid royalties and asked me to be patient, claiming he was facing financial difficulties. Now, it was time to take action. I contacted the German publisher and told him that Paul had broken our contract. Then, I reached out to several other authors published by Paul and discovered they also weren't receiving royalties. To make matters worse, Paul had created an eBook of *Summer with the Leprechauns,* which he had no legal right to produce, and he was selling it on both Amazon and Lightning Source.

I called Lightning Source and, while speaking with the CEO, asked him not to print Paul's books. The CEO presented this request to his board, but they refused because Paul had paid their invoices. This was disappointing. Not giving up, I contacted Amazon and sent them my publishing contract with Paul. They not only barred Paul from selling my book on Amazon but also removed his other 150 books. Yay, Amazon! I reached out to Lightning Source again and informed them that Amazon had decided not to sell any of Paul's books. Lightning Source, not to be outdone by Amazon, also chose to reject all of Paul's books. At last, legally free to republish *Summer with the Leprechauns,* we did so in 2012.

Initially, I only planned to end my contract with Paul. However, after talking with many other mistreated authors, I was glad to have helped them as well. This experience demonstrated that lying and mistreating others don't go unpunished. Spirit used my persistence and organizational skills to bring about justice. I sympathized with Paul's financial struggles and, in many ways, liked him, but something inside urged me to hold him accountable for his actions. It might sound strange, but it felt as if Spirit was using me as a tool to collect on his karma.

You might also relate to a difficult situation where you or others were unjustly treated, and you felt called to correct it even if it required a lot of time and energy. It takes courage to do this, knowing that you could face rejection or anger from others. Still, we must be willing to confront injustice, and in doing so, we strengthen our willpower and overcome many self-limiting fears.

*Summer with the Leprechauns* was not the only book we republished through Wayshower Enterprises. *Take Your Soul to Work*, published by Random House and a Canadian bestseller a decade earlier, was now out of print. It was surprising to discover  that most books have a short shelf life in bookstores and that publishers discard their extra stock. This happened to *Take Your Soul to Work;* however, the good news was that receiving the contract back, allowed us to republish this book. Spirit has perfect timing in all things, and we only need to embrace what comes to us without preferences or expectations. Writing and publishing books provided a continuous learning experience that reinforced this lesson.

The corporate examples in *Take Your Soul to Work* were outdated, and I was no longer interested in writing a book with examples of healthy workplaces. Instead, I wanted this book to help folks achieve their goals in both life and work. In fact, everywhere. And the information and modules on aligning with your soul to manifest your life's purpose were timeless. Re-editing the original book, I aimed to provide individuals with tools to achieve three concrete, practical goals: first, to balance their personality and soul needs; second, to develop a soul-infused personality; and third, to activate their seven chakras to succeed in reaching their goals. We published *Manifest Your Soul's Purpose: The Essential Guide for Life and Work* in 2012.

Writing books

Launch of *Take Your Soul to Work* supported by Dean Daly with The
Banff Centre for Management

The next book, *Hybrids: So You Think You Are Human,* explored a far-reaching topic. It discusses the 22 possible types of human hybrids, including elves, leprechauns, goblins, trolls, dolphins, whales, dragons, merpeople, and angels. Individuals from these lineages enter humanity with approval from the overseers of human destiny. I first learned about these hybrids in my counseling practice, as many people who seemed to have non-human ancestry sought assistance. The more I recognized this, the more types of hybrids I encountered.

In 2007, while leading a retreat in Germany, I discussed the possibility of human hybrids in a class setting. The participants were fascinated, and later, at lunch, Colin, one of the participants, said, "We'd like you to write another book, and we have the title for you. It's *Hybrids: So You Think You Are Human.*"

I began to laugh, realizing that Spirit was no longer prompting me directly to write books. Instead, it was communicating through a group.

"But I haven't even given workshops on that subject," I replied.

"We would all like a course on hybrids, wouldn't we?" Colin asked, turning to the group members, who nodded in agreement.

"What do you want in the course?" I asked, wondering how serious they were.

Others started to suggest ideas. "What kinds of hybrids are there?" one asked.

"Where did they come from, and when did they arrive on Earth?" another suggested.

"Relationships," said a third person succinctly. Noticing that we were waiting for her to continue, she added, "How do you get along with your parents, spouse, children, and friends if they are different hybrids from you?"

One woman had been quietly contemplating the discussion. "I'm interested in how hybrids enrich the planet and help humans," she said. Hearing her suggestion, many others agreed.

One of our more inventive participants volunteered, "I believe you should establish a support system for hybrids and rename your organization from The International Institute for Transformation to The Interstellar Institute for Transformation."

"The title of the book and all your ideas are great," I replied. "Even the idea of "Interstellar" for our organization is wonderful because it's exactly that. However, that title may not be viable in today's world. People might associate it with spaceships and UFOs. First, I'll begin by giving workshops on hybrids to develop the material and exercises. Additionally, it's necessary to conduct research on myths from around the world to evaluate whether my theory holds true. This is such a new concept that evidence is needed to encourage individuals to consider whether hybrids exist. Please be patient."

It took many years to fulfill this promise. *Hybrids: So You Think You Are Human* was finally published in 2015. The timing was perfect because readers might not have been receptive to the book earlier. Why? Because my other books in various languages needed to generate interest in hybrids. Furthermore, it was important to ensure the validity of my hypothesis and time was needed to conduct the research. As mentioned earlier, we are responsible for the errors in our words and actions. Making errors in spiritual judgment negatively affects our karma, so it's best to avoid them.

Writing books reflects my current interests. However, sometimes an unexpected theme may emerge. This happened with *The High Beings of Hawaii*. As you know by now, Lloyd, my leprechaun friend, often leads me along unknown paths. This incident occurred in January 2015 while I was vacationing in Hawaii. One day, Lloyd appeared and said he wanted me to meet the Menehune and another group. Since the Menehune are elementals, this made sense, so I agreed. The other group turned out to include various kinds of ancestors, such as water dragons, a fire goddess, and many others.

These encounters led me to a deep exploration of not only Hawaiian ancestors but also the significance of ancestors for everyone. I discovered that our core wounds stem from our ancestors and are downloaded at conception. By connecting with our physical and spiritual ancestors, we can heal these core wounds and ancestral traumas. Typically, our healing begins with our family's ancestors. Then, our focus broadens to our tribe, our nation, and eventually all beings on Earth. In the spiritual lineage, we often start by contemplating our life purpose. This leads us to past lives, then to our hybrid, and finally to our soul ancestors.

Writing *The High Beings of Hawaii*, I realized that my elemental and ancestor books, which resembled novels, were crafted on two levels. On the first level, they were engaging stories. On a deeper level, they provided spiritual insights to help seekers. I was amused at how, without realizing it, I had done this in each book. Clearly, I couldn't stop teaching!

The next book, *Good Morning Henry*, began on a flight to Florida in January 2018. It was the second time in a few months flying with a cold, and because my ear canals have been damaged by colds, I was concerned.

Closing my eyes, I journeyed within my body. "Why do I catch colds while flying?" I asked the body elemental, the intelligence of my body.

"Because the only time you speak with me is when you have a serious reason," the body elemental answered.

"Okay," I replied, ready to listen. "What do you want to communicate?"

"I want you to write a book with me and about me," the body intelligence said.

That was all I heard at that moment; however, sometime later, while sitting at the computer, the body elemental, Henry by name, resumed the conversation. Writing *Good Morning Henry* took many years of delving deeply into the link between physical, emotional, mental, and spiritual health. During those years, Henry revealed that he, she, or it was the same as the Holy Spirit, the Divine Mother, and the Divine sound Aum. This consciousness creates all forms in our physical, astral, and causal bodies. By working with this consciousness, we can not only heal our physical and mental illnesses but also learn to use our thoughts to fully manifest our purpose in this life.

Spirit's intention in co-writing the book was to help individuals apply its advice in their lives. In my opinion, *Good Morning Henry* is one of my most significant books. It might not be as entertaining as the novel-like leprechaun books or as serious as the spiritual self-help guides like *Decoding Your Destiny* and *Manifest Your Soul's Purpose,* but it bridges the gap between these two genres. *Good Morning Henry* was published in 2022.

The subsequent book, *The Leprechaun's Story,* was written by my leprechaun friend Lloyd, who, luckily for him, had this human taking his dictation. Years earlier, I traveled alone to Ireland and stayed in Keel. While wandering the hills and narrow lanes, Lloyd took me to all the places mentioned in our first book, *Summer with the Leprechauns.* I visited everyone in Keel who had memories of the "faerie cottage" to record what they knew. However, it wasn't until 2022 that Lloyd felt the time was right to tell the story of his life. The words flowed onto the page with ease, and the book was finished in just a few months. This was a sharp contrast to the many edits needed for other books.

As we approached the end of the story, I realized that this was our last book together. We continued to partner in co-creating workshops, but there would be no more books. Celebrating our wonderful years together, *The Leprechaun's Story* was published in January 2023. It was the easiest book I had ever written. Spirit, knowing that the next book would be a spiritual stretch, must have been giving me a gift.

One day, while meditating in 2022, I experienced a profound request from Mahavatar Babaji. He is a deathless guru who resides in the Himalayas and works with high-level initiates. He can appear and disappear at will and has given assignments to both Paramahansa Yogananda and Sri Yukteswar, who are gurus associated with my meditation practice. However, I had never had direct communication with Mahavatar Babaji until this encounter.

During meditation, he guided me into a high astral universe. I observed the physical Earth inhabited by humans, the elemental world existing in a slightly higher Earth vibration, and two other planets at even higher vibrations: one for dragons and another for merpeople.

Turning toward the dragon world, Babaji said, "You've done enough for the elementals. What about dragons?"

This request was shocking. Although both a profound dream about dragons and several mystical encounters had happened over the years, I had never considered writing about dragons. Also, I was hesitant to embark on another major topic, one I didn't feel qualified to tackle. Yet, it was both humbling and a great honor to receive a request from Babaji, and if he believed I could do it, it was important to release self-doubt. Nevertheless, with many projects to complete, I postponed starting the book for a year. In May 2023, while teaching in France, and tired of waiting, a dragon arrived.

Writing this book was easy, on one hand, because the information was readily available and Jake, my dragon brother, was fascinating. On the other hand, *The Dragon's Tale* was the most spiritually and energetically challenging book to write, as it required accessing the high astral and low causal vibrational frequencies of the dragon's homeworld. This was a spiritual stretch, akin to running a marathon. Spirit, working through Babaji, employed perfect timing in its request, as my vibrational frequency would not have been consistently high enough at a younger age to access this elevated realm. At one point in *The Dragon's Tale*, Jake, my dragon brother, mentions that my work is to build pathways between worlds, and looking back, it's surprisingly easy to see that this is what I have done in all the books. *The Dragon's Tale* was published in 2024.

Writing books has deepened my spiritual practice over the years. It has focused attention on what Spirit needs in the world. I am dedicated to this goal, and each book reflects my vibrational frequency at the time of writing. This is true for everything each of us says, does, or creates; however, this realization did not firmly impress itself upon my mind until this most recent book.

Self-publishing books wasn't my initial plan. But after submitting proposals and manuscripts to many publishers who declined to acquire my books, I realized that Spirit meant for me to handle the sale of these books by creating Wayshower Enterprises. During this endeavor, I've been deeply grateful for relationships with wonderful translators and publishers in different countries.

Writing books, editing, rewriting, facing mistreatment and rejection from publishers, and then having to self-publish and market your books may cause you to ask, "Why do people put themselves through this?" You might as well ask a painter, "Why paint?", a dog owner, "Why do it?" or a parent, "Why did you choose to have children?" Each of us possesses inborn creativity that seeks to birth something from ourselves. Humans are gods in training; we are creators.

# 20

# Yearning for God

Re-reading my journals over the years, several themes have become clear. I have mentioned before that the Void periods of Nothing were followed by bursts of creative energy. Another major theme was longing for a partner. To clarify, I never believed that a partner would replace devotion to the Divine, which remains my primary commitment. Still, couldn't there be both—commitment to God and to a man? I wasn't making lists of the "perfect man" or reciting daily affirmations and only occasionally wrote about this request in the journals.

This desire had many roots. It grew from wanting to share daily life with someone who genuinely cared about me, not just as a teacher. I love partnership, and had dear friends and had co-created with Merle for years, but it would be nice to live with a partner. This desire also partly stemmed from the responsibility of caring for Diamond Heart, an aging house and property that needed ongoing maintenance, and I was not a fix-it person. Living alone in the country without companionship was not easy. I expressed my loneliness and longing for a partner to our focalizers during their retreat at Diamond Heart in the summer of 2008.

One of them suggested, "You could make a list of the qualities you want and put it on the fridge."

"What about writing an affirmation and reciting it every day?" another said.

"Visualizing what you want is important," added a third person.

"There are a few dating sites I've been using," a fourth contributed.

"I appreciate that you're trying to help with ideas," I replied, "but if it's going to happen, it has to be easy. He will have to walk down the driveway."

A few weeks later, while on the phone inviting a neighbor to the barbecue I was hosting the next day, a car drove leisurely down the driveway. A man I had met recently emerged from the driver's side carrying a pizza. Hanging up the phone, I answered the door.

"I brought the pizza for your party," Simon said, beaming with delight.

"The party is tomorrow," I replied, amused by his poor timing.

"Well, if you haven't eaten, let's have the pizza," he said with a smile as he held out the box.

Sitting outside, we were tucking into the pizza when he leaned across the table, looked me in the eye, and asked, "Are you dating anyone?"

"No," I answered.

"You are now," he said, smiling and oblivious to the fact that his proposal hadn't been accepted...yet.

Simon and I shared some mutual friends, and he was a friendly person. However, things were happening too fast. "We should get to know each other better before we start dating," I replied. "I'm going to the mountains with the hiking group for three days."

"Great. I'll go too," he said.

"Okay," I agreed, adding, "but it's best if we go separately. We can see how we feel after we've had a chance to get to know each other better in the group."

That's what we did. Over the three days, it became clear that Simon had a great sense of humor, that both men and women liked him, and that he was both helpful and affectionate. After returning to Powell River, we started dating. His interests were quite different from mine. He was a sailor, while I often got seasick. He loved motorcycles, whereas I preferred walking. He was an extrovert who had spent more than a decade working for the United Nations World Food Program in war-torn countries, delivering food to starving people, so he was used to bullets flying and a fast-paced lifestyle. In contrast, I treasured peace and quiet. It might not sound like an auspicious beginning, but there were signs encouraging us to proceed.

First, the name Simon was also that of my first love in university, who was Welsh, while this new Simon was English. Second, Bill, with whom I had lived for 15 years, was Dutch by birth, and Simon had Dutch parents and spoke Dutch fluently. Perhaps the most significant indicator was his last name, Goede, which means "good man" in Dutch. He embodied that ideal, and what we seek in a partner while living in the country in our 60s may differ from what attracted us earlier when living in the city.

He was very independent, as was I, but we had some things we enjoyed doing together. We both loved nature, were fit, and enjoyed week-long hikes and trips to various countries. He had a curious mind and diverse interests, and we enjoyed visiting museums and events together. Gradually, our fondness for each other deepened, and Simon moved into Diamond Heart in 2011. He was the first man I had been with who embodied the hero archetype—something that would not have interested me when younger. What opened my heart more and more to him was not the exterior hero image but his soft, generous nature. He consistently sought ways to help me, his friends, and even strangers.

We faced numerous challenges over the years. He had never been in a committed relationship, which presented a steep learning curve for him and put pressure on me. He visited his mother in England at least twice a year, often for two months at a time, which also strained our relationship. However, as I let go of my need to be the most important person in his life, we grew closer. He faced serious health and financial difficulties, and as I supported him through these, he learned to trust me more. From his point of view, discovering that I wasn't always available to play because of my commitments to IIT and Spirit must have been difficult since he loved to play.

As I write, Simon and I have been together for 16 years. Our love and understanding of each other continue to grow deeper. People either grow in a relationship, whether with partners or friends, or they diminish. We have both grown. My heart continues to open to him, and with him, this love flows out to others. Being with Simon has helped me soften and become more yin, which I had been seeking. For this, I am very grateful.

I've had four significant partner relationships with men in my life, and each has been a teacher. My first relationship in university with Simon L was innocent. It was my first foray into learning how to love a partner. I had glimpses of potential ways to love, but as a young person, I didn't know how to be a lifelong partner. Next was Bill. He was comfortable, and with him, there was no need to prove anything or be different from who I was. He loved me unconditionally, which is a wonderful gift to receive. Bill was like a brother, and through him, I learned to love my brother, Mark, and other men better. Rod was different. I was deeply in love with him romantically, so much so that it took me a long time to relinquish my romantic fantasies of the ideal lover and partner. This, perhaps, was my greatest fantasy in this illusory world, and I am grateful to have awakened from that attachment. He also gifted me with three stepchildren which allowed me to love children more deeply.

Now, Simon Goede, my current partner, with his kind nature, helps open my heart more and more to loving all men. I see more clearly how men are wounded, feel compassion for them, and, even better, do not want to hurt them. It has always been easier for me to love and trust women deeply, so this was not the area where my heart and love needed to grow.

My mother once told me, "You have no type in men." That's true, and I thank these wonderful men who have taught me to love in so many ways, both in my personality and in my soul. They all opened my heart.

Having a loving, committed relationship with someone will never replace union with the Divine. Only the Divine can provide lasting happiness, and my commitment and love for the Divine continued to deepen. Over the next several years, I noticed that conversations with El Morya were replaced by those with Sri Yukteswar. This led to the realization that they are different aspects of the same being. In earlier years, I was not ready to know this. My spiritual journey has involved uncovering deeper and deeper layers of knowing about myself and others, and that was one instance of where this occurred.

In meditation, both Sri Yukteswar and his successor, Paramahansa Yogananda, helped answer questions regarding the direction of IIT. They supported the courses we offered, and we discussed practical ideas, such as upgrading our websites, using social media, and supporting both individuals and the community.

Sometimes, when we don't observe success in our daily lives or work, we may feel as though we are not making progress. Yet, if we remain committed to our spiritual journey, we do move forward. Even during difficulties, or especially during those times, if we stay the course, we grow. These subtle changes are recorded in the ether, and although we may not notice them, they accumulate over time.

The International Institute for Transformation served as a great teacher of this lesson. For the first 12 years of IIT, based on class enrollments and finances, our progress was so gradual that I often wondered if we could carry on. When we graduated the largest group of focalizers in January 2012, I questioned whether any of them would continue with IIT and if others would join. Nevertheless, through faith and love of Spirit, I kept teaching what would help them and others with their spiritual growth. The ultimate goal of spiritual transformation is service to all, and over time, this knowing became deeply rooted within me and influenced even daily decisions.

Spirit provided dramatic confirmation that I was correctly following its guidance in May 2013. I was in Germany conducting a soul reading for Katharina, one of our focalizers. It was Friday evening, two days before Pentecost—often a significant day in my life. During Katharina's reading, an ascetic-looking man, who referred to himself as John, appeared in my inner vision and requested to speak with her. This was unusual because normally, there are no intermediaries during the soul readings. In this instance, however, I intuitively knew it was St. John, the apostle, and that it was important to honor his request.

After John finished, another unexpected visitor arrived, calling himself Peter. He was a sturdy, middle-aged man holding keys in his left hand, and I realized he was St. Peter.

Peter, looking straight at me, said, "I have been sent by The Christ to deliver a message. You are being given more responsibility and Masters are coming to assist you. Embrace all that you are receiving. You struggle with low self-worth, and it is essential to trust yourself unconditionally."

Peter held me in a mental grip as he spoke. I was shocked not only that he was addressing me but also by what he was saying. In 13 years of conducting soul readings for focalizers, nothing like this had ever occurred.

Peter continued, "I came during Katharina's reading, because you would never have thought to speak with me otherwise."

He was right in his assessment. I had never been attracted to Peter, as he was portrayed in the Bible as patriarchal and fundamentalist. Mary Magdalene and the mystical interpretations found in the *Gnostic Gospels* resonated more with my path.

When Peter left, I retired to the bedroom to reflect on what had happened. Peter had been preparing me for something, but what exactly? I didn't have to wait long. Closing my outer eyes, I opened my third eye. Jesus the Christ, dressed in a shimmering white robe, stood at the end of a path. He was nearly translucent, with light radiating from him like a sparkler. He floated slightly above the path and began moving toward me.

Two thoughts raced through my mind. The first was, "I'm not ready." The second was, "I'm not worthy."

Neither of these projected thoughts deterred him. Jesus the Christ continued approaching, and my heart pounded with fear. The thought surfaced unbidden, "If he touches me, I'll probably die."

He kept coming and dissolved into my heart. As you might imagine, this was an incredibly powerful experience. No words can truly describe it. Writing about this minimizes...the opposite of the real transformative event.

The next morning, I sat down to meditate with Katharina and her kindhearted husband, Christoph, who had organized our IIT workshops in Europe for twenty years. I was still processing the enormity of what had happened and had no idea that even more would be revealed.

Closing my outer eyes, I observed Sri Yukteswar, Paramahansa Yogananda, and an unending line of Ascended Masters gazing at me. Yogananda stepped forward and placed a yellow ribbon on my left breast, over my heart. I felt, rather than heard, the words, "Congratulations," and all the Masters smiled, welcoming me into their group.

Feelings of being unworthy surfaced again. Since it was the second monumental event within a few hours, I began to wonder if this was a fantasy. I asked Yogananda, "Is Satan tempting me with pride?"

His response expressed a heartfelt, "No. This experience is true."

It's difficult to express the feeling and knowing I received from Yogananda. We were united in Spirit. In this soul union, he blessed me for my dedication to IIT and for supporting others through the stages of their spiritual growth.

Noticing Peter and John to my right, I asked, "What is my relationship with both of you?"

"You have devoted many lives to the Christian path, but your essence lies in the Eastern tradition," Peter explained. "You were part of the Rishi's lineage thousands of years before embracing the Christian path. However, both paths lead to the Christ Consciousness that Jesus and other enlightened Masters embodied."

As Peter spoke, he looked toward Yogananda, indicating that I go with him. I needed to commit to becoming a devotee of Paramahansa Yogananda, Sri Yukteswar, and that line of gurus. I was part of that lineage.

Later, when I spoke with Christoph about my experience, he remarked, "Paramahansa Yogananda represents love, Sri Yukteswar represents wisdom, and Peter represents will."

I hadn't noticed this until Christoph mentioned it. These are the three qualities of the Holy Trinity that we need to develop in our hearts to become conscious co-creators with the Divine. I was born with wisdom and a deep connection to the Holy Spirit, another name for the Divine Mother, the creator of all form in our universe. My life had been dedicated to becoming more loving and compassionate. When Jesus the Christ, the epitome of love, entered my heart, I felt fulfilled and at peace. The lifelong search was realized. Of course, continuing to develop each aspect of the Trinity—love, wisdom, and will—is essential, and my focus now shifted to my weakest area. The last aspect of the Trinity, the Divine Father, the omniscient Source of All, was still unknown. This would be the focus in the next stage of my spiritual transformation.

Left to right Lahiri Mahasaya, Mahavatar Babaji, Jesus Christ, Bhagavan Krishna, Paramahansa Yogananda, Swami Sri Yukteswar

Christoph Wasser has been organizing IIT European
courses for over two decades

Simon and Tanis after 16 years

Mark's sons, my nephews: Top left to right, Ben, Jason. Bottom, Eric, Zenon

My brother Mark

A joyful time swimming with a sea turtle

The spiritual journey often involves two steps forward and one step back. This has definitely been true in my life. At first glance, life seemed much the same until that autumn when Simon and I took a road trip through the Northwestern United States. As night fell, we were driving home on a major highway. We were in the passing lane when a car in the next lane bounced off the end of a large truck, spinning us off the road. My airbag deployed, knocking me out. When I regained consciousness, I sat dazed in the smoke-filled car. Simon was in better shape and got out to talk with the other driver, who, fortunately, had not been hurt.

Confused, I stayed seated in the smoky car until the ambulance arrived.

"Are you hurt?" one of the paramedics inquired.

"I'm fine," I replied, giving my standard answer.

"What is your name?"

"Tanis." That answer was easy.

More questions followed. I must have sounded coherent because, when the tow truck arrived, the ambulance left. Our car was a write-off, so the tow truck driver took us to a motel. Simon later said that he had asked me to call the insurance company while he spoke with the tow-truck driver. In a blank, non-thinking state, I did nothing. When Simon returned, he found me in bed, shaking and not lucid. The next year and a half were not the best of times. I had a concussion and often did strange things, such as putting food in the oven instead of the fridge and misnaming objects. One day, I even awoke from my foggy state to find myself standing in the middle of a downtown street. I also had severe sciatica and couldn't sit without discomfort. Making matters worse, the young man who had crashed into us didn't have insurance. Since our car was a write-off and we had medical bills, we needed to work with a lawyer to receive compensation. This situation added to the overwhelming stress.

During the physically painful and confusing year that followed, another emotional event broke my heart. Although I had many acquaintances and good friends, I had few soul friends. A soul friend is someone who connects with you on a soul level. You are at the same stage in your spiritual transformation. While your personality traits and interests may differ, your intuition, consciousness, and dedication to the Divine are relatively the same.

A soul friend dear to my heart, with whom I'd journeyed for over a decade, ended our relationship. We were both going through a heart-wrenching time, and our needs no longer aligned. While I needed silence and solitude to recover from my back and brain injury, she, being more extroverted, wanted to visit and talk about her situation. We were both drained and had nothing left to give each other. Still, it was heartbreaking when our deep friendship ended. Before this experience, I believed our bond would grow and evolve throughout our lives.

Now, many years later, our relationship is somewhat healed but, sadly, lacks the unconditional trust we once had. At the same time, we both know we are profoundly connected from past lives and will be again in future lives. So, what do we learn from the ending of a significant relationship? The lesson remains the same throughout my life: to be free of all attachments, even to soul friends. Thank you soul friend for teaching me this.

On the path of spiritual transformation, we undergo many Dark Nights of the Soul. Previously, I had experienced numerous spiritual dark nights. Because of the accident, I faced both physical and mental struggles, and the loss of my soul friend was a profound emotional blow. Dark Nights of the Soul can arise at any time. Often, their impact is greatest in the areas where our ego is most attached, resulting in liberating our soul from its entrapment by our ego. Viewed in this light, Dark Nights of the Soul are a blessing.

Recovering from injuries sustained in the car accident and from the emotional pain of losing my soul friend, I turned more intensely to the spiritual path. This led to dedicating much of 2014 to studying Paramahansa Yogananda's Self-Realization Fellowship (SRF) lessons. Yogananda's wisdom radiated from every page, drawing me deeper into commitment to him and his lineage. Before that time, I felt more aligned with Sri Yukteswar, who, like me, was an El endowed with wisdom. Sri Yukteswar had a reputation as a strict disciplinarian, yet he was gentle with me. Through studying the SRF lessons, I realized that Sri Yukteswar had entrusted me to his closest disciple to cultivate devotion, which was Yogananda's strength.

My commitment to Paramahansa Yogananda continued to grow. On April 16, 2016, I received the Kriya initiation, at which point I accepted him as my guru. A guru is an enlightened being who guides and supports a devotee in achieving Self-realization, no matter how many lifetimes it takes. Enlightenment, or Self-realization, ultimately happens when we surrender our individual identities to unite with the Divine. Then, as Jesus said in John 10:30 of the Bible, "I and the Father are One."

I have been fortunate to study with many excellent teachers from Buddhist, Native American, and mystical Western traditions. Although none of these paths became my ultimate path, I honor all the teachings and teachers and discovered many commonalities among different spiritual traditions. Yet, I never felt a deep commitment to any of those paths or teachers. Most of these teachers, like me, were wayshowers on the path. A time comes on the spiritual path when your soul yearns to commit to one Self-realized Master who can guide you to the Divine.

Choosing Paramahansa Yogananda and his lineage, which includes Sri Yukteswar, Babaji, and Jesus, brought all the Masters I felt close to together in one place.

Reinforcing this knowing was a vision I had of an ancient life in a forest in India. Sri Yukteswar was Yogananda's and my guru, but bored with continuous meditation, I left to pursue a more active path. Yogananda said nothing at that time but looked at me with deep sadness. The way he looked at me in that Indian life triggered the memory of the way The Great One looked at me in Atlantis. Through this look, I realized Yogananda had been supporting me for thousands of years. A guru never leaves you until you achieve enlightenment. The only way I can repay Sri Yukteswar and Yogananda's commitment to me through these eons is to stay the course.

Synchronicities confirmed my choice of a guru and his lineage. One spring day in 2016, I was reading *The Autobiography of a Yogi* by Paramahansa Yogananda, a book I had first read about 30 years earlier.

Coming across a passage about his guru, I was riveted. In that passage, Sri Yukteswar, who had already passed away, appeared to Yogananda in a resurrected physical form and gave him instructions. Yogananda asked Sri Yukteswar what he was doing in this resurrected life. Sri Yukteswar replied that he was working in the astral universe, which is "peopled with millions of astral beings…and with myriads of fairies, mermaids, fishes, animals, goblins, gnomes, demigods, and spirits, all residing on different astral planets." [8]

Reading those words, my soul knew that Sri Yukteswar had overseen my entire life. He guided me to meet Lloyd, my leprechaun friend, and through this, he encouraged me to write many books about elementals. Furthermore, it was Sri Yukteswar who wished for a book to be written on *Hybrids,* which had been published a year earlier. Discovering this was a humbling experience that brought me closer to him.

# 21

# The Journey Continues...

From 2017 to 2019, life largely remained the same, focused on teaching courses for IIT, writing books, and enjoying time with friends and Simon. Then, in 2020, the pandemic hit, giving me several years at home and time to finish writing two books. Also, gardening, especially in May and June, was a real treat, since I usually worked in Europe during that time.

However, not everything was joyful. My brother, Mark, grew increasingly unwell due to a lung condition that was eventually diagnosed as caused by asbestos. Mark's lung problems coincided with my battle with COVID in the fall of 2022, leaving me with lingering lung congestion for another year and a half. I intuitively felt that my lung issues were linked not only to pneumonia earlier in this life and tuberculosis in previous lives but also to Mark dying of lung disease. I grieved for my brother. He was my only sibling, and I had memories of other lives we shared.

There might have been another reason for my lung problem. Now, in my 70s, with energy waning, the productive life of writing books and teaching was winding down. In fact, life itself was coming to an end. For several decades, I had a strong intuition of dying at age 76. My father passed away at that age, and approaching the end of my 76th year, I wondered if I would also die. Deciding to prepare, I revised my will. However, I didn't die; my dear brother did.

As Mark became weaker, I accompanied him in the astral world through my dreams. One night, while traveling with Mark on a bus, he got off and I couldn't follow. There was a young woman who, noticing my concern, guided me to a house filled with young men with feathered wings. We waited together until their father arrived. Even in the dream, I realized the men were angels and that their father was God. This seemed normal, as strange events often do in dreams. The father allowed me to speak with Mark, and I saw that he was in a halfway house, a liminal space between life and death. That's why it was impossible to follow him.

Mark was a born-again Christian who had accepted Jesus as his savior. Over the following weeks, I witnessed Jesus drawing closer to him, and one day, Jesus said, "Your brother will be going soon. It's time to practice non-attachment." I followed Jesus's instructions and practiced non-attachment during daily meditation so my brother could leave peacefully. Meanwhile, during our phone calls, Mark mentioned that he had nothing more to say and that it wasn't necessary to call every day. He was intentionally helping me practice non-attachment as he withdrew from the world. Not long after, Mark suffered a stroke and lay dying in the hospital with three of his sons by his side.

On the other side of Canada, during meditation, I saw Jesus standing beside my brother. Turning to me, Jesus said, "You can let go now; I am holding him."

One of Mark's sons, Eric, called 30 minutes later. When I asked what time their father had passed, it was exactly when Jesus had spoken to me.

"I was singing hymns to Dad," Eric said. "Then Ben and Zenon joined in, and we sang Dad's favorite song, Puff the Magic Dragon. That was when Dad relaxed."

Hearing that Mark had passed away while listening to a song about a dragon living forever, I realized that my brother in this life was Jake, my dragon brother in the dragon world. To reinforce this knowing, I remembered that during the last months of Mark's life, he had mentioned several times that he was trying to get in touch with an old friend, Jake, with whom he had not spoken for decades. It's no wonder we were so close, and that I wrote *The Dragon's Tale* while being so preoccupied with my brother.

Through this realization, I knew that relationships with significant people in our lives may exist not only in our past lives but also in other worlds. By liberating ourselves from our concepts of time and space, we open up to this possibility. This awareness grounds itself as truth within my body, and I see a portal to a multi-dimensional universe calling to me and others to explore. This is our human destiny.

So, where are we in this story now? I feel closer to Spirit than ever, yet I also recognize how little I know of the Divine plan. Piece by piece, parts of the grand design have revealed themselves. Still, these are only glimpses. My life has been a continual unfolding of knowing. The journey does not end. Two things currently call me.

The first is to meditate more often and for longer periods. This is an area calling for improvement. Although I have followed Spirit's guidance and strengthened many weak areas in my life, boredom, restlessness, and insufficient meditation still remain challenges. We make the greatest progress in any area of our lives when we correct the weakest area that continually holds us back. If I don't correct this pattern in this lifetime, it will keep repeating in the next...and the next. Changing a long-standing habit isn't easy. Willpower is necessary. Advanced spiritual masters, like Yogananda and Sri Yukteswar, have this one-pointed focus to unite with the omniscient Divine, the Source of All. In doing this, masters completely surrender their self-identity.

Thinking of the Divine as God and the Father raises resistance in me due to concerns about patriarchal religions and organizations that have inflicted a lot of suffering. Instead, it's helpful to reframe my understanding of the triple aspect of the Divine in terms of Vedic-Hindu concepts like Sat-Chit-Ananda, which represent the three aspects of the Divine: eternal unchanging being, consciousness-wisdom, and bliss. It also helps to remember that Jesus valued women and included them in his inner circle, and that Paramahansa Yogananda also valued women, naming them as his successors in his organization.

Just saying I need to increase my willpower and maintain one-pointed focus to unite with the Source of All isn't enough of an incentive. Even knowing that Yogananda and many trusted masters emphasize the importance of meditation isn't enough. I need daily rewards to motivate myself until I form a new positive habit and see progress.

When I was a child, I learned to reward myself for doing homework, which was boring but necessary if I wanted to pass in school. I would tell my parents after dinner, "I'm going to do my homework now. Don't let me watch TV unless I've done it."

If I came out of my room to watch TV, they would ask, "Have you done your homework?"

I would answer honestly. This system worked well, and I've used rewards throughout my life to stay focused and complete difficult or unpleasant tasks.

A healthy reward that works well for me is anything in nature. Nature restores us to harmony because it aligns with spiritual laws. I want to spend more time listening to the birds sing, smelling the flowers, and feeding the goldfish in my pond. Walking, gardening, swimming in the ocean, and sleeping under the stars all nurture my soul and body.

To increase time in nature and meditation, I have decided to reduce doing time. Spirit encourages and supports this. I am in the process of letting go of teaching, an activity I am still attached to, to embrace the next step of not knowing. Sometimes, I wonder if there will be another book, maybe about the merpeople. The answer remains in the ether, as Spirit has not yet called for this. As for more courses, who can say? The most important thing is to surrender attachment to all roles and to any and all "doing." As always, I am guided by Spirit's will.

Embarking on this story, I initially hoped to conclude that I had achieved my primary purpose—union with the Divine. I haven't. Is it still possible? Yes. In my view, it's the only intention worth pursuing. Still, I realize that my journey isn't over and it may or may not happen in this lifetime. I'm grateful for the life and opportunities I've received and remain patient with the process, knowing each step has been a wonderful learning experience.

I thank Spirit, God, the Source of All, for my life.

# Endnotes

### Chapter 9 – Spiritual Allies

1. Alma Bell Brown created this virtual church with charitable legal status, but I believe it disbanded after her death.

2. I don't know if The New Age Church of the Christ still exists.

### Chapter 12 – Soul, Sirius, and Krishnamurti

3. Several years later, in 1988, I self-published five thousand copies and all copies were sold. Yet, I never taught from *Decoding Destiny* until the year 2000, when the information had moved from theory to embodiment in my own life. Over the next decade, I re-edited *Decoding Destiny* to more thoroughly anchor the information on Earth and make it accessible for more people. *Decoding Your Destiny: Keys to Humanity's Spiritual Transformation* was republished in 2011.

### Chapter 14 – Summer with the Leprechauns

4. Mr. Douglas and Mrs. Toolis are the pseudonyms for Mr. Davidson and Mrs. O'Toole in my book *Summer with the Leprechauns*.

5. In my book, *Summer with the Leprechauns*, published in 1997, I recount my summer with Lloyd the leprechaun.

6. I have written about the body elemental in *Good Morning Henry: An In-Depth Journey with the Body Intelligence*, published in 2022.

### Chapter 15 – Sacred Sites and Magical Mystery Tours

7. We visited many significant sacred sites in England, Ireland, and Scotland on the Magical Mystery Tours. I detail the numerous sacred sites in Ireland in my book *Pilgrimage with the Leprechauns*.

### Chapter 20 – Yearning for God

8. Paramahansa Yogananda, *The Autobiography of a Yogi*, Self-Realization Fellowship, printing 2011, p. 355.

# Acknowledgments

When I was 46, I wrote my autobiography. A good friend, Joe Fisher, who was also a writer and a published author, kindly edited it. I then gave it to Patrick Crean, a well-respected editor at a major publishing house, who appreciated my work for his appraisal. He tactfully recommended waiting until I was famous to write an autobiography. Of course, he was right. Famous or not, now, 30 years later, being at the no-time-to-wait stage of life, I decided to finish the book.

Thanks for re-reading it, Patrick, and for your supportive thumbs-up.

I want to thank Merle Dulmage, who reviewed the first half of the book and encouraged me to keep going. I am grateful to my partner, Simon Goede, who let me read the entire book to him and offered continuous suggestions before anyone else saw it.

Rilla Clark, who has known me since we were both 19, was very helpful with her high-level comments, sharp intelligence, and psychological insight. Next, I am grateful to Donna Minielly, who has edited several of my books and kindly edited this memoir as well, and to Monika Bernegg, my generous and excellent German translator of books, courses, newsletters, and much more, who, with her eagle eye, caught other points that were overlooked. Finally, I appreciate Rory Hill for his perceptive feedback in a genre and topic he seldom reads. My thanks to Melany Hallam who masterfully did the layout and finished the cover. In the last stages, Janet Rouss came to the rescue to help find the subtitle, as did Jenny Lou Linley, who, by changing things in the final book layout, got me editing again. Ugh. I'm grateful to Nita Kay Alverez for all the book covers over the years. She started the process for us to discover the cover Spirit wanted.

The acknowledgments would not be complete without thanking the many people who have studied with me over the decades, trusting and encouraging me to guide them on their spiritual journey.

Lastly, this book would not have been written without my parents and brother, Mark, who supported and loved me even when they didn't fully understand the mystical path I was on.

# About the Author

TANIS HELLIWELL has seen higher realms and spoken with Masters, angels and elementals since childhood. Walking in many worlds, she led tours to sacred sites for two decades, was a management consultant working with universities, government, and business for over 30 years, and conducted a psychotherapy practice specializing in spiritual transformation.

In 2000, she founded the International Institute for Transformation (IIT), which offers programs to assist individuals in becoming conscious creators to work with the spiritual laws that govern our world. Her gift is assisting others to develop a soul-infused life in harmony with the Earth.

Her knowledge and understanding of other worlds and spiritual realms can be found in some of her most popular books: *Summer with the Leprechauns, The Dragon's Tale, Hybrids: So You Think You Are Human, Decoding Your Destiny: Keys to Humanity's Spiritual Transformation, and Good Morning Henry: An In-depth Journey with the Body Intelligence.*

She is committed to helping individuals to develop right relationships with themselves, others and the Earth.

To write to the author, order books, audio recordings or for self-study courses to assist with your spiritual transformation, please contact:

Tanis Helliwell

tanis@tanishelliwell.com

https://www.tanishelliwell.com/

facebook.com/Tanis.Helliwell